THE
COMPLETE
ALL-IN-THE-OVEN
COOKBOOK

THE COMPLETE
All-in-the-Oven
COOKBOOK

Dolores Riccio
&
Joan Bingham

STEIN AND DAY/*Publishers*/New York

To our husbands, Rick and Don

With loving thanks
for your patience
in testing, approving, and proofreading

First published 1981
Copyright © 1981 by Dolores Riccio and Joan Bingham

All rights reserved.
Designed by Louis A. Ditizio
Printed in the United States of America
Stein and Day/*Publishers*/
Scarborough House,
Briarcliff Manor, N.Y. 10510

Contents

Introduction

For years we lifted lids, checked temperatures, stirred, scraped, tested, and hovered over the range top as we prepared meals. While everyone else was resting in the living room, we were watching pots in the kitchen. We arrived at the dinner table hot and harried, just when we wanted to appear cool and relaxed. There must be an easier way, we decided, and that's how we came to develop a system of meal preparation that has taken the hassle out of cooking for us. It's called all-in-the-oven cookery.

Little of that last minute agonizing is actually necessary. Most of the dishes we used to labor over can be effortlessly cooked in the oven, everything for one meal at one time. Oven cooking is easier because it doesn't require the attentive supervision of the range-top method. It's cheaper, too, because it makes more efficient use of fuel.

Of course, the foods still need some slicing, dicing, ricing, or other work, but this can be done when the cook has a bit of spare time. Then, an hour or so before the meal, the dishes are taken out of the refrigerator and placed in the oven according to a timetable previously planned. There's nothing to do but take it easy while they cook!

We find this marvelously convenient, and we think you will, too. If you're off to work each day, you might elect to prepare foods the night before in a leisurely fashion. After a hard day, you can pop the meal into the oven, kick off your shoes, and enjoy a soothing beverage or a visit with your family while dinner readies itself. When the weatherman predicts 90-degree temperatures, you can prepare meals in the cool of the early morning without having to resort to feeding your family a diet of salads. With company, you can entertain more confidently, knowing that your sumptuous dinner, assembled ahead of time, can now safely be left in the oven.

You'll find additional benefits to oven cooking. Cheaper cuts of meat can be used; they will shrink less and tenderize more. Foods which are usually pan fried will be moister and much less greasy when cooked in the oven. Also, you won't have to stand there waiting to turn the cutlets, fearing they will stick or burn.

Oven cookery is by no means restricted to casseroles (although there are recipes for some delectable casseroles in our menus). We've devised dinners that include everything from soup to savoury! By adjusting times and temperatures, they can all be cooked in the oven.

Many vegetables which are traditionally boiled on top of the range may be oven-steamed in a covered dish (aluminum foil can serve as a cover) with herbs and seasonings that make the vitamin-rich juices taste delicious.

Fruit sauces (apple, rhubarb, cranberry) can be similarly covered and steamed while the oven is in use.

Not only potato dishes, but rice pilaf and other starch substitutes can also be oven-cooked.

For extra points with the family, or when you're having dinner guests, a dessert can be tucked right into the oven along with dinner.

In other words, practically anything you've been keeping an eye on while it cooked on top of the range can be just as successfully cooked in that magical, all-purpose oven.

What are the tricks to complete oven cooking? The standard size oven of 30 inches will accommodate three to four items at the same time, as long as the foods share a common temperature requirement. Heat must be allowed to circulate freely throughout the oven. That means placing pans so that there is at least an inch between them and an inch away from the oven's sides.

Pans on the top shelf will reflect extra heat onto the foods below them. For this reason, uncovered foods are placed on the top shelf, which prevents them from over-browning.

Another important step is to fill the pans correctly, if you want to avoid messy spills. Since many foods expand and bubble up when they bake, fill pans only three-quarters full.

Naturally, no oven is going to do the job properly if it's not in proper working order. A surprising number of people have turned out failure after failure without ever suspecting that the oven was the culprit. A burnt-out or weak element or a thermostat gone haywire can ruin a delicate dish. A simple way to make sure that your oven's working right is to check it with an inexpensive oven thermometer. Is the temperature the same on the thermometer as the temperature you have set on the oven control?

Timing is a critical factor, since we certainly don't want limp vegetables or dried-out fish fillets. That's why we've provided a timetable for every menu in this book. After you've followed these for a while, you may be inspired to experiment with your own favorite range-top recipes, converting them to easy oven dishes.

We think of the oven as the greatest cooking invention since fire. Its versatility enables you to produce meals from budget fare to foods fit for a Roman banquet. Meats can be roasted or stewed or oven-fried. Vegetables can be simply steamed, or cooked in elegant sauces. Breads can be crisp or tender. Desserts can be as homespun as apple pie or as exotic as mocha-rum soufflé. To sum it up, there's not much worth cooking that you can't cook in an oven.

A Potpourri of Pots and Pans

When it comes to selecting the utensils for oven cooking, the choice is a broad one because so many different foods can be cooked in an oven, each ideally suited to a particular type of pan. The heavyweight material that would be perfect for a braised-beef pot would not be desirable for making lady fingers; these delicate cakes require lightweight metal that heats and cools off quickly. But there are a few general watch points which we will outline here.

Handles should be sturdy and grippable, situated on both sides of the pan and close to the top. Although many handles and knobs are called ovenproof, some of them weaken from repeated exposure to heat that's over 350 degrees. Metal and ovenproof glass are better at withstanding high heat than handles of other materials.

In heavyweight pots, the physique of the cook is a consideration. In other words, if you can't lift the pot in the store, don't buy it. You won't be able to lift it any better when it's filled with hot food. Safety first!

Because we often use the make-ahead method of cooking, doing what preparation is involved in our spare moments and refrigerating the dishes until oven time, we prefer ovenproof glass utensils. They go beautifully with our lazy way of cooking—the same casserole from refrigerator to oven to table. What a way to cut down on dirty dishes! Although glass is a bit slower to heat up than metals, it heats evenly, holds the heat well, and is inexpensive. Glass and glass-ceramics are materials which really lend themselves to the refreigerator-to-oven method we find so convenient. Metals will warp at such drastic temperature changes.

There's a design of glass ovenware to suit every lifestyle and table decor. If you really want to be elegant, you can buy sets which include wicker, or even silver, serving baskets that you slip the dishes into before setting them on your table, pretty enough for the poshest party!

Glass pans clean easily, too. A swish of the soapy sponge and a rinse in hot water is all that's required to make them sparkle again. If there is some stubborn, baked-on food, you can fill the dish with a solution of half water and half ammonia, let it stand for an hour, and then wash. This method is effective for stainless steel, enamel, and non-stick finishes as well. But don't use ammonia on aluminum. To clean aluminum, use a soap-filled steel wool pad.

Stainless steel, particularly pans with a dull black finish, is our choice for baking cakes, pies, cookies, breads and the like. Pans with release surfaces that are not a coating and therefore will not wear off are excellent for these foods. For oven "frying," too, choose a shallow stainless steel pan.

Porcelain ware or enamel-coated steel are fine for covered roasting pans used for braising or pot roasting meats, or for any food that requires long, slow moist cooking at a bare simmer. Close-fitting covers are a must!

Some imported or handmade pottery baking dishes contain harmful chemicals that are released into the food contained in them. We are wary of this material.

We use a well-seasoned cast iron frying pan for oven omelets and upside-down cakes, two foods that might stick in a round pan of lighter metal. This is the kind of pan that gets better with age. The longer you own it, the more that seasoned surface works for you. Also, you become rather fond of it.

Which brings us to our last point. In general, we find that a beloved old pan, not beautiful perhaps, but predictable and efficient, is a friend to be trusted and usually better than any newfangled item on the market.

Company's Coming!

A dinner party is supposed to be a pleasure for all, and the purpose of this chapter is to help make your dinner parties more fun for you with menus and recipes that are memorable for the guests without being tension-producing for the cook. All can be prepared with little last-minute fussing, but timing is of the essence in whole-oven cooking. Be prepared to keep an eye on your watch and an ear out for the timer bell in the kitchen. (That's better than having to *be* out in the kitchen, now isn't it?)

We like to do as much of the work as possible in advance. Some of the menus in this chapter are even cooked in advance and simply reheated later (also in the oven) which is a special boon when company is expected after you've had a full work day.

Do make a list of every detail: shopping needs, menu, guests—and, after the party, keep it on hand for future reference, if only to prevent your serving the same dishes to the same people at a later date. Organization is probably the single most important ingredient in every successful dinner party.

Not only the cooking, but many other details of dinner party preparation can be checked off your list in advance. If you are serving drinks, have the bar area stocked and ready. Don't forget to have plenty of ice cubes emptied out of their trays, waiting in a plastic container in the freezer, and the trays refilled. Get coffee-making equipment all set to turn on when needed, and set out cups, saucers, sugar bowl, dessert plates, and utensils on a side table, too. Fill the cream pitcher, and put it in the refrigerator.

If you're naturally artistic, a beautifully decorated table adds to the joys of fine dining. Even if you're all thumbs, you can aspire to a simple floral centerpiece and attractive table settings. In any case, all this can and should be done well in advance. Keep centerpieces and other decorations low so as not to inhibit the free flow of dinner conversation.

Buffets are casual and practical, but sit-down dinners are comfortable. Consider not only the number of people you wish to feed but also their age and dexterity is deciding between these two options. If buffet is your choice, select a menu that can be served all on one plate and eaten with the fork alone, to cut down on the number of things a guest will have to hold.

It is in preparing company dinners that an oven is most liable to be crowded, so it is quite important that you assemble the casseroles and baking dishes you plan to use, and check to see that they will fit into the oven as you intend, with the shelves adjusted as needed. It is much easier to work this out with the empty dishes in a cold oven when you have plenty of time.

Whenever possible, use deep rather than shallow casseroles of the same capacity. Eliminating the rack under roasting meats also saves space and usually doesn't make any difference in the results of the dish.

On the chance of an unexpected guest (or one with an unexpectedly large appetite), we don't like to count any food too closely. There's always a little extra in the kitchen which, if unneeded, will provide good lunches for the cook.

If you know your guests' needs and preferences, it does make it easier to choose a menu. We always try to cater to those idiosyncrasies insofar as practical, diligently trying not to serve meat to vegetarians, strawberries to the allergic, carrot soufflé to carrot-haters, escargot to the unadventurous, and cream puffs to dieters. When the number of guests precludes full consideration of individual preference, offer sufficient choice so that no one will go hungry if he skips one dish. A filling side dish of ample proportions is helpful in this regard.

We believe it is cruel to expect guests to drink and nibble for over an hour before dinner and still remain affable, mannerly, and politely hungry. The only thing worse is over an hour's drinking *without* nibbles. (But remember that appetizers should whet not satiate the taste buds!) Using the timed menus in this chapter, dinner can be expected to be ready according to your schedule. If one guest is detained, you are not obligated to hold dinner beyond a reasonable time, in consideration of your other guests.

Avoid over-crowding serving dishes in presenting your dinner, and make full use of color-contrasting garnishes to enhance its appearance. If you want some ideas for garnishes, our best recommendation is to study the Japanese presentation of food—simple, bold, and colorful. They are masters of the art!

Most of all, enjoy yourself at your own dinner parties, and give your guests the pleasure of a relaxed hostess as well as a superb dinner!

CHICKEN BREASTS WITH RICOTTA

A relaxed dinner for six to eight with one of the world's easiest pies for dessert.

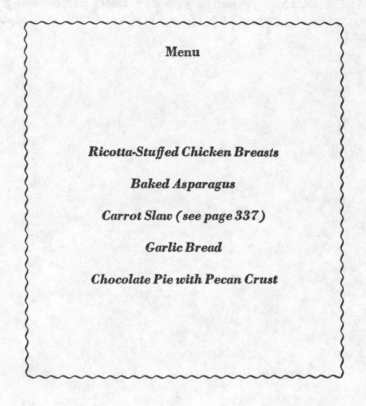

Menu

Ricotta-Stuffed Chicken Breasts

Baked Asparagus

Carrot Slaw (see page 337)

Garlic Bread

Chocolate Pie with Pecan Crust

Total Cooking Time: 1 hour

Plan of Action

Heat oven to 325° F. Place chicken on lower shelf, pie on top shelf. Cook them for 35 minutes. Remove pie; add asparagus, placing it on lower shelf beside chicken. Continue cooking for 25 minutes, a total time of 1 hour for the chicken. During the last 15 minutes, bake garlic bread on the top shelf of the oven.

Ricotta-Stuffed Chicken Breasts

1-pound container ricotta cheese
¼ cup grated Parmesan cheese
2 tablespoons minced fresh flat parsley
¼ teaspoon salt
¼ teaspoon white pepper
4 whole chicken breasts (8 halves)
Salt and pepper
Olive oil
2 cups seasoned bread crumbs (see page 361),
  or butter cracker crumbs
Paprika

Mix together cheeses, parsley, ¼ teaspoon salt, and white pepper. If not already cut, cut whole chicken breasts in half, but leave the skin on. Prepare pockets in chicken by pushing your fingers between skin and flesh. Stuff each pocket with ¼ cup of the cheese mixture. Lay the chicken breasts in an oiled baking pan, skin side up. Salt and pepper the breasts, and drizzle olive oil on top. Sprinkle them with crumbs and paprika. Bake for 1 hour at 325° F.

Baked Asparagus

2½ to 3 pounds fresh asparagus
¼ cup (½ stick) butter
Salt and pepper

Trim off tough, woody ends of asparagus. Lay the stalks in a large sheet of foil, and dot them with pieces of butter. Seal the foil into an airtight package, and place the package on a baking sheet. Bake the asparagus in a 325° F. oven for 25 minutes. (Squeeze a stalk through the foil to test if it is tender.) Carefully transfer asparagus and melted butter to a warm serving dish. Season the vegetable with salt and pepper.

Garlic Bread

½ cup (1 stick) butter, melted
1 clove garlic
1 large loaf Italian or French bread

Press the garlic clove through a garlic press into butter. Cut bread in half lengthwise, and spread the cut side with the butter. Bake for 15 minutes in a 325° F. oven.

Note: If making this recipe at another time, the bread can be baked at 400° F. for 10 minutes. In this case, a lower temperature is used for the convenience of the menu.

Chocolate Pie with Pecan Crust

½ cup (1 stick) butter
2 ounces unsweetened chocolate
¾ cup pecans
3 eggs
2 tablespoons milk
1 teaspoon vanilla
½ cup granulated sugar
½ cup brown sugar
2 tablespoons all-purpose flour
6 or 8 pecan halves

Melt butter and chocolate together, and cool them slightly. (This can be done in the oven, while it is heating, or in the top of a double boiler over hot water.) In a blender or processor fitted with steel blade, grind the ¾ cup pecans. Generously butter a 9-inch pie pan, and pat the nuts over the bottom and sides of the pan. In a blender or processor, blend eggs, milk, vanilla, sugars, and flour. Blend in butter and chocolate. Pour the filling into the pie shell. Bake in a 325° F. oven for 35 minutes or until the filling is set at the center. Garnish with pecan halves. Serve at room temperature.

ROAST CHICKEN WITH APPLES

A real fruit stuffing in this savory chicken. Serves six.

Menu

Roast Chicken with Apple-Pecan Stuffing

Acorn Squash Filled with Peas

Spinach-Bacon Salad (see page 344)

*Steamed Chocolate Fudge Pudding
with Coffee Cream*

Total Cooking Time: 3 hours and 15 minutes

Plan of Action

Coffee cream and spinach for salad can be prepared in advance.

Heat oven to 350° F. Steam pudding on lower shelf for 30 minutes. Place chicken beside pudding. Baste chicken occasionally while it is cooking. Continue baking 1½ hours longer. Remove pudding, and place squash beside chicken. Continue baking for 1 hour. Remove chicken and squash. Add peas to squash cavities, and cook them for 15 minutes while chicken is resting.

Roast Chicken with Apple-Pecan Stuffing

2 cups thin apple slices, closely packed
1 cup pecan meats
¼ cup (½ stick) butter, melted
2 tablespoons sherry
1 tablespoon sugar
¼ teaspoon salt
¼ teaspoon ground thyme, divided
5 to 6 pound roasting chicken
Additional butter
Salt and pepper

Mix together apples, pecans, melted butter, sherry, sugar, and ¼ teaspoon salt to make stuffing. Salt the chicken cavity, and sprinkle it with ⅛ teaspoon thyme. Spoon in stuffing. Place the chicken in an oiled baking pan just big enough to accommodate it without crowding. Tuck wings under, and tie legs together. Rub the chicken skin with butter, sprinkle it with the remaining ⅛ teaspoon thyme, salt, and pepper. Bake the chicken in a 350° F. oven, basting occasionally with additional butter, melted, or pan juices, for 2½ hours or until the leg meat shrinks away from the bone and juices run clear not pink when thigh is pierced with a fork. Remove trussing string. Let chicken rest for 15 minutes before carving.

Note: Firm, fresh pear slices can be substituted for all or some of the apples, if desired.

Acorn Squash Filled with Peas

3 acorn squash, 1 to 1¼ pounds each
Salt
1 small onion, chopped
6 tablespoons butter, divided
1 16-ounce bag frozen peas

Cut the squash in half lengthwise, and scoop out the seeds. Place squash, cut side up, in a roasting pan, and fill the pan to the depth of 1 inch with water. Salt squash, and place a pat of butter (about ½ tablespoon) in each cavity. Divide onion between squash halves. Bake for 1 hour in a 350° F. oven or until tender. If water dries out of squash pan during cooking time, add more. Remove squash from oven. Spoon peas into each cavity, and stir them into juices. (The peas separate quite readily while frozen. Put unused peas back into freezer, tightly closing bag.) Place a pat of the remaining butter on each. Cover the squash quite loosely with a sheet of foil. Bake them for 15 minutes more, or until peas are just tender.

Steamed Chocolate Fudge Pudding with Coffee Cream

3 ounces unsweetened chocolate
⅓ cup butter
1 cup sugar
2 eggs, room temperature
⅔ cup milk, room temperature
2 teaspoons vanilla
2 cups all-purpose flour
3 teaspoons baking powder
½ teaspoon salt
½ cup chocolate chips
Coffee Cream (recipe follows)

Melt unsweetened chocolate and butter in a small heavy casserole in the oven while heating it to 350° F. Generously butter two empty, well washed 1-pound coffee cans. Scrape chocolate-butter mixture into the small bowl of an electric mixer. Beat in sugar, then eggs, one at a time, then milk and vanilla. Remove from mixer. Stir flour to lighten it before measuring. Add flour, baking powder, and salt to liquid ingredients, and stir with a spoon until well blended, but don't overbeat. Fold in chocolate chips. Divide batter between coffee-can molds. Make a dome-shaped lid for the mold out of foil, and tie it in place with twine. Place the molds in a casserole of the same height. Half-fill the casserole with boiling water, but don't add enough to make the molds tip or float. Bake the puddings for 1½ hours. Cool in cans for 10 minutes. Remove with a spatula. (If you have trouble removing pudding, you can always open the bottom end of can with a can opener.) Serve at room temperature with cold coffee cream.

Coffee Cream: Whip ½-pint heavy cream until stiff. Beat in 1 tablespoon sugar and 1 teaspoon instant (not freeze-dried) coffee.

FRUITED CORNISH HENS

Fruit sauce provides the garnish and the glaze for these festive little birds. Buy small ones (under one pound each) so that you can realistically serve each person a whole bird. This menu serves six.

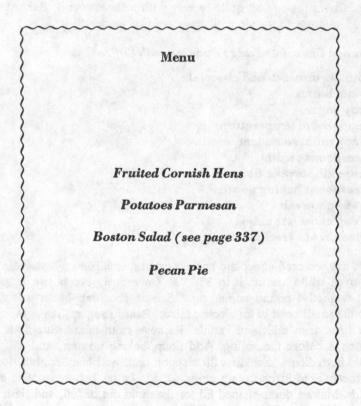

Menu

Fruited Cornish Hens

Potatoes Parmesan

Boston Salad (see page 337)

Pecan Pie

Total Cooking Time: 1 hour and 10 minutes

Plan of Action

Preheat oven to 450° F. Make fruit sauce and keep it warm. Bake the pie on the top shelf of the oven for 10 minutes. Reduce heat to 325°

F. Place birds on lower shelf, potatoes on top. After 30 minutes, remove pie. Baste birds occasionally, and continue cooking birds and potatoes for 30 minutes more, until birds are cooked through and potatoes are tender. Toss salad when ready to serve. Glaze and garnish birds with fruit sauce.

Fruited Cornish Hens

6 **Cornish hens, ¾ to 1 pound each**
Salt
6 **tablespoons butter**
1 **teaspoon dried rosemary or 6 sprigs fresh rosemary**
1 **teaspoon dried thyme or 6 sprigs fresh thyme**
1 **teaspoon ground cloves**
3 **small onions, halved**
3 **tablespoons butter, melted**
6 **ounces chicken fat**
1 **teaspoon paprika**
Blender Blond Cumberland Sauce with Fruit (see page 354)

Rinse and drain hens. Salt each cavity, and place in each 1 tablespoon butter and a pinch of rosemary, thyme, and cloves. Add half an onion. Tuck in wings, and tie the legs together with kitchen twine. Place the birds in a shallow roasting pan, and brush them with melted butter. Cut the chicken fat into 6 pieces, flatten each piece, and lay the chicken fat over the breastbones of the birds. Sprinkle birds with paprika and additional salt. Roast them for 1 hour at 325° F., basting occasionally with pan juices, or until they are cooked through. Remove twine. Pour the sauce over and around birds on platter as a glaze and garnish.

Note: If you buy larger birds, extend cooking time to 1 hour and 15 to 30 minutes. If you wish, you may serve a half bird to each person.

Potatoes Parmesan

2 pounds (6 medium-large) potatoes
2½ cups half-and-half
½ cup grated Parmesan cheese
1 tablespoon flour
1 teaspoon salt
Several dashes of white pepper
1 cup seasoned crumbs (see page 361)
Paprika

Peel and slice potatoes into very thin slices. Put them in a large bowl with half-and-half, cheese, flour, salt, and pepper; mix thoroughly. Spoon the mixture into a buttered 2-quart casserole. Top with crumbs and a sprinkling of paprika. Bake for 1 hour at 325° F. or until all liquid is absorbed and potatoes are tender.

Pecan Pie

¼ cup (½ stick) butter, softened
¾ cup sugar
1 teaspoon vanilla
3 eggs, beaten
1 cup dark corn syrup
1½ cups pecan meats (if possible, use halves)
Pastry for single crust 9-inch pie (see page 359)

Cream butter and sugar. Gradually add the next 3 ingredients. Sprinkle pecan meats in unbaked 9-inch pie shell. Pour the filling over all. Bake on the top shelf of a preheated 450° F. oven for 10 minutes. Reduce heat to 350° F., and continue cooking pie for 30 to 35 minutes or until set. A table knife inserted 1 inch from the center should come out clean. Cool the pie on a wire rack.

VEAL IN CREAM

Prepare the sauce for the veal as soon as you have mixed the cake, to minimize your time in the kitchen. (The sauce can be kept warm over hot water in a double boiler.) This menu serves six.

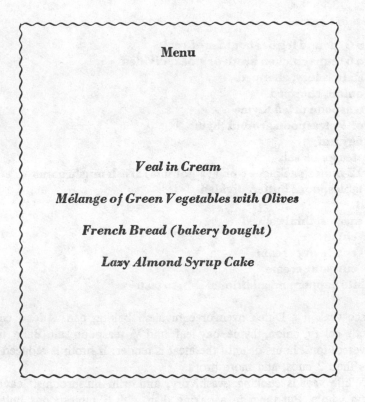

Menu

Veal in Cream

Mélange of Green Vegetables with Olives

French Bread (bakery bought)

Lazy Almond Syrup Cake

Total Cooking Time: 2 hours and 30 minutes

Plan of Action

Bake veal at 300° F. for 2 hours. During this time, brown mushrooms in a separate baking dish in oven for 20 minutes. Remove and reserve mushrooms. After 2 hours, drain veal juices. Reserve 2 cups juice for the sauce. Raise oven temperature to 350° F. Add carrots, mushrooms, and 1 cup juice to the veal and return it to the oven. At the same time, place vegetable casserole and cake on top shelf to bake 30 minutes. Prepare veal sauce and cake topping, and add topping to cake while it is warm.

Veal in Cream

5 to 6   pound leg or shoulder of veal
5 to 6   cups chicken broth or stock, divided
1   stalk celery, chopped
1   onion, chopped
1   teaspoon dried thyme
   or ¼ teaspoon ground thyme
1   bay leaf
½   teaspoon salt
2   12-ounce packages (or 1½ pounds) fresh mushrooms
7   tablespoons butter, divided
Salt
3   carrots, thinly sliced
¼   cup flour
½   cup heavy cream
½   cup sour cream
White pepper and additional salt, to taste

Place veal in a Dutch oven or equivalent baking pan. Add 4 cups broth, celery, onion, thyme, bay leaf, and ½ teaspoon salt. Bake, uncovered, for 2 hours or until the meat is tender. If broth is reduced to less than 2 cups, add more broth.

While veal is cooking, wash, dry, and trim mushrooms, leaving them whole. Put them in a baking dish with 3 tablespoons butter, and let them brown in the oven for about 20 minutes. Remove the mushrooms, and salt them lightly.

After the veal has cooked for 2 hours, remove the pan from the oven. Pour out the juices and strain them; reserve 2 cups of this stock for the sauce. Put the veal back in the oven, adding 1 cup broth, carrots, and mushrooms. Cover the pan, raise temperature to 350° F. and bake for 30 minutes longer or until carrots are tender.

To make the sauce, melt the remaining 4 tablespoons butter in a saucepan. Stir in flour, and cook this roux over low heat, stirring constantly, for 2 minutes. Add the 2 cups hot reserved stock all at once, whisking until thick and smooth. Cook 5 minutes over lowest heat, stirring occasionally. Remove from heat. Whisk in heavy cream and sour cream until smooth. If necessary, strain sauce. Add white pepper and additional salt, to taste. Keep the sauce warm over hot water in a double boiler.

To serve, pour some of the sauce over the veal, and pass the rest in a gravy boat.

Note: A less expensive, homelier version of this dish can be made using about 8 pounds of veal breast.

Mélange of Green Vegetables with Olives

1   pound fresh green beans, trimmed and cut into thirds
2   medium zucchini, scrubbed and sliced ¼ inch thick
1   green pepper, seeded and chopped
1   stalk celery, sliced thin
2   scallions with green tops, chopped
2   tablespoons chopped fresh parsley
½   cup small stuffed green olives
2   tablespoons olive oil
½   cup chicken broth or stock
½   teaspoon salt

Combine all ingredients in a 2-quart casserole. Cover and cook at 350° F. for 30 minutes or until vegetables are tender.

Lazy Almond Syrup Cake

2 eggs
½ teaspoon almond extract
1 cup sugar
1½ cups all-purpose flour
1 teaspoon baking powder
¼ teaspoon salt
½ cup buttermilk
   or ½ cup milk (see page 362)
1 tablespoon butter, melted
⅓ cup apple jelly
2 tablespoons butter
¼ cup Amaretto (or other almond-flavored liqueur)
1 cup blanched, lightly toasted almonds (see page 361)

Beat eggs and almond extract in the small bowl of an electric mixer until light and thick. Continue beating, and gradually add sugar. Blend well. Stir flour to lighten it before measuring. Mix together flour, baking powder, and salt. Stir these ingredients into the egg mixture on low speed or by hand. Add buttermilk or soured milk and melted butter. Pour the batter into a buttered, floured 9-inch square pan. Bake 25 to 30 minutes in a preheated 350° F. oven or until a cake tester inserted in the center comes out dry. Remove cake from oven and cool it in the pan on a wire rack. In a small saucepan, heat jelly with remaining 2 tablespoons butter until the mixture boils. Remove from heat. Add Amaretto and almonds. Pour the syrup evenly over the cake. Serve the cake from the pan.

STUFFED, BRAISED VEAL WITH TOMATOES

Easy-to-make French bread loaves accompany this elegant dinner for six.

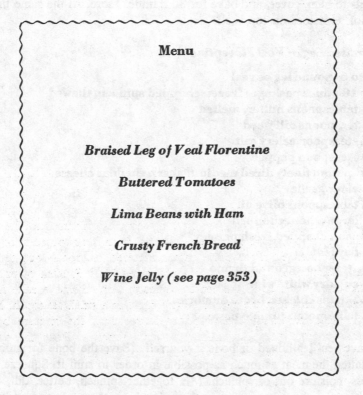

Menu

Braised Leg of Veal Florentine

Buttered Tomatoes

Lima Beans with Ham

Crusty French Bread

Wine Jelly (see page 353)

Total Cooking Time: about 2 hours and 25 minutes

Plan of Action

Make jelly in advance and chill it to set. Prepare bread and allow it to rise.

Preheat oven to 400° F. Bake veal with onion, uncovered, on

lower shelf for 15 minutes. Add liquids to veal, and place bread on top shelf. Bake 30 minutes or until bread is golden brown. Remove bread, and cover braising pan. Reduce heat to 350° F., and continue cooking veal for 1 hour. Place casserole with ham (for lima beans) beside veal to oven-sauté for 10 minutes. Add the remaining ingredients to ham, cover, and bake for 30 minutes more. At the same time, cook tomatoes on top shelf.

Braised Leg of Veal Florentine

5 to 6 pound leg of veal
2 10-ounce packages frozen chopped spinach, thawed
2 tablespoons butter, melted
2 teaspoons dill weed
½ teaspoon celery salt
¼ teaspoon pepper
¼ pound finely diced medium-sharp cheddar cheese
1 clove garlic
2 tablespoons olive oil
1 large onion, chopped
¼ cup chopped fresh parsley
1 bay leaf
¼ teaspoon ground thyme
1 cup dry white wine
2½ cups chicken broth or stock
2 tablespoons tomato paste

Have veal leg boned or bone it yourself. (Save the bone for stock.) Flatten the meat as much as possible in order to stuff it. Squeeze excess moisture out of spinach. Mix together spinach, butter, dill, celery salt, and pepper. Arrange the spinach on the veal, and sprinkle the stuffing with the diced cheese. Roll up veal, and tie it in several places with twine. Cut the garlic in half, and insert the halves into 2 slits in the veal. Place the veal in a Dutch oven, pour the oil over it, and add the onion to the pan. Bake, uncovered, for 15 minutes in a 400° F. oven. Add all the remaining ingredients to the pan, and continue cooking, uncovered, for 30 minutes. Cover veal, reduce heat to 350° F., and braise the meat for 1½ hours or until tender. Remove twine, garlic, and bay leaf. Save the pan juices for soup or gravy. Let the stuffed veal rest for 10 minutes before slicing. Garnish the platter with buttered tomatoes. (Recipe follows.)

Buttered Tomatoes

6 large ripe but firm tomatoes
3 tablespoons butter
Salt and pepper
2 tablespoons minced fresh chives or scallion tops

Submerge the tomatoes in boiling water for 1 minute. Peel off skins. Place the tomatoes in a baking dish that will just hold them. Dot them with butter. Sprinkle with salt and pepper. Bake for 30 minutes in a 350° F. oven. Use the tomatoes to garnish braised veal. Sprinkle them with minced chives or scallions before serving.

Lima Beans with Ham

1 cup chopped ham
2 tablespoons butter
2 10-ounce packages frozen lima beans, thawed just to separate
⅓ cup water
Freshly ground black pepper

In a 3-quart casserole, oven-sauté ham in butter for 10 minutes in a 350° F. oven. Add lima beans, water, and pepper. Cover and cook for 30 minutes or until tender.

Crusty French Bread

1½ packages dry yeast
1 teaspoon sugar
1½ cups very warm water
3½ cups Pillsbury bread flour,
    or other high gluten flour
1½ teaspoons salt

Dissolve yeast and sugar in water. Let the mixture stand in a warm place for 10 minutes. Yeast should bubble up to prove that it is active. Stir in flour and salt to form dough. Knead the dough on a floured surface for 10 minutes (if using a processor, process for 20 seconds). Divide the dough in thirds, form each into a loaf. Oil a baking sheet, and sprinkle it with a little cornmeal or bread crumbs. Make a slash in four places on the top of each loaf (use a very sharp knife, or even a single-edged razor blade). Place the loaves on the sheet, 2 inches apart, and allow them to rise until doubled, about 1 hour. Place the loaves on the top shelf of a 400° F. oven, and bake for 30 minutes or until they are golden brown and sound hollow when tapped on the bottom.

Note: Steam from the braising veal will help make the loaves crusty. If using this recipe at another time, put a pan of hot water below the loaves to achieve the same effect.

Let the loaves cool to room temperature on wire racks while finishing veal. Serve each person a half loaf wrapped in a napkin with plenty of sweet butter on the side.

EASY EYE ROAST OF BEEF

A simple, dependable dinner for six that cooks in an hour. The mousse, which makes this menu festive and interesting, could also be the feature of a meatless meal on another occasion.

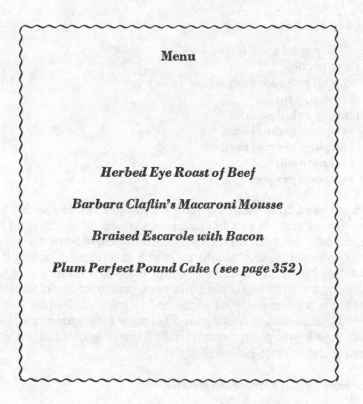

Menu

Herbed Eye Roast of Beef

Barbara Claflin's Macaroni Mousse

Braised Escarole with Bacon

Plum Perfect Pound Cake (see page 352)

Total Cooking Time: 1 hour

Plan of Action

Heat oven to 450° F. Place roast and bacon on lower shelf. Cook for 10 minutes. Reduce heat to 350° F. Place mousse on top shelf.

Remove bacon when it is brown (20 to 25 minutes total cooking time) and finish escarole casserole with it. Place escarole on lower shelf. For medium rare, the roast will take 1 hour; the mousse cooks in 45 to 50 minutes or until set at the center; the escarole will be braised in 30 minutes.

Dessert may be prepared in advance and refrigerated.

Herbed Eye Roast of Beef

3 to 3½ pound eye roast of beef
1 clove garlic
¼ cup all-purpose flour
1 teaspoon paprika
1 teaspoon chili powder
¼ teaspoon ground sage
¼ teaspoon ground thyme
½ teaspoon salt
¼ teaspoon pepper

Remove roast from the refrigerator 30 minutes before cooking. Cut the clove of garlic in half and insert it under the fat on the roast in 2 places. Mix the flour with all the remaining ingredients on a large sheet of waxed paper. Coat the roast with this mixture, patting it on all sides. Put the roast, fat side up, in a shallow roasting pan, one that is just a little bigger than the roast, and bake it on the lower shelf of a preheated 450° F. oven for 10 minutes. Reduce heat to 350° F., and continue cooking for 50 minutes longer for medium rare (less time if you prefer really rare!). Remove garlic. Let the roast stand a few minutes before slicing it.

Barbara Claflin's Macaroni Mousse

2 cups cooked elbow macaroni
2 cups soft bread crumbs
2 tomatoes, seeded and chopped
1 onion, grated or chopped fine
3 cups grated sharp cheddar cheese, loosely packed
2 tablespoons minced fresh parsley
5 large eggs
1 teaspoon salt

¼ teaspoon pepper
3 cups scalded milk
¼ cup (½ stick) butter, melted, slightly cooled

Use an oblong casserole about 11-inch by 8-inch that will fit into a larger roasting pan.

Mix together macaroni, crumbs, tomatoes, onion, cheese, and parsley in casserole. Beat eggs with salt and pepper. *Gradually* add scalded milk to eggs while continuing to beat with whisk or hand-held electric mixer. Add butter. Pour this mixture over the casserole ingredients. Place the baking dishes, one inside the other, on the top shelf of a 350° F. oven. Pour hot water into the outer pan. Cook for 40 to 50 minutes or until the mousse is set at the center.

Braised Escarole with Bacon

1 head escarole
3 slices bacon
½ cup water
1 chicken bouillon cube
Freshly ground black pepper to taste

Wash escarole well. Tear leaves into pieces. Cut the bacon slices in half and place in a 3-quart casserole or baking dish (with cover) and cook, uncovered, at 450° F. for 10 minutes. Reduce heat to 350° F. and continue cooking until bacon is brown and crisp, about 20 minutes total cooking time. Remove the bacon in casserole and cool it slightly. Place escarole in the casserole with bacon and bacon fat. Add water, chicken bouillon cube, and pepper. You may have to press the escarole leaves down to fit them all into the casserole, but they will soon wilt in the cooking. Cover tightly, and braise the dish at 350° F. for 30 minutes. Include a half slice of bacon with each serving.

BEEF AND PORK IN BEER

This rustic dinner for six, which comes to us from France and Belgium, is traditionally served with beer.

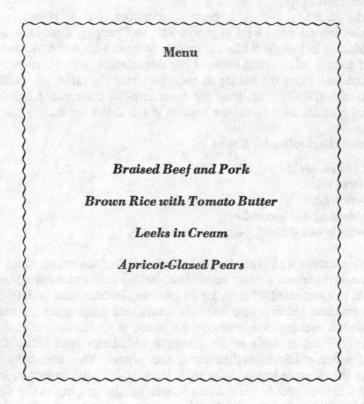

Menu

Braised Beef and Pork

Brown Rice with Tomato Butter

Leeks in Cream

Apricot-Glazed Pears

Total Cooking Time: 2½ hours

Plan of Action

Oven-sauté onion and garlic for stew at 375° F. until sizzling. Add floured meat and bake on lower shelf, uncovered, for 15 minutes. Add the remaining ingredients, cover, and braise for 2 hours or until the meat is quite tender. After 1 hour, place rice casserole and pears on top shelf of oven. Cook leeks on lower shelf during the last 30 minutes of cooking time. Stir cream into leeks, and pour apricot sauce over drained pears.

Braised Beef and Pork

6   onions, chopped
1   clove garlic, minced
3   tablespoons salad oil
4   pounds lean beef and pork, cubed
¼   cup flour
12   ounces beer
½   cup water
1   tablespoon chopped fresh parsley
2   bay leaves
¼   teaspoon ground thyme
½   teaspoon Gravy Master
1   teaspoon salt
¼   teaspoon pepper

Heat oven to 375° F. Oven-sauté onions and garlic in oil until sizzling. Add meat and stir to coat with oil. Bake, uncovered, for 15 minutes. Add all the remaining ingredients, cover, and braise on lower shelf for 2 hours or until the meat is quite tender. Remove bay leaves.

Brown Rice with Tomato Butter

1½   cups brown rice
1   teaspoon salt
3   tablespoons butter, cut into pieces
2   tomatoes, peeled, seeded, and chopped
3¼   cups boiling water

Combine rice, salt, butter, and tomatoes in a 3-quart casserole. Cover tightly and bake on top shelf for 1 hour at 375° F. Fluff the rice with a fork before serving.

Note: If possible, use a glass casserole for cooking rice in the oven so you can see when all the water has been absorbed and the surface of the rice is "dimpled," indications that cooking is complete.

Leeks in Cream

6 leeks
½ cup beef or chicken broth
Salt and white pepper to taste
8-ounce container of sour cream, slightly warmed in saucepan
1 tablespoon minced fresh parsley

Trim ends from leeks, and cut off green tops. Slice leeks in half lengthwise, and wash them well under cold running water. Place them in a 2 or 2½-quart casserole with broth, salt, and white pepper. Cover and bake on lower shelf in a 375° F. oven for 30 minutes. Drain juice and blend it with sour cream. Spoon this mixture over the leeks. Garnish with parsley.

Apricot-Glazed Pears

6 large ripe but firm fresh pears
2 cups apple juice
1 teaspoon vanilla
1 tablespoon butter
1 cinnamon stick
12-ounce jar apricot preserves

Peel pears, but leave them whole with stems on. Place them in a casserole that will hold them snugly. Add the remaining ingredients, except apricot preserves. Cover and bake the pears for 1 hour on the top shelf of a 375° F. oven. Remove pears (drained) to 6 dessert dishes. Heat apricot preserves to melt them, and top each of the pears with some of this sauce. Serve pears at room temperature.

A REHEATABLE ROAST BEEF DINNER

Specifically planned for two-stage cooking, this dinner may be cooked in the morning, then reheated when ready to serve. Serves six to eight people.

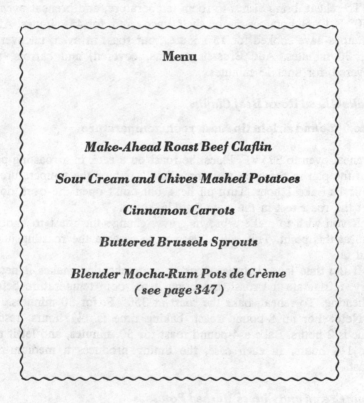

Menu

Make-Ahead Roast Beef Claflin

Sour Cream and Chives Mashed Potatoes

Cinnamon Carrots

Buttered Brussels Sprouts

Blender Mocha-Rum Pots de Crème
(see page 347)

Total Cooking Time: earlier in day—1 hour and 50 minutes
to reheat—45 minutes

Plan of Action

Preheat oven to 375° F. Cook potatoes and Brussels sprouts for 10 minutes, lower shelf. Place carrots on top shelf, and continue cooking all dishes for 40 minutes. Remove all dishes from the oven. Drain potatoes.

Place room-temperature roast in the oven on lower shelf and immediately reduce heat to 350° F. Bake 1 hour. Turn off heat, but don't open oven door. Leave roast in the oven for 1½ hours. Finish preparing vegetables. Prepare and chill the *pots de crème*.

To reheat, bring dishes to room temperature, and preheat oven to 350° F. Cook potatoes on top shelf, uncovered, for 45 minutes. After potatoes have cooked for 15 minutes, put roast in oven, uncovered, for 30 minutes. Add Brussels sprouts, covered, and carrots, uncovered, for final 15 minutes.

Make-Ahead Roast Beef Claflin

5 to 6 pound sirloin tip roast, room temperature

Preheat oven to 375° F. Place the roast on a rack in a roasting pan. Put the pan in the oven and immediately reduce the temperature to 350° F. Bake 1 hour. Turn off heat, but don't open the oven door! Let the roast rest in the oven for 1½ hours.

If you wish to make a brown gravy, change the roast to another pan at this point. This will allow you to reserve the roasting juices and fat.

If the time lapse between cooking and reheating makes it necessary, refrigerate the roast, but bring it to room temperature before reheating. To reheat, bake the roast at 350° F. for 30 minutes.

Note: For an 8-pound roast, baking time is 1½ hours, resting time is 2 hours. Bake a 4-pound roast for 50 minutes, and let it rest for 1½ hours. In each case, the timing produces a medium-rare roast.

Sour Cream and Chives Mashed Potatoes

3 pounds (9 medium or medium-large) potatoes
2 cups water
½ teaspoon salt
1 teaspoon vinegar
8-ounce (1 cup) container sour cream
3-ounce package cream cheese, softened
1½ teaspoons salt

White pepper
¼ cup snipped chives or 2 scallion tops, minced
¼ to ½ cup milk
3 tablespoons bread crumbs
2 tablespoons grated Parmesan cheese
2 tablespoons butter
Paprika

Peel and cut potatoes into thirds (roughly, the size of an egg). Place them in a 2-quart casserole with water, ½ teaspoon salt, and vinegar. (Vinegar keeps potatoes from darkening.) Cover tightly and bake in a 375° F. oven for 50 minutes, or until just tender. *Drain immediately.*

Rice or mash potatoes. Cream together sour cream, cream cheese, 1½ teaspoons salt, a few generous dashes of white pepper, and chives or scallions. Beat this mixture into the potatoes. Add enough milk to whip potatoes until they are fluffy, either by hand or with an electric mixer. Butter the 2-quart casserole, and spoon the potatoes into it lightly. Sprinkle with crumbs and Parmesan cheese. Dot with butter, and sprinkle with paprika.

If refrigerated, bring the casserole to room temperature before reheating. To reheat, place on top shelf of a 350° F. oven, uncovered, for 45 minutes.

Cinnamon Carrots

2 pounds carrots
½ cup water
2 tablespoons butter
½ teaspoon salt
¼ teaspoon cinnamon
2 tablespoons honey or light corn syrup
2 tablespoons lemon juice

Scrape carrots and cut into ½-inch diagonal slices. Place them in a 2-quart casserole with water, butter, and salt. Cover, and bake 40 minutes in a 375° F. oven. Remove from oven and stir in cinnamon, honey or corn syrup and lemon juice.

To reheat, bake, uncovered, for 15 minutes at 350° F.

Buttered Brussels Sprouts

1½ pounds fresh Brussels sprouts
¾ cup water
½ teaspoon salt
½ teaspoon sugar
3 tablespoons butter

Place all ingredients in a 2-quart casserole. Cover, and bake 50 minutes at 375° F.

To reheat, bake 15 minutes, covered, in a 350° F. oven.

Note: If frozen Brussels sprouts are substituted, use 2 10-ounce packages. Do not thaw before cooking. Reduce baking time by 10 minutes.

PORK CHOPS AND SWEET POTATOES

This dinner for six is a perfect choice for fall when the main ingredients are seasonably plentiful and inexpensive.

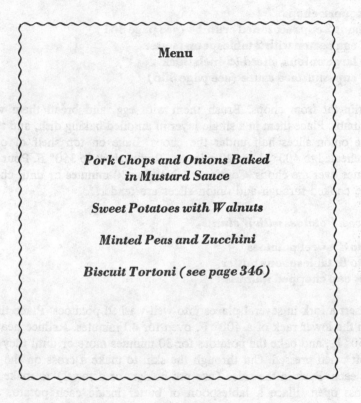

Menu

*Pork Chops and Onions Baked
in Mustard Sauce*

Sweet Potatoes with Walnuts

Minted Peas and Zucchini

Biscuit Tortoni (see page 346)

Total Cooking Time: 1 hour and 10 minutes

Plan of Action

Prepare the tortoni in advance. Keep them frozen until ready to serve.
Preheat oven to 400° F. Place the potatoes on lower shelf. Bake
20 minutes. Place pork chops (without sauce) on top shelf. Cook 20

minutes. Add sauce to chops, and place peas and zucchini casserole on lower shelf beside potatoes. Reduce heat to 350° F. Cook everything 30 minutes longer. Add lemon juice to peas and zucchini.

Pork Chops and Onions Baked in Mustard Sauce

12 pork chops
About 2 cups seasoned crumbs (see page 361)
1 egg beaten with 2 tablespoons water
4 large onions, sliced ½-inch thick
3 cups mustard sauce (see page 356)

Trim fat from chops. Brush them with egg, and bread them with crumbs. Place them in a single layer in an oiled baking dish, and tuck the onion slices half under the chops. Bake on top shelf of oven preheated to 400° F. for 20 minutes. Reduce heat to 350° F. Pour the sauce over the chops. Continue baking for 30 minutes or until chops are cooked through and onion slices are tender.

Sweet Potatoes with Walnuts

6 to 8 sweet potatoes
6 to 8 tablespoons butter
½ cup chopped walnuts

Insert a fork in several places into well-washed potatoes. Place them on the lower rack of a 400° F. oven for 40 minutes. Reduce heat to 350° F., and bake the potatoes for 30 minutes more or until they are soft when pressed. Cut through the skin to make a cross on the top of each. Push in the sides (use pot holders or a towel) to make the cross open. Place a tablespoon of butter inside each potato, and sprinkle each pat of butter with a tablespoon of chopped walnuts.

Minted Peas and Zucchini

2 10-ounce packages frozen peas, thawed to separate
2 small or 1 large zucchini, scrubbed and diced
½ cup water
3 tablespoons butter
2 teaspoons sugar

¼ **teaspoon dried mint**
½ **teaspoon salt**
¼ **teaspoon pepper**
Juice of ½ lemon

Combine all ingredients except lemon juice in a 2-quart casserole. Cover and bake the vegetables for 30 minutes in a 350° F. oven. Toss the peas and zucchini with lemon juice before serving.

A MAKE-AHEAD ROAST PORK EN CROÛTE

Sometimes it's more convenient to do the major portion of the cooking a day ahead, as with this menu. Then you can turn out this dazzling dinner for six straight from the refrigerator in about 30 minutes whenever you are ready to serve. The dessert cooks during the dinner hour.

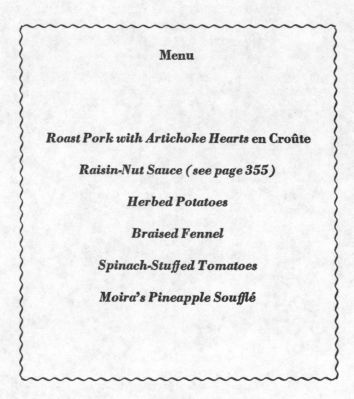

Menu

Roast Pork with Artichoke Hearts **en Croûte**

Raisin-Nut Sauce (see page 355)

Herbed Potatoes

Braised Fennel

Spinach-Stuffed Tomatoes

Moira's Pineapple Soufflé

Total Cooking Time: day before—2 hours
to reheat—30 minutes
to cook soufflé during dinner—40 to 50
minutes

Plan of Action

Heat oven to 375° F. Bake pork, uncovered, for 2 hours or until a meat thermometer inserted in the center registers 180° F. During this time, bake potatoes, uncovered, on top shelf for 1 hour or until tender. Braise fennel for 30 minutes. Cool and refrigerate everything. Defrost spinach; make and refrigerate stuffed tomatoes and raisin-nut sauce.

The next day, finish preparing roast in pastry. Assemble soufflé. Preheat oven to 400° F. Place pork, uncovered, on lower shelf. Place tomatoes, uncovered, on top shelf. Bake these dishes for 10 minutes. Place fennel, covered, on lower shelf and potatoes, uncovered, on top shelf. Cook everything 20 minutes longer or until pastry is golden brown and potatoes are heated through.

While dinner is being served, reduce oven heat to 350° F., and bake soufflé for 40 to 50 minutes.

Roast Pork with Artichoke Hearts en Croûte

3½ to 4 pound boned, rolled pork roast
1 clove garlic
½ teaspoon dried rosemary
¼ teaspoon ground sage
Salt and pepper
1 7½-ounce can artichoke hearts, well-drained
1-pound package frozen puff pastry sheets
1 egg, beaten

Heat oven to 375° F. Cut garlic in half and insert into 2 small slits in the meat. Rub the meat with rosemary, sage, salt, and pepper. Roast it, uncovered, for 2 hours or until a meat thermometer inserted in the center registers 180° F. Remove garlic. If there are any strings around the roast, remove those also. Trim off skin and fat. Cool meat completely, and keep it refrigerated, covered, until ready to finish it.

Slice each artichoke heart into thirds, and dry them well with paper towels. Allow the puff pastry to thaw at room temperature for 20 minutes only. Form the 2 sheets of pastry into one square or oblong, whichever will best fit the shape of the roast. Use a little cold water where sheets must be seamed together. Lay the artichoke hearts close together on the pastry in a square at the center. Put the roast upside down on the artichokes. Enclose roast in pastry, pinch the ends together neatly and turn the package, seam side down, into an oiled shallow roasting pan that can double as a server. Use left-over pieces of pastry to decorate the package. (Place the decorations where they will do the most good; i.e., over any patched surfaces.) Make slits to allow steam to escape during baking. Brush the pastry with beaten egg. Bake the package in a preheated 400° F. oven for 25 to 30 minutes, or until it is beautifully golden brown. Let it rest a few minutes before slicing into inch-thick slices with a sharp carving knife.

Note: The pastry should still be cold to the touch when it is put into the oven.

Herbed Potatoes

2 to 2½ pounds (7 to 8) potatoes, peeled
¼ cup olive oil
1 teaspoon dried basil
½ teaspoon dried marjoram
Salt and pepper

Slice the potatoes in half lengthwise. Place them in one layer in a shallow baking dish. Pour on oil evenly. Sprinkle the potatoes with basil, marjoram, salt, and pepper. Bake them 1 hour on the top shelf of a 375° F. oven or until they are tender. Stir at least once during cooking. Loosen them carefully from the pan to keep crust intact. Potatoes can be cooled and refrigerated at this point.

Put the potatoes and their oil into a 3-quart casserole that can double as a server. (This will save space when all these dishes are being reheated at one time.) To reheat, bake for 20 minutes in a 400° F. oven. Cut one potato to be certain they are piping hot throughout.

Braised Fennel

1 large or 2 small onions, chopped
¼ cup (½ stick) butter
½ cup water
1 chicken bouillon cube

White pepper
2 bulbs fennel, trimmed of hair

Combine onion and butter in a 3-quart casserole, and oven-sauté the onion until it sizzles. Quarter the fennel bulbs and cut out the cores. Place fennel on onion, and add the remaining ingredients. Cover tightly, and braise the fennel in a 375° F. oven for 30 minutes, or until it is just tender.

To reheat, bake the dish, covered, for 20 minutes in a 400° F. oven.

Spinach-Stuffed Tomatoes

6 large ripe but firm tomatoes
10-ounce package frozen chopped spinach, completely thawed
1 cup seasoned bread crumbs (see page 361)
1 teaspoon dried dill weed
½ teaspoon salt
¼ teaspoon pepper
¼ cup (½ stick) butter melted
6 tablespoons grated Parmesan cheese

Cut the tops off the tomatoes, scoop out the seeds, and turn tomatoes upside down to drain for 15 minutes. Drain spinach well and squeeze out as much moisture as possible. Mix spinach with crumbs, dill, salt, pepper, and melted butter. Stuff the tomatoes with spinach, and place them in a non-metal baking dish that will just fit them and hold them upright. At this point, they can be refrigerated until needed.

To cook, bake the tomatoes in a preheated 400° F. oven for 25 minutes.

Moira's Pineapple Soufflé

½ cup butter, softened
1 cup sugar
4 eggs
1 20-ounce can crushed pineapple, drained
5 slices white bread, crusts removed, cubed

Cream butter until light. Gradually beat in sugar, then eggs, one at a time. Fold in pineapple, then bread. Spoon the mixture into a buttered 1½-quart soufflé dish or casserole. Bake 40 to 50 minutes on the middle shelf of a 350° F. oven or until puffed and set. Serve warm, with or without an ice cream topping.

Note: In mixing, the batter may appear to be curdled, but the cooking process will correct this.

ZESTY CREOLE DINNER

The word "gumbo" is taken from the African name for okra, the chief thickening agent of this flavorful, dark brown stew. Ladle it into soup plates, and put a generous spoonful of rice in the center of each. Serves six.

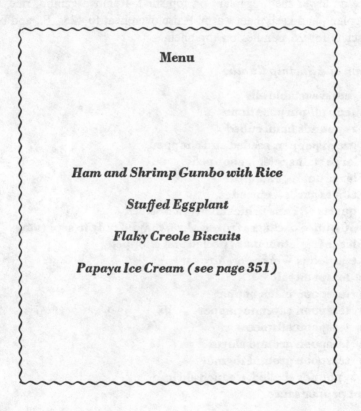

Menu

Ham and Shrimp Gumbo with Rice

Stuffed Eggplant

Flaky Creole Biscuits

Papaya Ice Cream (see page 351)

Total Cooking Time: 2 hours and 25 minutes

Plan of Action

Heat oven to 350° F. Precook the roux for gumbo for 20 minutes and the eggplant for 15 minutes. Remove and cool eggplant. Add ham and vegetables for sautéing to roux. Oven-sauté this mixture for 10 minutes. Add remaining ingredients except shrimp and hot pepper sauce, and bake the gumbo, covered, on the lower shelf in the oven. Meanwhile, stuff eggplant. After the gumbo has cooked for 1 hour, add shrimp, and bake it another 30 minutes. At the same time, bake rice on lower shelf, eggplant on top shelf. Remove gumbo, rice, and eggplant, and keep them warm. Raise oven heat to 425° F., and bake biscuits for 25 minutes on top shelf.

Ham and Shrimp Gumbo

¼ cup vegetable oil
¼ cup all-purpose flour
1½ pounds ham, cubed
1 green pepper, seeded and chopped
2 large stalks celery, chopped
1 large onion, chopped
2 cloves garlic, minced
2 quarts (8 cups) chicken broth or stock
2 10-ounce packages frozen okra, thawed only to separate
4 large fresh tomatoes, peeled and chopped
2 teaspoons Worcestershire sauce
½ teaspoon salt
¼ teaspoon black pepper
¼ teaspoon cayenne pepper
¼ teaspoon allspice
¼ teaspoon ground cloves
¼ teaspoon ground thyme
1½ pounds shelled, cleaned shrimp
Hot pepper sauce

In a Dutch oven, combine oil and flour. Let the mixture cook in a 350° F. oven until the roux is dark brown but not burned, about 20 minutes. Add ham, green pepper, celery, onion, and garlic, and oven-sauté these ingredients for 10 minutes. Stir in all the remaining ingredients except shrimp and hot pepper sauce. Cover and bake 1 hour. Add shrimp, and bake the gumbo 30 minutes longer. Serve the gumbo in soup plates with a big spoonful of white rice (recipe follows) in the center. Pass hot pepper sauce at the table.

Oven-Baked White Rice

A touch of vinegar in the cooking water keeps rice or potatoes white without changing their flavors.

1½ cups long grain, converted rice
2 tablespoons butter
1 teaspoon vinegar
¾ teaspoon salt
3 cups boiling water

In a 2-quart casserole, combine rice, butter, vinegar, and salt. Add boiling water. Immediately cover casserole, and bake it in a 350° F. oven for 30 minutes, or until all the water is absorbed and the surface of the rice is dimpled. Let stand, covered, for 5 minutes (or longer). Fluff the rice with a fork before serving.

Stuffed Eggplant

3 small eggplants
1 clove garlic, very finely minced
2 tablespoons chopped parsley
½ teaspoon salt
¼ teaspoon pepper
3 tablespoons lemon juice
1½ cups seasoned bread crumbs (see page 361)
⅓ cup olive oil
¼ pound gruyere cheese, coarsely grated

Cut the eggplants in half lengthwise. Place them, cut sides down, on an oiled baking sheet. Bake in a preheated 350° F. oven for 15 minutes or until eggplant pulp is tender enough to be scooped out. When eggplant cools enough to handle, spoon pulp into a bowl, leaving shells ¼ inch thick. Chop eggplant, and mix it with garlic, parsley, salt, pepper, lemon juice, and bread crumbs. Place the shells in a shallow casserole that will hold them in place snugly and also double as a server. Stuff eggplant shells, pour 1 tablespoon oil over each, and sprinkle cheese on top. To finish, bake eggplant for 30 minutes on the top shelf of a 350° F. oven.

Flaky Creole Biscuits

4 cups all-purpose flour
2 tablespoons baking powder
1 teaspoon baking soda
2 tablespoons sugar
⅔ cup cold butter or other shortening
About 1½ cups buttermilk
3 tablespoons butter

Stir flour to lighten it before measuring. Sift together dry ingredients. With 2 knives or a pastry blender, cut in ⅔ cup butter or shortening until the mixture resembles oatmeal. Gradually stir in enough buttermilk to form a soft but manageable dough. On a floured surface, knead the dough gently just two or three times to smooth it out. Pat the dough into a square 1 inch thick. With a floured knife, cut the dough into 12 to 16 square biscuits. Place them in a buttered baking pan, and dot the tops with the remaining 3 tablespoons butter. Bake on the top shelf of a preheated 425° F. oven for 25 minutes or until the biscuits are golden brown on top.

A DINNER PARTY FOR TWELVE

Giving a dinner party can be fun for the hostess, or it can be an exhausting experience. This menu is designed with fun in mind.

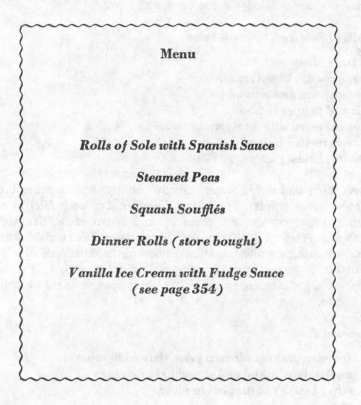

Menu

Rolls of Sole with Spanish Sauce

Steamed Peas

Squash Soufflés

Dinner Rolls (store bought)

*Vanilla Ice Cream with Fudge Sauce
(see page 354)*

Total Cooking Time: 1 hour and 10 minutes

Plan of Action

Assemble sole in advance (except for drizzling butter over top) and refrigerate, covered. Make Spanish sauce, fudge sauce, and prepare tomatoes. Cover each and refrigerate. About 1 hour and 30 minutes before serving time, prepare soufflés. Place them on bottom shelf of preheated 350° F. oven. Remove other dishes from refrigerator. When soufflés have been cooking for 30 minutes, place peas on middle shelf of oven. In another 10 minutes, add sole to middle shelf, and continue cooking for 30 minutes more. During this time, heat Spanish sauce and fudge sauce on top of stove.

Rolls of Sole with Spanish Sauce

12 sole fillets
1½ cups dry bread crumbs
⅛ teaspoon garlic powder
Salt and pepper to taste
3 eggs beaten with 3 teaspoons water
½ cup melted butter
Spanish Sauce (see page 357)

Wash fillets under cold water. Gently pat dry. Mix together bread crumbs, garlic powder, and salt and pepper. Dip each fillet in egg, then in bread crumbs, roll them up and fasten each fillet with a toothpick. Place rolls in large, shallow, buttered baking dish. Drizzle melted butter over fillets, and bake them on middle shelf of a preheated 350° F. oven for 30 minutes. Remove from baking dish to large platter, discarding excess butter. Pour Spanish sauce over them and serve.

Steamed Peas

3 10-ounce packages frozen peas, thawed to separate
2 small onions, sliced and separated into rings
½ cup (1 stick) butter, cut in pieces
½ cup water
1 teaspoon oregano
1 teaspoon salt

Combine all ingredients in a 2½-quart casserole. Cover and cook on the middle shelf of a preheated 350° F. oven for 40 minutes. Do not drain.

Squash Soufflés

5 tablespoons butter
1 medium-sized onion, chopped
5 tablespoons flour
2 teaspoons salt
2 cups milk
½ pound Swiss cheese, grated
4 large potatoes, boiled, peeled, and mashed
2 10-ounce packages winter squash, thawed
⅛ teaspoon nutmeg
⅛ teaspoon cinnamon
8 eggs, separated

Melt butter in large saucepan. Add onion and cook until transparent but not brown. Add flour to form paste. Gradually add milk, stirring constantly until mixture starts to thicken. Add cheese, and stir constantly until it has melted. Stir in potatoes, squash, nutmeg, and cinnamon. Heat through. Remove from heat. Beat egg yolks, and stir them into mixture. Beat egg whites to peak stage. Fold them into squash mixture. Pour into 2 greased 1½-quart casseroles, and bake on bottom shelf of preheated 350° F. oven for 1 hour and 10 minutes. Soufflé should be puffy when done.

FESTIVE FISH DINNER

A fresh shrimp filling redolent of garlic and lemon makes this fish dinner for four delectable fare. So easy to get ready, it's a good menu choice for weekend company or whenever you're especially busy.

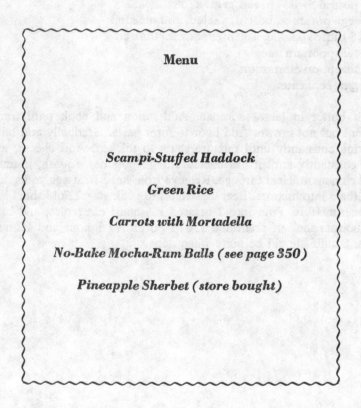

Menu

Scampi-Stuffed Haddock

Green Rice

Carrots with Mortadella

No-Bake Mocha-Rum Balls (see page 350)

Pineapple Sherbet (store bought)

Total Cooking Time: 30 minutes

Plan of Action

Make mocha-rum balls at least one day ahead.

Preheat oven to 375° F. While oven is heating, oven-sauté onions for rice. Place rice and carrot casseroles on lower shelf. Cook 10 minutes. Place fish, uncovered, on top shelf. Cook everything 20 minutes longer. Fluff rice with a fork before serving.

Scampi-Stuffed Haddock

Use fresh, not frozen, fish for best results. If large fillets cannot be obtained, use smaller ones (totaling 2 pounds) and stuff them as roll-ups.

4 large haddock fillets, at least 2 pounds total weight
¾ to 1 pound fresh cooked, shelled, cleaned shrimp, coarsely chopped
2 tablespoons finely chopped fresh parsley
¼ teaspoon grated lemon rind
¼ teaspoon salt
¼ teaspoon pepper
Juice of 2 lemons, divided
¼ cup (½ stick) butter, melted, divided
1 cup seasoned crumbs (see page 361)
 or butter-cracker crumbs
Paprika
Salt and pepper
Lemon wedges
Watercress (optional)

Generously oil a shallow baking dish that will double as a serving dish, and lay 2 fillets in it. (Fillets should fit pan without too much extra space.) Mix together shrimp, parsley, lemon rind, ¼ teaspoon salt, ¼ teaspoon pepper, and the juice of 1 lemon. Layer this stuffing on top of fillets. Drizzle on half the butter. Top with remaining fillets. Pour the remaining lemon juice over fish. Sprinkle with crumbs, paprika, salt, and pepper. Evenly pour remaining butter on top. Bake on top shelf of a preheated 375° F. oven for 20 minutes or until fish fillet on the bottom flakes apart easily with a fork. Garnish with lemon wedges and watercress sprigs.

Green Rice

1 **large onion, chopped**
2 **tablespoons olive oil**
½ **cup chopped fresh parsley**
A few celery leaves
4 **scallions with green tops, coarsely chopped**
1 **teaspoon salt**
¼ **teaspoon pepper**
½ **cup cold water**
1½ **cups long grain rice**
2 **tablespoons butter**
2¾ **cups boiling water**

Heat oven to 375° F. While it is heating, oven-sauté onion in oil in a 2-quart casserole. In a blender, or processor fitted with steel blade, purée parsley, celery leaves, scallions, salt, and pepper in ½ cup cold water. When onions are sizzling, take the casserole out of the oven, and stir in rice. Stir purée into rice. Add butter and boiling water. Cover and bake on the lower shelf for 30 minutes or until all the water is absorbed. Fluff rice with a fork before serving.

Carrots with Mortadella

1 **pound fresh carrots, scraped and thinly sliced**
¼ **pound sliced mortadella, chopped**
⅓ **cup water**
2 **tablespoons butter**
½ **teaspoon salt**
½ **teaspoon sugar**
⅛ **teaspoon pepper**

Combine all ingredients in a 2-quart casserole, cover, and bake on the lower shelf of a 375° F. oven for 30 minutes.

Cooking with Love: Everyday Meals

The average cook creates a great many meals per year, most of them for the family. It's easy to become lax when it comes to this everyday meal preparation, either serving convenience foods, taking undesirable short cuts that result in lackluster meals, or serving the same old dishes over and over again. It's sad but understandable that we're tempted to save our best for company instead of giving it to those we love most.

But few people want to spend all day in the kitchen. And the good news is that it's not necessary.

Cooking with love means having time left to spend with your family. The menus in this chapter are designed to give maximum results for minimum effort. So you can cook delicious meals for your family without spending your days chained to the kitchen stove. Since the recipes need little if any attention once they're in the oven, you will be able to spend that time with your loved ones. In many busy households that hour or so before dinner is the only time everyone is at home.

Some of the dishes in this chapter must be made ahead of time. Some may be assembled either well in advance or just prior to cooking. Still others require last minute preparation just before oven time, but all allow for freedom while they oven cook.

These menus are all designed for four people—patterned after the "boy for you, girl for me" average American family. If your family is larger or smaller you may want to adjust the recipes. Bear in mind that if you increase amounts, you may have to increase cooking time, too. So you may have to experiment a bit the first time you try adding to a dish. Of course, little people have little appetites, and young children may not eat a full helping of everything. But most of these dishes can be either reheated or eaten cold.

Cooking with love also means serving good, nourishing, tasty meals without spending exorbitant amounts of money which could go for other family pleasures.

And cooking with love means helping those we love stick to their diets; not encouraging them to put on unwanted pounds by serving rich foods. If dieting is called for in your family, trim all the fat from meats before you cook them. Substitute low-fat cheeses for the cheeses called for in the recipes. Make your sauces from skim milk instead of cream or whole milk. Cut down on the amount of pasta or other starchy foods called for in recipes, and serve fresh fruits for desserts.

Cooking with love means sometimes setting the table with the best dishes and silver, a fancy tablecloth or special placemats, and even flowers in the center of the table when it's no special occasion, and the only diners will be the people for whom you cook every day. When you cook with love, you try and spare the dish washer (especially since it may be you). Many of the recipes in this chapter can be mixed up in the dishes in which they cook—a real help at clean-up time.

Cooking with love can be a challenge, but with a little thought and preplanning, and an average-sized oven, it's a challenge that's not hard to meet.

PERFECT POT ROAST DINNER

The company flavor in this family roast comes from V-8 juice. As a base for the gravy, it mingles with the other ingredients to offer a delightfully different taste. Serves four.

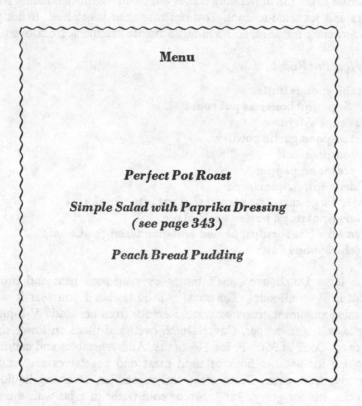

Menu

Perfect Pot Roast

Simple Salad with Paprika Dressing
(see page 343)

Peach Bread Pudding

Total Cooking Time: 2½ to 3 hours

Plan of Action

You can make these dishes by preparing the vegetables and meat for the pot early in the day, or you can wait to start your preparations until just before it's time to pop them into the oven. Three hours before serving time, place covered Dutch oven containing pot roast (but not vegetables) on bottom shelf of cold oven. Turn it to 350° F. and cook for 1½ hours. Drain vegetables, add them to Dutch oven, and re-cover it. Place bread pudding on same shelf of oven and continue cooking everything for another 50 to 60 minutes or until knife inserted in middle of pudding comes out clean. Remove pudding from oven and set aside to cool. Test pot roast and vegetables. If not yet tender, cook for another 30 minutes before removing from oven.

Perfect Pot Roast

2 tablespoons butter
2 to 3 pound boneless pot roast
1½ cups V-8 juice
¼ teaspoon garlic powder
½ teaspoon salt
¼ teaspoon pepper
1 large onion, quartered
4 to 6 large carrots, scraped and cut into chunks
4 large potatoes, peeled and halved
4 small white turnips, peeled and quartered (optional)
2 tablespoons flour

In a large Dutch oven, melt butter over medium heat and brown meat in it on all sides. The roast will be tastier if you sear it well, forming an almost crusty exterior. Remove from heat, add V-8 juice, garlic, salt, and pepper. Cover Dutch oven and place on lower shelf of oven. Cook at 350° F. for 1½ hours. Add vegetables and continue cooking for another hour or until meat and vegetables are tender. Remove from oven. Drain meat and vegetables, reserving liquid in Dutch oven for gravy. Put 1 cup of cold water in a jar with a tight-fitting lid. Add flour, cover, and shake until flour and water are well mixed. Over medium heat, gradually add flour mixture to the V-8 gravy in Dutch oven, stirring constantly until it has thickened to a smooth gravy. Slice pot roast. Arrange meat on a large platter surrounded by vegetables, and serve gravy in separate gravy dish.

Note: If you prepare vegetables ahead of cooking time, keep them in cold water until it's time to add them to the roast.

Peach Bread Pudding

6 slices white bread
1 16-ounce can sliced peaches
Peach juice
2½ cups milk
2 tablespoons butter
2 eggs, slightly beaten
½ cup sugar

Tear bread (including crusts) into small chunks, and put them in a medium-sized, well-greased casserole. Drain peaches, reserving juice, and cut each slice into 3 or 4 pieces. Combine peach juice, milk, and butter in medium-sized saucepan, and heat over medium heat until milk is scalding and butter is melted. Pour over bread. Mix eggs and sugar, and blend into bread-milk combination. Add peaches, and stir to distribute them evenly. Bake uncovered on bottom shelf of pre-heated 350° F. oven for 50 to 60 minutes, or until knife inserted in center comes out clean. Serve warm or cold.

BEAUTIFUL BEEF BIRDS DINNER

Because the stuffing stretches the meat, this is a budget meal, but it tastes like company cuisine. Serves four.

Menu

Beautiful Beef Birds

Mock Saffron Rice

Plain Green Beans

Butterscotch Bars

Total Cooking Time: 1 hour

Plan of Action

Everything except the rice can be prepared ahead of time. Sixty minutes before dinner time, put butterscotch bars on middle shelf of preheated 350° F. oven. Prepare rice. Fifteen minutes after starting beans and butterscotch bars, put beef birds on middle shelf and rice on lower shelf of oven. In another 5 minutes, add beans to lower shelf. When bars have cooked for 25 minutes, remove them from oven, score them with a knife for cutting and put them aside to cool slightly. They should be a good temperature for eating by dessert time. Continue to cook other dishes for another 35 minutes. Drain beans, adding butter, and fluff rice before serving.

Beautiful Beef Birds

The raisins in this dish not only add flavor, they're good for your family, too.

6 slices bread
2 tablespoons butter
1 medium-sized onion, finely chopped
1 egg, slightly beaten
¼ cup raisins
Salt and pepper to taste
1 teaspoon allspice
1 pound sirloin tips, no thicker than ⅛ of an inch
1 tablespoon oil
½ beef bouillon cube dissolved in ½ cup water

Crumb bread. Melt butter in oven in a small ovenproof dish, add onion, and cook about 5 minutes. Remove from oven, pour over bread crumbs and blend well. Mix in egg, and add enough water to make stuffing the desired consistency. Stir in raisins, salt and pepper, and allspice. Lay pieces of meat flat, and put a heaping spoonful of stuffing on each piece. Roll meat around stuffing into individual birds. Heat oil in skillet, and brown birds in hot oil on all sides. Remove to large covered casserole. Pour beef bouillon over birds, cover, and put on middle shelf of preheated 350° F. oven for 45 minutes.

Mock Saffron Rice

Saffron is touted as the world's most expensive spice, and while we love our families, it is a bit costly to buy saffron for an everyday meal. So unless it happens to be in the kitchen cabinet, we use turmeric in its place. It gives an almost-saffron flavor.

1 tablespoon butter
1 cup long-grained converted rice
1 small onion, grated
2½ cups boiling water
1 teaspoon salt
½ teaspoon turmeric

Dissolve butter in boiling water, and pour it over rice in large casserole. Mix in other ingredients, stirring with a fork. Cover and place on bottom shelf of preheated 350° F. oven for 45 minutes. Fluff rice with a fork before serving.

Plain Green Beans

1 pound fresh beans
½ cup water
Salt and pepper to taste
2 tablespoons butter

Wash beans. Cut off ends, and cut them into 1½ to 2 inch pieces. Put in medium-sized casserole, add water, salt and pepper. Cover, and place on lower shelf of 350° F. preheated oven for 40 minutes. Drain and add butter.

Butterscotch Bars

3 ounces butterscotch bits
¼ pound butter
⅔ cup all-purpose flour
½ teaspoon baking powder
½ teaspoon salt
2 eggs
1 cup sugar
½ teaspoon vanilla
½ cup chopped walnuts

In top of a double boiler over hot water, melt butterscotch and butter together. Sift next 3 ingredients together. In a large mixing bowl, beat eggs well with an electric beater set on low, gradually adding sugar, butterscotch mixture, and vanilla until blended. Continue to beat while slowly adding dry ingredients. Stir in nuts. Pour batter into greased, 8-inch square, glass baking dish. Cook on middle shelf of preheated 350° F. oven for 25 minutes. Mark for cutting while still hot.

A STEAK DINNER WITH STYLE

Yes, you can roast steak, and the U.S. Department of Agriculture's Consumer and Food Institute recommends it, based on their series of taste and cost tests. Roasted steaks require less attention, cause less spattering in the oven, use only half the fuel, and are juicier and more flavorful than the broiled variety. Serves four.

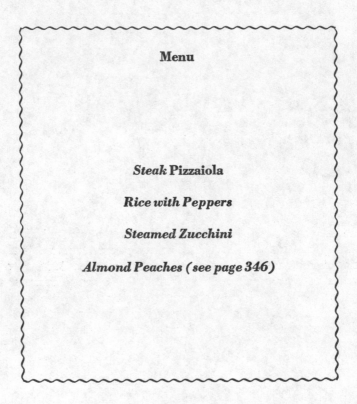

Menu

Steak **Pizzaiola**

Rice with Peppers

Steamed Zucchini

Almond Peaches (see page 346)

Total Cooking Time: 45 minutes

Plan of Action

Preheat oven to 325° F. Put rice on bottom shelf of preheated oven.

Make steak sauce, if you haven't made it ahead of time. Prepare steak, and zucchini. When rice has been in oven for 15 minutes, place steak on top shelf, sauce and zucchini on bottom shelf, and continue to cook for another 30 minutes. While they're cooking, assemble almond peaches and tuck them in the refrigerator until serving time.

Steak Pizzaiola

2 pounds London broil steak, 1½ inches thick
Salt to taste

for sauce

3 tablespoons butter
1 clove garlic, halved
⅓ cup red wine
¾ cup tomatoes, drained, seeded, and finely chopped (canned or fresh)
½ teaspoon dried basil
¼ teaspoon salt
⅛ teaspoon black pepper, freshly ground
Fresh parsley, chopped

Score fat on steak to prevent curling, and place it on oiled rack in shallow pan. Put all sauce ingredients except parsley into a small flat baking dish. Place steak on top shelf of preheated 325° F. oven. Place sauce on bottom shelf, uncovered. Cook for 30 minutes, stirring the sauce once to mix ingredients. This amount of time will give you a medium rare steak. Test for doneness by making a small cut near the center. Place steak on a warm platter, salt to taste, and cut into serving pieces, thin slices crossgrain for London broil. Remove garlic from sauce, then pour it over steak and sprinkle liberally with parsley.

Rice with Peppers

1 cup long-grain converted rice
1 cup chopped green peppers
2½ cups beef broth
½ teaspoon salt
1 tablespoon butter

Put rice into large casserole. Stir in peppers. Bring remaining ingredients to a boil in small saucepan. Pour them over rice, cover tightly, and cook on bottom shelf of preheated 325° F. oven for 45 minutes. Fluff with a fork before serving.

Steamed Zucchini

2 medium-sized zucchini
½ medium-sized onion, chopped
½ cup beef broth

Scrub zucchini skin, and cut off and discard ends. Slice zucchini into thin pieces and place slices in casserole with onion. Pour broth over all. Cover and cook on bottom shelf of preheated 325° F. oven for 30 minutes.

MEAT LOAF SURPRISE DINNER

Families expect to be served meat loaf. It's an old standby in most homes. But this one has a surprise filling that makes it different. The meal is an economical one to serve because you can use the least expensive ground beef. Serves four.

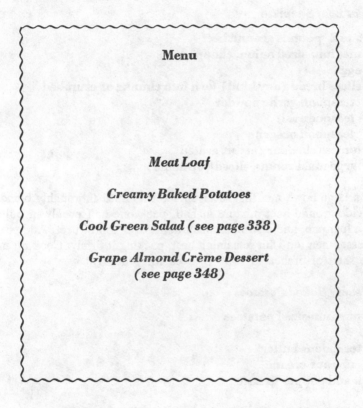

Menu

Meat Loaf

Creamy Baked Potatoes

Cool Green Salad (see page 338)

Grape Almond Crème Dessert
(see page 348)

Total Cooking Time: about 1 hour and 20 minutes

Plan of Action

Place potatoes on bottom shelf of preheated 375° F. oven. When potatoes have cooked for 20 minutes, place meat loaf on middle shelf.

Continue to cook for another 50 minutes. During this time make salad and dessert. Remove potatoes from oven. Turn off oven and leave meat loaf in it to keep warm while you prepare potatoes (about 5 minutes). Return potatoes to oven, remove meat loaf, and let it rest for 5 minutes, then drain off excess fat. Remove potatoes from oven and serve meal.

Meat Loaf Surprise

1½ to 2   pounds ground beef
1   medium-sized onion, chopped
2   eggs
2   slices bread (any kind) torn into chunks or crumbed
⅛   teaspoon garlic powder
¼   teaspoon salt
½   teaspoon oregano
4   ounces cheddar cheese, grated
6   large mushrooms, sliced (optional)

In a large bowl, mix first seven ingredients until thoroughly blended. Divide ground beef mixture in half, pack one-half evenly in bottom of a loaf pan, and distribute mushrooms over top of beef. Add grated cheese, then top with remaining beef, packing it firmly. Cook on middle shelf of preheated 375° F. oven for 1 hour.

Creamy Baked Potatoes

4   medium-sized potatoes
Oil
4   teaspoons butter
1   cup sour cream
Salt and pepper to taste

Oil potato skins and prick with a fork. Put potatoes on bottom shelf of preheated 375° F. oven; cook for 1 hour and 15 minutes. Turn off oven and remove potatoes. Split potatoes in halves, scoop out pulp, and set skins aside. In a bowl, mash potato with butter until butter has melted. Add sour cream and salt and pepper, mixing well. Return to potato skins. Place on preheated cookie sheet, skin side down, on bottom shelf of oven for 5 minutes or until heated through.

ALOHA MEATBALLS

Everything in this delicious dinner except the cheese sauce for the cauliflower can be prepared ahead of time. Serves four.

Menu

Aloha Meatballs

Cauliflower au Gratin

Potato Biscuits

Sliced Herb Tomatoes (see page 343)

Chocolate Rice Pudding

Total Cooking Time: 45 minutes

Plan of Action

Forty-five minutes before dinner time, put rice pudding on bottom shelf of oven preheated to 375° F. Put meatballs on middle shelf of oven. Cook for 20 minutes. Put biscuits on middle shelf and cauliflower on bottom shelf, and continue to cook everything for 25 minutes. Make cheese sauce while cauliflower is cooking. When it has been in the oven for 20 minutes, drain off water, pour cheese sauce over vegetable, re-cover and return to oven for another 5 minutes.

Aloha Meatballs

1 pound ground beef
1 small onion, finely chopped
2 eggs
1 7-ounce can crushed pineapple, well-drained, juice reserved
Salt and pepper to taste
½ teaspoon cinnamon
¼ cup oil
Pineapple juice from crushed pineapple
¼ cup cornstarch
⅓ cup water

Put ground beef in large mixing bowl. Add onion, eggs, pineapple, salt and pepper, and cinnamon, mixing well. Divide meat into 12 parts and make into firm meatballs. Oven-brown meatballs in oil for 20 minutes in a casserole they will fit in one layer. Put juice drained from pineapple into small saucepan. Add ⅓ cup water, and blend in cornstarch, stirring constantly over low heat until juice thickens. Pour over meatballs, cover, and bake on middle shelf of preheated 375° F. oven for 45 minutes.

Cauliflower au Gratin

1 10-ounce package frozen cauliflower florets, thawed to separate
⅓ cup water
2 tablespoons butter
2 tablespoons flour
½ teaspoon salt
⅛ teaspoon white pepper
¾ cup milk
4 ounces orange cheddar cheese, grated

Put cauliflower in casserole with water. Cover, and place on lower shelf of preheated 375° F. oven for 25 minutes or until cauliflower is soft but still crisp. While it is cooking, make sauce.

Cheese Sauce

In a medium-sized saucepan, melt butter over medium heat. Blend in flour, salt, and pepper with the back of a wooden spoon. Gradually add milk, stirring constantly until sauce is smooth. Stir in cheese. Continue to cook until sauce has thickened and cheese has melted. Remove cauliflower from oven after 20 minutes, drain it, pour cheese sauce over it, cover and return to oven for another 5 minutes.

Potato Biscuits

1 large, boiled potato, peeled
¾ cup flour
1 tablespoon baking powder
1 teaspoon salt
1 tablespoon butter
½ cup milk

Mash potato and set it aside. In a large mixing bowl, blend next 3 ingredients. Using 2 knives, cut butter into flour mixture. Add potato and milk, blending to make batter. Drop in 12 spoonfuls on nonstick cookie sheet. Bake on top shelf of 375° F. oven for 25 minutes or until nicely browned on top. Serve hot with gobs of butter.

Chocolate Rice Pudding

2 cups cooked rice
1 cup milk
⅓ cup sugar
1 tablespoon cocoa
1 teaspoon vanilla
2 eggs

Put rice into a greased, medium-sized casserole. Heat milk to scalding. Mix sugar, cocoa, vanilla and eggs and add milk to this mixture a little at a time, stirring constantly. Pour over rice, blending well with a fork. Place on bottom shelf of preheated 375° F. oven for 45 minutes. Let pudding cool slightly while you eat dinner. It's delicious plain or topped with either ice cream or half-and-half.

PORK CHOPS WITH CELERY SAUCE

All the dishes in this meal go into the oven at the same time and come out at the same time. This gives the cook time to relax, put her feet up, and reflect on the day's activities before dinner. But best of all, it's the sort of meal most kids seem to gobble up. Serves four.

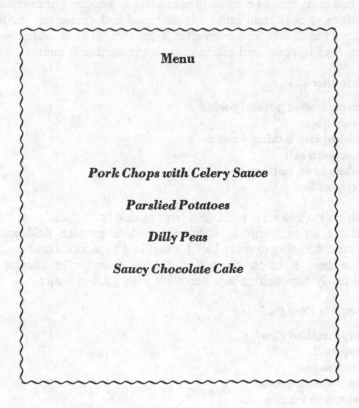

Menu

Pork Chops with Celery Sauce

Parslied Potatoes

Dilly Peas

Saucy Chocolate Cake

Total Cooking Time: about 45 minutes

Plan of Action

Preheat oven to 350° F. Prepare all dishes starting with chops, then potatoes, peas, and cake—in that order. Everything except the cake should be covered. Place chops and potatoes on bottom shelf of oven, and peas and cake on middle shelf. In 20 minutes mix peas with a fork. Continue cooking all dishes for another 25 minutes.

Pork Chops with Celery Sauce

½ cup flour
¼ teaspoon salt
⅛ teaspoon pepper
1 egg, beaten
2 teaspoons water
3 tablespoons butter
4 thick pork chops
3 tablespoons flour
1 cup milk
Chicken broth
1 teaspoon celery salt

In a medium-sized mixing bowl, combine first 3 ingredients. In a smaller bowl, mix egg and 2 teaspoons water. Coat each chop with flour, then dip into egg. In a large skillet, melt butter and brown chops over low heat. Remove browned chops from skillet. Blend flour into butter in skillet, adding more butter if necessary to make a paste. While stirring constantly over medium heat, add milk slowly and, when gravy begins to thicken, add broth, using just enough to make a gravy of medium consistency. Stir in celery salt. Put chops in large casserole, pour gravy over them, cover, and put on bottom shelf of preheated 350° F. oven for 45 minutes.

Parslied Potatoes

4 medium-sized potatoes, peeled and halved
Water to cover
½ teaspoon salt
1 tablespoon crushed parsley
1 tablespoon butter

Place potatoes in medium-sized casserole. Pour water over them. Cover and place on lower shelf of preheated 350° F. oven. Cook for

45 minutes. Drain, add salt and butter, sprinkle with parsley and turn potatoes until they are well-coated.

Dilly Peas

2 tablespoons butter
¼ cup water
1 10-ounce package frozen peas, thawed
Salt and pepper to taste
½ teaspoon dried, crushed dill

Put butter and peas in casserole. Sprinkle on seasonings, cover, and place on middle shelf of preheated 350° F. oven for 45 minutes, stirring with a fork after 20 minutes.

Saucy Chocolate Cake

1 cup all-purpose flour
½ cup sugar
2½ teaspoons baking powder
3 tablespoons cocoa
2 tablespoons mild-tasting vegetable oil
½ cup milk
½ teaspoon almond extract
1 cup brown sugar, firmly packed
3 tablespoons cocoa
2 cups very hot water
Vanilla ice cream

With a fork mix first four ingredients together in an 8-inch square glass pan. Add oil, milk, and almond extract and mix thoroughly, spreading to sides of pan. Distribute brown sugar and remaining cocoa over top. Pour hot water evenly over all, and bake on middle shelf of preheated 350° F. oven for 45 minutes. Serve warm topped with vanilla ice cream.

HAM AND SWISS SUPPER

This light supper hits the spot on those nights when no one feels like eating a big, heavy meal. If your family doesn't care for luncheon meat, substitute cubed, cooked ham. Serves four.

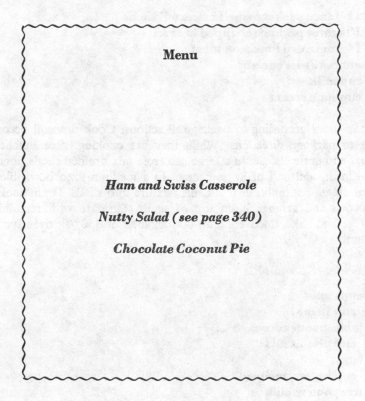

Menu

Ham and Swiss Casserole

Nutty Salad (see page 340)

Chocolate Coconut Pie

Total Cooking Time: about 40 minutes

Plan of Action

Preheat oven to 350° F. Assemble pie and place on middle shelf of oven. While pie is cooking, make ham and Swiss casserole. Put it on bottom shelf of oven. When pie has cooked for 25 minutes, remove it from oven and set aside to cool. Continue to bake ham and Swiss until it has been in oven for 25 minutes. During last 5 minutes of cooking time, put together salad.

Ham and Swiss

1 16-ounce package small macaroni shells
1 10-ounce package chopped broccoli
1 14-ounce can luncheon meat
8 ounces Swiss cheese
1 cup milk
1 cup sour cream

Cook shells according to package directions. Cook broccoli according to package directions. While they are cooking, dice luncheon meat and grate cheese. In a large casserole mix drained shells, luncheon meat, and half of Swiss cheese. In a medium-sized bowl, blend sour cream and milk, then stir this mixture into shells. Drain cooked broccoli and arrange it on top of shells. Sprinkle with remaining cheese and bake, uncovered, on bottom shelf of 350° F. oven for 25 minutes.

Chocolate Coconut Pie

2 cups milk
¾ cup sugar
2 tablespoons cocoa
½ cup biscuit mix
3 eggs
¼ cup butter, melted
1 teaspoon vanilla
1 cup shredded coconut

Grease 9-inch glass pie plate. In a blender, combine all ingredients except coconut. Blend on low for 1 or 2 minutes. Pour into prepared pie plate. Allow to set for a few minutes, then top with coconut. Bake on middle shelf of preheated 350° F. oven for 35 minutes or until knife inserted in center of pie comes out clean. Can be served warm or cold.

SAUSAGE SYMPHONY

This is more than just tasty—it's nutritious. The spinach offers iron, and the peanuts protein. Serves four.

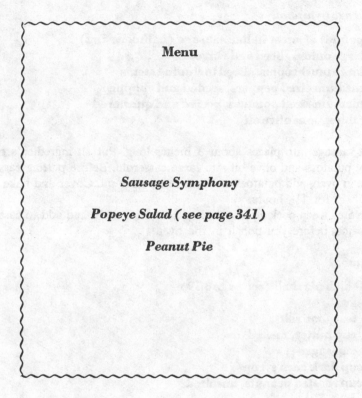

Menu

Sausage Symphony

Popeye Salad (see page 341)

Peanut Pie

Total Cooking Time: 1 hour and 30 minutes

Plan of Action

Put together Popeye salad and dressing, keeping them separate. Chill. Preheat oven to 350° F. Bake pie shell for 5 minutes. Remove from oven. Assemble sausage symphony and place on bottom shelf of 350° F. oven. (The sausage symphony can be made ahead except for potatoes, which must be added just before oven time.) Fill pie shell. When sausage has been in oven for 45 minutes, put pie on middle shelf of oven and continue cooking for 45 minutes or until knife inserted in middle comes out clean.

Sausage Symphony

2 pounds of sweet Italian sausage (in link casing)
1 large onion, sliced and ringed
6 large mushrooms, sliced including stems
2 medium-sized peppers, seeded and chopped
4 medium-sized potatoes, peeled and quartered
3 tablespoons olive oil

Cut sausage into pieces about 3 inches long. Put all ingredients except potatoes and olive oil into large casserole. Before putting casserole in oven, add potatoes and drizzle on olive oil. Cover and bake at 375° F. for 1½ hours.

Note: Keep peeled potatoes in cold water; drain and add to casserole just before you pop it in the oven.

Peanut Pie

1 9-inch pie shell (see page 359)
3 eggs
¼ teaspoon salt
¼ cup butter, melted
¾ cup sugar
1 cup dark corn syrup
1 cup roasted peanuts, unsalted

Prick pie shell with a fork and bake for 5 minutes in a preheated 350° F. oven. Beat eggs, salt, butter, sugar, and cornstarch together with an electric beater set on low. Stir in peanuts, and pour mixture into pie shell. Return to top shelf of oven and continue to bake at 350° F. for 45 minutes, or until a knife inserted in the middle comes out clean. Serve warm topped with coffee ice cream.

SUPER SUNDAY CHICKEN DINNER WITH STUFFING

This dish is a perfect Sunday dinner treat for the family. It tastes rather special, but that's what cooking with love is all about. Serves four.

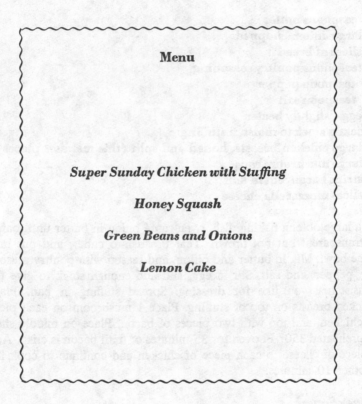

Menu

Super Sunday Chicken with Stuffing

Honey Squash

Green Beans and Onions

Lemon Cake

Total Cooking Time: 1 hour

Plan of Action

Place halved squash cut side down in a shallow pan of water and place on bottom shelf of preheated 350° F. oven. Put beans on bottom shelf. After 15 minutes, put chicken and lemon cake on middle shelf. When squash has cooked for 45 minutes, drain it, put skin side down in same pan, add other ingredients and return it to oven. Ten minutes before chicken is done (when it has been in oven for 35 minutes) add cheese to it.

Super Sunday Chicken with Stuffing

4 teaspoons butter
1 large onion, chopped
8 slices of bread
2 teaspoons poultry seasoning
⅛ teaspoon pepper
¼ teaspoon salt
2 eggs, slightly beaten
Chicken stock to moisten stuffing
2 large chicken breasts, boned and split (this makes 4 pieces)
4 large mushroom caps
4 strips bacon, cut in half
4 slices mozzarella cheese

In a large oblong baking dish, oven-sauté onion in butter until onion is transparent but not brown. Tear bread into cubes, and put in a large bowl. Mix in butter and onion, and season with poultry seasoning, pepper, and salt. Stir in egg, and add enough stock to give the consistency you like for dressing. Spread stuffing in pan. Place chicken breasts on top of stuffing. Place 1 mushroom on each piece of chicken, and top with two pieces of bacon. Place on middle shelf of preheated 350° F. oven for 35 minutes or until bacon is crisp. Add a piece of cheese to each piece of chicken and continue to cook for another 10 minutes.

Honey Squash

2 butternut squash
4 tablespoons butter
4 tablespoons honey

Halve squash, and clean out seeds and stringy pulp. Put squash cut side down in rectangular pan. Add an inch or so of water, and place pan on lower shelf of preheated 350° F. oven. In 45 minutes, drain off water, and place squash skin side down in same pan. Put 1 tablespoon of butter and 1 tablespoon of honey in hollow of each squash. Return squash to oven and bake for another 15 minutes.

Green Beans and Onions

1 10-ounce package frozen French cut beans
1 small bag frozen pearl onions, slightly thawed
2 tablespoons butter
¼ teaspoon marjoram
⅛ teaspoon salt
⅛ teaspoon pepper

Place vegetables in a casserole dish. In a small saucepan, melt butter over low heat. Add marjoram, salt, and pepper, and pour over vegetables. Cover tightly and place on lower shelf of oven preheated to 350° F. In 30 minutes stir mixture to blend, re-cover and continue to cook another 30 minutes.

Lemon Cake

1½ cups all-purpose flour
⅛ teaspoon salt
2 teaspoons baking powder
¾ cup sugar
2 eggs, beaten
½ cup milk
½ teaspoon vanilla extract
½ teaspoon lemon extract
½ teaspoon grated lemon peel
¼ cup butter, melted
½ pint heavy cream
2 tablespoons confectioners' sugar

Sift first four ingredients together. Combine next six ingredients, and add to dry ingredients. Beat with an electric beater on medium for about 1 minute. Grease 8-inch square glass pan. Pour in batter. Bake on middle shelf of preheated 350° F. oven for 45 minutes.

Beat heavy cream with electric beater until it forms soft peaks. Add sugar and beat to mix in. Top each serving of cake with a dollop of whipped cream.

FRIED CHICKEN LEGS PARMESAN

(Oven fried, that is!) Kids and drumsticks seem to go together, and this meal provides enough of them so everyone can eat their fill. If you grate the cheese just before you use it, rather than buying the pre-grated variety, the flavor will be ever-so-much better. Serves four.

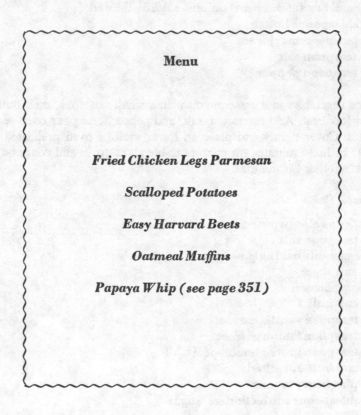

Menu

Fried Chicken Legs Parmesan

Scalloped Potatoes

Easy Harvard Beets

Oatmeal Muffins

Papaya Whip (see page 351)

Total Cooking Time: 1 hour

Plan of Action

Make papaya whip ahead of time and refrigerate. Preheat oven to

375° F. Prepare chicken legs and potatoes. Place chicken, covered, on bottom shelf, and potatoes, covered, on middle shelf of oven. Assemble beets, and when chicken and potatoes have been in oven for 10 minutes, put beets, covered, on bottom shelf. Make muffins. When chicken and potatoes have been in oven for 40 minutes remove their covers, and put muffins on middle shelf of oven. Continue to cook everything for another 20 minutes.

Fried Chicken Legs Parmesan

½ cup all-purpose flour
¼ cup grated Parmesan cheese
½ teaspoon paprika
½ teaspoon salt
2½ to 3 pounds chicken legs

Combine flour, cheese, paprika, and salt in a bag. Wash chicken legs, patting off excess water with paper toweling but leaving them still damp. Shake each piece of chicken individually in bag of flour mixture until well coated. Place chicken legs in a large rectangular casserole. Cover with foil, and put on bottom shelf of preheated 375° F. oven for 40 minutes. Remove foil, and continue to cook another 20 minutes until chicken is browned.

Scalloped Potatoes

4 medium-sized potatoes
1 large onion
½ cup flour
1 teaspoon celery salt
⅛ teaspoon pepper
¼ cup butter
Milk
1 teaspoon parsley flakes

Wash, peel, and thinly slice potatoes into a bowl of cold water. Peel and thinly slice onion, and separate into rings. Combine flour, celery salt, and pepper. Put a layer of potatoes (drained) on bottom of greased, medium-sized casserole. Dot with butter, and sprinkle with flour. Add a layer of onion rings. Continue until casserole is three-quarters full. Pour milk just to top of potatoes. Sprinkle with parsley, and bake, covered, on middle shelf of preheated 375° F. oven for 40 minutes. Remove cover, and continue to cook for another 20 minutes until potatoes are golden on top.

Easy Harvard Beets

1 bunch fresh beets
1 cup water
½ teaspoon salt
1 tablespoon butter
2 tablespoons honey
1 tablespoon vinegar

Wash, peel, and thinly slice beets, and place in medium-sized casserole. Add water and salt. Cover and put on bottom shelf of preheated 375° F. oven for 50 minutes. Remove from oven and drain. Mix butter into beets. When butter has melted, mix in honey and vinegar. Serve immediately.

Oatmeal Muffins

1½ cups quick oats
1 cup all-purpose flour
⅓ cup brown sugar, packed
⅓ cup white sugar
½ teaspoon salt
1 tablespoon baking powder
⅓ cup vegetable oil
¾ cup milk
2 eggs, beaten

Mix quick oats, flour, brown sugar, white sugar, salt, and baking powder together in a large mixing bowl. Add oil, milk, and eggs to dry ingredients. Mix enough to moisten. Fill a well-greased, 12-cup muffin tin with batter. (Don't fill cups more than two-thirds full.) Bake on middle shelf of preheated 375° F. oven for 20 to 25 minutes, or until muffins are a nice even brown.

CHICKEN LIVERS AND ONIONS WITH ALL THE FIXINGS

Liver and spinach are two good-for-you foods that it's so difficult to get most people to eat. But we've seen liver and spinach haters eat this meal with relish. Chicken livers, if good and fresh, tend to be sweeter than other forms of liver. And spinach soufflé lacks that real spinachy taste. Serves four.

Menu

Chicken Livers and Onions

Spinach Soufflé

Baked Tomatoes

Paprika Potatoes

Lime Ice Cream Pie (see page 350)

Total Cooking Time: 1 hour

Plan of Action

Make lime ice cream pie in advance. Preheat oven to 375° F. Prepare potatoes and put them on middle shelf of oven. Assemble spinach soufflé. After potatoes have been in oven for 15 minutes, place soufflé on middle shelf. Prepare livers. When potatoes have been cooking for 30 minutes, place livers on bottom shelf. Prepare tomatoes (this may be done in advance if you prefer). When potatoes have been in oven for 40 minutes, put tomatoes on middle shelf and move potatoes to bottom shelf. Continue to cook everything for another 20 minutes.

Chicken Livers and Onions

3 tablespoons butter
1 large onion
½ cup flour
Salt and pepper
1½ pounds chicken livers

Put butter in large casserole to melt in oven set at 375° F. Peel, slice, and ring onion. Oven-sauté in butter until sizzling but not brown. Mix flour with salt and pepper, and dredge chicken livers in the mixture, shaking off excess. Place the livers on the onions, and stir to coat livers with butter. Place on bottom shelf of preheated oven for 30 minutes.

Spinach Soufflé

1 cup milk
¼ cup flour
1 teaspoon salt
2 eggs, beaten
1 10-ounce package spinach, thawed and drained

Grease medium-sized casserole. To blend flour and milk without lumps, mix them first in jar with tight-fitting lid, shaking vigorously. In a large bowl, mix together all ingredients thoroughly. Pour into casserole and put on middle shelf of preheated 375° F. oven for 45 minutes. Cover top with foil if soufflé starts to brown too soon.

Baked Tomatoes

4 large, ripe tomatoes
1 cup fresh bread crumbs
½ teaspoon salt
⅛ teaspoon pepper
1 tablespoon grated onion
¼ cup grated cheddar cheese

Cut tops off tomatoes, scoop out and reserve pulp. In a medium-sized bowl, mix other ingredients adding enough tomato pulp to moisten. Fill tomatoes with mixture. Place them in lightly greased shallow pan. Put on middle shelf of 375° F. oven and cook for 20 minutes.

Paprika Potatoes

4 medium-sized potatoes
3 tablespoons butter
2 tablespoons water
½ teaspoon paprika

Set oven at 375° F. Put butter in medium-sized casserole, and place into oven until butter is melted. While butter is melting, peel and halve potatoes. Put potatoes in melted butter and turn to coat on all sides. Add water to casserole. Sprinkle with paprika, cover and put casserole on middle shelf of preheated 375° F. oven for 40 minutes. Move to bottom shelf and continue to cook for another 20 minutes.

HERB BAKED FISH

Gone are the days when fish was a real bargain and a budget meal. But this fish dish is still inexpensive enough to serve as everyday fare. Your blender or food processor will crumb the saltine crackers for you in a matter of seconds. Serves four.

Menu

Herb Baked Fish

Luscious Lima, Corn, and Potato Bake

Red Cabbage Slaw (see page 342)

Applesauce Cake

Total Cooking Time: 45 minutes

Plan of Action

Make slaw ahead of time and refrigerate. Place lima, corn, and potato bake on bottom shelf of preheated 350° F. oven. Prepare fish, and when lima bake has been cooking for 10 minutes, place fish on middle shelf of oven. Assemble applesauce cake, and when fish has been in oven about 15 minutes put applesauce cake on top shelf of oven, and continue to cook for another 20 minutes. Cake will cool slightly while you eat the rest of the meal.

Herb Baked Fish

¼ pound butter
1 cup saltine cracker crumbs
¼ teaspoon garlic powder
1 teaspoon Italian seasoning
⅛ teaspoon pepper
1½ pounds fillet of sole
1 lemon, cut into wedges

Set oven at 350° F. Place butter in large, shallow baking pan, and put it in oven until butter melts. Combine cracker crumbs, garlic powder, Italian seasoning, and pepper. Pat fillets with paper toweling to remove excess moisture. Dip each fillet first into melted butter, then in crumb mixture. Arrange in remaining butter in pan. Place on middle shelf of preheated oven for 30 to 35 minutes. Serve garnished with lemon wedges.

Note: A simple tartar sauce can be made by combining well-drained pickle relish with mayonnaise.

Luscious Lima, Corn, and Potato Bake

1 chicken bouillon cube
1½ cups boiling water
4 medium-sized potatoes
1 10-ounce package frozen baby lima beans, thawed
1 10-ounce package frozen corn niblets, thawed

Dissolve bouillon cube in boiling water. Peel and cube potatoes. Combine lima beans, corn, and potato cubes in a large casserole. Pour chicken bouillon over vegetables. Cover and cook on bottom shelf of preheated 350° F. oven for 45 minutes. Drain before serving.

Applesauce Cake

½ cup butter, softened
2 cups fresh white bread crumbs
½ teaspoon cinnamon
½ teaspoon nutmeg
1½ cups applesauce

Turn oven to 350° F. Put butter into 8-inch square casserole and melt in oven as it heats. Remove from oven. In a mixing bowl, combine crumbs with butter. Put half of crumb-butter mixture on bottom of pan in which butter was melted. Pat it in place firmly. Mix cinnamon and nutmeg into applesauce and spread over crumbs in casserole. Sprinkle remaining crumbs on top, and bake on top shelf of preheated 350° F. oven for 20 to 25 minutes. Spoon into serving dishes and enjoy it while it's still warm.

Thirty-Minute Magic

Cooking quick and easy meals with no sacrifice of quality is an art that looks surprisingly like magic. In this chapter, we've gathered some speedy alternatives to the store-bought-instant variety of fast food—menus for hasty family feasts and for dinners fancy enough to impress an important guest. You'll find this chapter especially helpful if you work full time and would like to streamline dinner preparations at the end of a tiring day. All the recipes cook in the oven in thirty minutes or less, and that half hour can be a good time in which to relax and "shift gears." Just rely on your timer to do the pot-watching for you!

Some advance preparation will enhance your ability to work culinary magic in short order. The following time-saving tips are all little things that mean a lot of time saved just when you need it most.

Fast food from your own kitchen can be raised from the ranks of the ordinary by the imaginative use of herbs and spices, so have a full range of these on the shelf. For easy locating, store them in alphabetical order. If your spice cabinet is deep, consider an inexpensive plastic turntable to keep every last herb at your fingertips.

Prepare frequently used ingredients in large batches. Consider the advantages of having on hand "kitchen-ready" chopped onions and green peppers, refrigerated or frozen; and snipped parsley, hard-boiled eggs, crumbled cooked bacon, freshly grated cheese, flavored butters, chopped nuts, bread crumbs seasoned as you like them; frozen soup stocks, gravies, and sauces; your own special salad dressings. These are the kinds of basics that make possible *le cuisine vite*. Of course, you may not have all of these helpers in stock all of the time but, once you get into the spirit of the thing, you won't find it much more difficult to chop four green peppers instead of just one. The extra will pay off later!

Keep in mind that anything small cooks faster than the same thing in large quantity. Speed up cooking time by cutting meat small or putting casserole mixtures into individual-serving baking dishes.

How about a planned program of useful leftovers? Previously cooked rice, potatoes, or macaroni, for instance, are like money in the bank to the time-pressured cook. Cook too much today, and reap the benefits tomorrow!

Make your own mixes for favorite biscuits, breads, and other baked foods, anything you find yourself making often. There's no mystery to it—just a minimum of mathematical effort. Simply pre-measure and sift together all the dry ingredients in a triple-or-more batch. Solid shortening, if used, can be cut in at this point. (When butter is used, the mix must be refrigerated.) If you wish, you can plan to use dry milk, a real money saver; for every cup of milk the recipe calls for, add a quarter cup of dry milk to the dry ingredients, and add three-quarters of a cup of water later. When ready to bake, measure out the total amount of dry ingredients for one batch, then add the liquid and/or perishable ingredients such as eggs.

But the best time-saving technique of all requires the least effort. Just make it a practice to plan menus, assemble recipes if needed, and buy the required ingredients for several days at one time. Once you have done that, super speedy meals are almost as easy as "abracadabra"!

CONTINENTAL DRUMSTICKS

Tasty little chicken rolls made from boned drumsticks cook in just thirty minutes. Serves four.

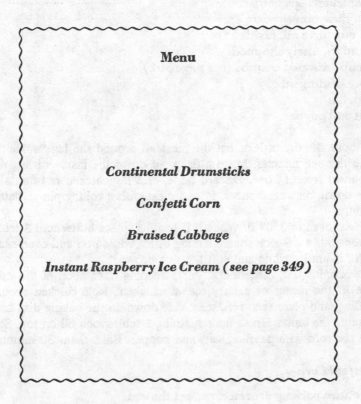

Menu

Continental Drumsticks

Confetti Corn

Braised Cabbage

Instant Raspberry Ice Cream (see page 349)

Total Cooking Time: 30 minutes

Plan of Action

Place drumsticks on top shelf, vegetables on lower shelf of a pre-heated 350° F. oven. Cook everything 30 minutes. Just before serving dinner, remove frozen raspberries from package. Allow them to defrost just enough to break the solid block into pieces. Whip up ice cream when ready for dessert. Serve immediately.

Continental Drumsticks

8　chicken legs, boned
2　tablespoons butter
¼　cup olive oil, divided
1　onion, finely chopped
1　cup seasoned crumbs (see page 361)
　　or stuffing mix
Paprika
Salt and pepper

To bone the drumsticks, cut the meat all around the leg "ankle" to slice through muscles. Make a deep slit down the inside of leg, and cut meat free of bone. Discard bone, and lay chicken out flat, skin side down, on waxed paper. Pound meat with a rolling pin to flatten slightly.

Heat oven to 350° F. While it is heating, place butter and 3 table-spoons oil in a 9-inch square baking dish. Add onion and oven-sauté it in fat until sizzling and soft but not brown.

Mix onion, fat, and crumbs. Put 1 heaping tablespoon of this mixture in the center of each piece of chicken. Roll chicken around stuffing, and place each roll, seam side down, in the baking dish used to sauté the onion. Brush the remaining 1 tablespoon oil on top. Season the rolls with paprika, salt, and pepper. Bake them 30 minutes.

Confetti Corn

10-ounce package frozen corn, not thawed
⅓　cup water
2　tablespoons butter
¼　teaspoon salt
⅓　cup sliced stuffed green olives

Combine all ingredients in a 1½-quart casserole. Cover tightly, and cook for 30 minutes in a preheated 350° F. oven. Stir.

Braised Cabbage

1 to 1¼   pounds shredded cabbage (about ½ large head)
½   cup water
1   chicken bouillon cube
2   tablespoons butter
⅓   cup diced or shredded ham (optional)
Freshly ground black pepper to taste

Combine all ingredients in a 3-quart casserole. Cover and cook for 30 minutes in a preheated 350° F. oven. Stir.

CHAMPAGNE CHICKEN

Simple elegance for four people.

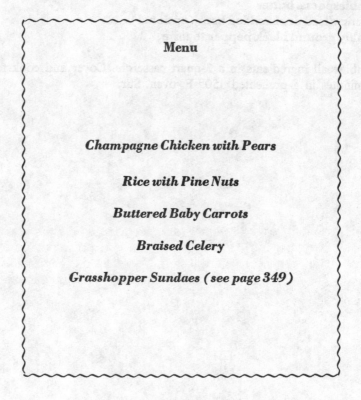

Menu

Champagne Chicken with Pears

Rice with Pine Nuts

Buttered Baby Carrots

Braised Celery

Grasshopper Sundaes (see page 349)

Total Cooking Time: 30 minutes

Plan of Action

Whip cream for sundaes sometime before dinner, and refrigerate it, covered. Place all baking dishes in the oven, chicken on top shelf. Bake 30 minutes. Remove all dishes, and let rice rest, covered, for 5 minutes, then fluff it with a fork, stirring in pine nuts.

Champagne Chicken with Pears

⅓ cup butter, divided
1 onion, finely chopped
8 chicken breasts, skinned and boned
Salt
1½ cups seasoned crumbs (see page 361)
4 D'Anjou pears
1 cup champagne (dry vermouth or dry white wine could be substituted)
Ground cloves

Heat oven to 375° F. While it is heating, oven-sauté the onion with ¼ cup butter until sizzling in an oblong non-metal baking dish which can double as a serving dish. Do not let the onion brown. Place the chicken between 2 pieces of waxed paper, and pound lightly with a bread board or rolling pin to flatten meat. Remove top sheet of waxed paper. Salt the chicken, and sprinkle each piece with 2 tablespoons of the seasoned crumbs. Roll up chicken breasts, and lay them, seam side down, in the baking dish. Peel and cut the pears into eighths, and place them around roll-ups. Pour champagne over all. Sprinkle the pears lightly with cloves. Sprinkle the chicken rolls with the remaining crumbs, and dot them with the remaining 2 table-spoons butter. Bake for 30 minutes, uncovered.

Rice with Pine Nuts

1½ cups raw rice
1½ tablespoons butter
2 chicken bouillon cubes
½ teaspoon salt (optional—the bouillon cubes contribute some salt)
3 cups boiling water
½ cup lightly toasted pine nuts

Combine rice, butter, bouillon cubes, and salt, if using, in a 2-quart casserole. Pour boiling water over all. Immediately cover the casserole, and bake it in a 375° F. oven for 30 minutes. Let the dish rest, covered, for 5 minutes, then fluff the rice with a fork, stirring in pine nuts.

Buttered Baby Carrots

16-ounce bag frozen baby carrots, partly thawed (30 minutes
   at room temperature)
3 tablespoons butter
1 tablespoon dried parsley
   or 2 tablespoons minced fresh parsley
½ teaspoon sugar
¼ teaspoon salt
½ cup water

Combine all ingredients in a 2-quart casserole and cover tightly.
Bake for 30 minutes in a 375° F. oven.

Braised Celery

10 stalks celery
2 tablespoons butter
1 cup well-flavored chicken stock or broth

Peel strings from celery stalks with a vegetable peeler. Cut the stalks
into ½-inch diagonal slices. Combine all ingredients in a 1½-quart
casserole. Cover and bake for 30 minutes in a 375° F. oven.

VERSATILE VEAL AND VEGETABLES

Easy to prepare, this menu for four can be expanded as needed simply by doubling amounts and using larger baking dishes.

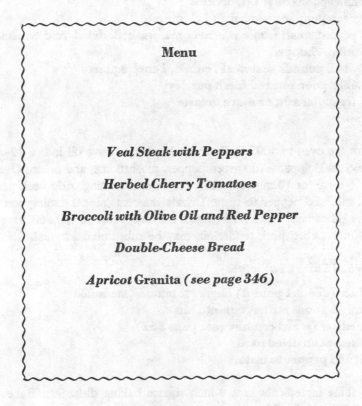

Menu

Veal Steak with Peppers

Herbed Cherry Tomatoes

Broccoli with Olive Oil and Red Pepper

Double-Cheese Bread

Apricot Granita *(see page 346)*

Total Cooking Time: 30 minutes

Plan of Action

Make apricot granita 3 hours in advance and freeze it. Heat oven to 400° F., and while it is heating oven-sauté the vegetables for the veal dish. Place veal and broccoli casseroles on lower shelf. Bake 20 minutes. Stir veal. Place tomatoes and cheese bread on top shelf. Cook everything 10 minutes longer.

Veal Steak with Peppers

3 tablespoons olive oil, divided
2 green peppers, seeded and chopped
½ pound small whole mushrooms, washed, dried, and trimmed
1 onion, chopped
1½ to 2 pounds veal steak, cubed, 1-inch squares
1 tablespoon minced fresh parsley
¼ teaspoon salt, or more to taste
Pepper

Turn the oven to 400° F. Pour 2 tablespoons olive oil into a 12- by 8-inch baking pan. Add green pepper, mushrooms, and onion. Oven-sauté them for 10 minutes while the oven is heating. Add veal, parsley, salt, and pepper to taste. Drizzle the remaining 1 tablespoon of olive oil on top. Bake 20 minutes. Stir and bake 10 minutes longer.

Note: Cubed pork tenderloin may be substituted for veal.

Herbed Cherry Tomatoes

1 box (about 1 pound) cherry tomatoes, stemmed
3 tablespoons butter, cut into bits
½ cup seasoned crumbs (see page 361)
½ teaspoon dried basil
Salt and pepper to taste

Combine ingredients in a 9-inch square baking dish. Stir. Bake 10 minutes at 400° F.

Broccoli with Olive Oil and Red Pepper

1 small bunch fresh broccoli
½ cup water
2 tablespoons olive oil
½ teaspoon garlic salt
¼ teaspoon crushed red pepper flakes

Wash and trim broccoli spears. Cut through stem and head lengthwise into ½-inch thick sticks. Place them in a 3-quart casserole with the remaining ingredients. Cover and cook at 400° F. for 30 minutes.

Double-Cheese Bread

1 small loaf Italian bread, unsliced
2 cups coarsely grated cheddar cheese
¼ cup Parmesan cheese
½ cup mayonnaise

Slice the bread in half lengthwise. Mix together the remaining ingredients, and spread the mixture on the bread. Bake uncovered for 10 minutes in a 400° F. oven.

HASH IN FANCY DRESS

Hash *can* be special—when it's homemade and served with flair. Eggs and anchovies give this version its sophisticated touch. A supper for four.

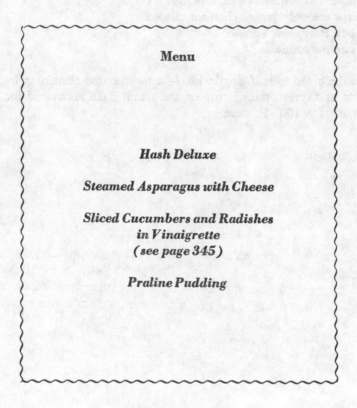

Menu

Hash Deluxe

Steamed Asparagus with Cheese

*Sliced Cucumbers and Radishes
in Vinaigrette
(see page 345)*

Praline Pudding

Total Cooking Time: 30 minutes

Plan of Action

Place all baking dishes in a preheated 350° F. oven, hash and pudding on top shelf, asparagus on lower shelf. Bake 30 minutes. Place anchovy fillets on eggs, and sprinkle parsley on hash.

Hash Deluxe

3 cups cubed cooked beef
  (roast beef, steak, pot roast, corned beef—whatever you have
  left over)
2 large potatoes, cut up
1 onion, cut up
¼ cup gravy or beef broth
2 tablespoons chili sauce
1 tablespoon steak sauce
½ teaspoon Gravy Master
½ teaspoon salt (reduce amount if corned beef is used)
Pepper to taste
1 tablespoon vegetable oil
4 eggs
4 anchovy fillets (optional)
1 tablespoon chopped fresh parsley

Grind beef, potato, and onion to a coarse texture, or chop them in a
food processor using steel blade with on-off turns. Mix chopped meat
and vegetables thoroughly with gravy or broth, chili sauce, steak
sauce, Gravy Master, salt, and pepper. Oil a baking dish (9-inch
square or 11- by 7½-inch) with 1 tablespoon oil. Press the hash into
the dish, and make four indentations in it with the back of a tablespoon. Leave at least ½ inch of hash at the bottom of the indentations, and shape each large enough to hold an egg. One at a time,
break eggs into a cup and pour them into hollows in hash. Bake the
hash for 30 minutes in a preheated 350° F. oven. Before serving, lay
an anchovy fillet over each egg, if desired, and sprinkle the hash with
parsley.

Steamed Asparagus with Cheese

1½ pounds fresh asparagus
⅓ cup water
¼ teaspoon salt
2 tablespoons seasoned crumbs (see page 361)
2 tablespoons butter, cut into bits
1 cup coarsely grated cheddar cheese

Wash asparagus and trim off woody ends. Cut the stalks into 2-inch lengths. Put the asparagus into a 2-quart casserole. Pour in water, and sprinkle asparagus with the remaining ingredients in the order given. Cover tightly, and steam the dish for 30 minutes in a preheated 350° F. oven.

Praline Pudding

1 cup all-purpose flour
1 cup dark brown sugar
½ cup chopped pecans
2 teaspoons baking powder
½ teaspoon salt
½ cup milk
3 tablespoons butter, melted and cooled slightly
1½ teaspoons vanilla
1⅔ cups hot water

Mix together flour, sugar, nuts, baking powder, and salt. In another bowl mix milk, melted butter, and vanilla. Blend the liquid ingredients except water into the dry, and spoon the mixture into a buttered 8-inch square baking dish. Pour the hot water evenly over the top. Do not mix. Bake in a preheated 350° F. oven for 30 minutes or until a cake tester inserted in the center comes out clean.

MINI-MEAT LOAVES

Smaller is faster! Small meat loaves cook in less time than a larger meat loaf. This easy dinner serves eight.

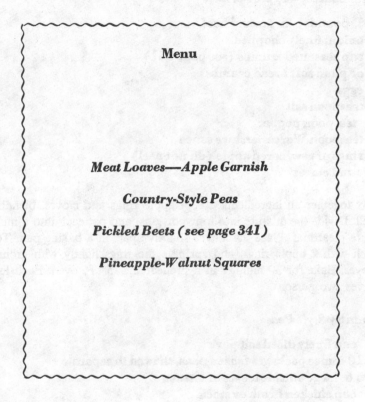

Menu

Meat Loaves—Apple Garnish

Country-Style Peas

Pickled Beets (see page 341)

Pineapple-Walnut Squares

Total Cooking Time: 30 minutes

Plan of Action

Prepare and refrigerate pickled beets. Preheat oven to 375° F. While oven is heating, melt butter for squares in baking dish. Mix up squares, then meat loaves, place on top shelf. Place peas and salt pork for peas (in separate dishes) on bottom shelf. After 10 minutes of cooking, check salt pork for golden brown color. If necessary, cook salt pork longer. Cook squares, meat loaves, and peas a total of 30 minutes.

Meat Loaves—Apple Garnish

2½ pounds lean ground beef
1 onion, finely chopped
1 cup seasoned crumbs (see page 361)
   or plain soft bread crumbs
2 eggs
1 teaspoon salt
½ teaspoon pepper
1 teaspoon Worcestershire sauce
8 rings of raw, cored apple (do not peel)
Ground cloves

Mix together all ingredients except apple rings and cloves, blending well. Divide the mixture into four portions, and pat each into a miniature meat loaf. Place the loaves slightly apart in a baking pan. Top each with 2 apple rings, and sprinkle the rings lightly with ground cloves. Bake for 30 minutes in a preheated 375° F. oven. Each loaf serves two persons.

Country-Style Peas

½ cup finely diced salt pork
3 10-ounce packages frozen peas, thawed to separate
4 to 6 large outside leaves of lettuce
¾ cup chicken broth or stock
½ teaspoon dried basil
½ teaspoon salt
½ teaspoon sugar
Pepper to taste

Place salt pork in a pie pan, and cook it in a 375° F. oven until it is golden brown, 10 to 20 minutes. Line a 3-quart casserole with lettuce. Add peas, broth or stock, basil, salt, sugar, and pepper. Cover and bake in a 375° F. oven for 20 minutes. Sprinkle salt pork on peas before serving.

Pineapple-Walnut Squares

⅓ cup butter
⅔ cup all-purpose flour
½ teaspoon baking soda
½ teaspoon cinnamon
¼ teaspoon salt
1½ cups quick-cooking oats
⅔ cup firmly packed brown sugar
Juice from pineapple
8-ounce can crushed pineapple, drained
½ cup coarsely chopped walnuts

Melt butter in 9-inch square baking pan while oven is heating to 375° F. Stir flour to lighten it before measuring. Sift together flour, baking soda, cinnamon, and salt. Combine flour mixture with oats, sugar, butter, and pineapple juice, blending well. Pat about half this mixture into a single layer in the baking pan you used to melt butter. Make another layer of pineapple and walnuts. Spoon the remaining flour-oat mixture on top, and pat it gently into a third layer. Bake for 30 minutes or until lightly browned.

JAMBALAYA IN A JIFFY

This spicy taste of New Orleans cuisine serves six.

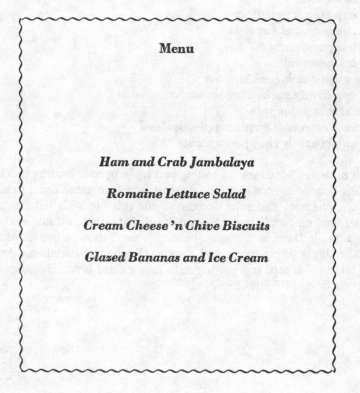

Menu

Ham and Crab Jambalaya

Romaine Lettuce Salad

Cream Cheese 'n Chive Biscuits

Glazed Bananas and Ice Cream

Total Cooking Time: 30 minutes

Plan of Action

Oven-sauté the vegetables for the jambalaya while oven is preheating to 400° F. Place the jambalaya on lower shelf. Bake for 10 minutes. Place the two pans of biscuits on top shelf, bananas on lower shelf beside the jambalaya, and continue cooking for 20 minutes. Remove all dishes from the oven. Let the jambalaya and biscuits rest for 10 minutes. Fluff the jambalaya with a fork, and recut biscuits before serving.

Ham and Crab Jambalaya

1 large onion, chopped
1 clove garlic, minced
1 green pepper, seeded and chopped
2 tablespoons vegetable oil
1½ cups raw rice
6-ounce package frozen crabmeat, thawed
1½ to 2 pound ham slice, fully cooked
12 shucked or canned oysters, drained (optional)
2 cups chicken broth
   or 1 cup chicken broth and 1 cup clam juice
1 cup drained canned tomatoes, chopped
¼ cup dry sherry or dry vermouth
1½ teaspoons chili powder
½ teaspoon marjoram
½ teaspoon paprika
¼ teaspoon ground thyme
¼ teaspoon salt (or more if you want, but the ham is salty)
¼ teaspoon pepper

Heat oven to 400° F. While it is heating, combine onion, garlic, green pepper, and oil in a 2-quart casserole, and let them sauté in oven until they are sizzling, about 5 minutes. Remove casserole from oven. Stir in rice, crabmeat (diced), ham (trimmed of fat and diced), and oysters, if using. In a saucepan, combine all the remaining ingredients, and bring the mixture to a boil. Pour it into the casserole, cover tightly, and bake for 30 minutes. Remove the casserole from the oven, and let it rest for 10 minutes without uncovering it. Fluff the jambalaya well with a fork before serving.

Cream Cheese 'n Chive Biscuits

3 cups all-purpose flour
2 tablespoons baking powder
½ teaspoon baking soda
2 tablespoons sugar
2 4-ounce packages cream cheese with chives
¼ cup butter and ¼ cup lard
    or ½ cup vegetable shortening
½ to ⅔ cup buttermilk
¼ cup fresh chives, or 2 scallion tops, minced

Stir flour to lighten it before measuring. Mix together flour, baking powder, soda, and sugar. Cut in cheese, butter, and lard or shortening with two knives or a pastry blender until the texture is like oatmeal. Add minced chives or scallions. Stir in enough buttermilk to make a dough that leaves the sides of the bowl. Sprinkle the dough with a little flour, and knead it once or twice in the bowl to smooth it. Divide the dough in half. Pat the dough into two buttered 8-inch pie pans. Score each circle into six wedges, not quite cutting through. Bake 20 minutes in a preheated 400° F. oven. Let rest 10 minutes. Cut apart before serving.

Glazed Bananas and Ice Cream

⅓ cup brown sugar
⅓ cup apple jelly
2 tabespoons rum
2 tablespoons butter, melted
6 bananas
Vanilla ice cream

Mix the first four ingredients until well blended. Peel and slice the bananas in half lengthwise, then cut each piece in half again. Lay the bananas in slightly overlapping rows in a buttered 9-inch baking dish (not metal). Brush the bananas evenly with the sauce. Bake 20 minutes in a preheated 400° F. oven. Serve warm or at room temperature with ice cream as a topping.

Hasty, Tasty Haddock

Baked fish is always fast. Fish can be fresh or frozen and thawed, but fresh is best. Serves four.

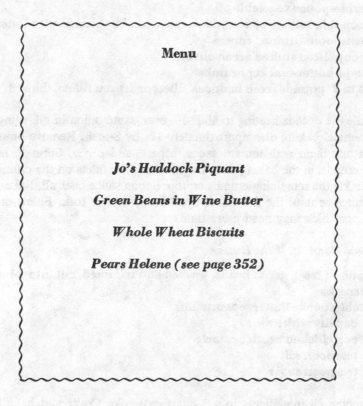

Menu

Jo's Haddock Piquant

Green Beans in Wine Butter

Whole Wheat Biscuits

Pears Helene (see page 352)

Total Cooking Time: 30 minutes

Plan of Action

While oven is heating to 400° F., oven-sauté onion for the haddock casserole. Place green beans in the oven, lower shelf. Cook 10 minutes. Place biscuits and fish on top shelf. Cook all 3 dishes 20 minutes longer or until fish flakes apart easily with a fork and biscuits are lightly browned.

Jo's Haddock Piquant

1 large onion, chopped
2 tablespoons vegetable oil
1 cup thin tomato sauce (thick sauce can be thinned with water)
2 teaspoons drained capers
¼ cup sliced stuffed green olives
2 cups butter-cracker crumbs
1½ to 2 pounds fresh haddock fillets or frozen fillets, thawed

While the oven is heating to 400° F., oven-sauté onion in oil, using a non-metal baking dish approximately 12- by 8-inch. Remove onions and mix them with tomato sauce, capers, and olives. Sprinkle half the crumbs in the baking dish. Lay the haddock fillets on the crumbs. Sprinkle the remaining crumbs on top. Spoon sauce over all. Bake 20 minutes or until the fish flakes apart easily with a fork. Fillets over ½ inch thick may need more time.

Green Beans in Wine Butter

1 pound fresh green beans, washed and trimmed, cut into 1-inch lengths
3 tablespoons butter, cut into bits
¼ cup dry white wine
½ cup chicken broth or stock
¼ teaspoon salt
¼ teaspoon sugar

Combine all ingredients in a 3-quart casserole. Cover and bake 30 minutes in a preheated 400° F. oven.

Whole Wheat Biscuits

2 cups whole wheat flour
4 teaspoons baking powder
½ teaspoon salt
1 tablespoon sugar

¼ cup (½ stick) butter, plus 1 tablespoon
¼ cup lard
½ to ⅔ cup buttermilk or soured milk (see page 362)

Thoroughly mix flour with baking powder, salt, and sugar. With a pastry blender or 2 knives, cut in ¼ cup butter and the lard until the mixture resembles coarse meal. Stir in enough buttermilk or soured milk to make a soft dough. Turn out onto a lightly floured surface, and knead until just smooth. Pat the dough into a square, and cut the square into nine or twelve square biscuits. Place them in a buttered baking dish. Cut the remaining 1 tablespoon butter into thin slices and place on each biscuit. Bake the biscuits for 20 minutes on the top shelf of a preheated 400° F. oven.

A FEAST OF FRIED SCALLOPS

Oven-frying is both easier and less greasy. A very relaxed dinner for four.

Menu

Oven-Fried Scallops

Spinach and Onion Casserole

Corn and Tomatoes

Triple Coffee (see page 352)

Total Cooking Time: 20 minutes

Plan of Action

Preheat oven to 525° F., and be sure it has reached that heat before timing the dishes. Place spinach and onion casserole, and corn and tomatoes on lower shelf. Bake 10 minutes. Place scallops on top shelf. Continue baking for 10 minutes or until scallops are lightly browned. Assemble the dessert after dinner.

Oven-Fried Scallops

1½ cups seasoned crumbs (see page 361)
3 tablespoons vegetable oil, divided
1½ pounds fresh scallops
   (extra-large scallops should be cut in half)
½ cup undiluted evaporated milk

Mix crumbs thoroughly with 2 tablespoons oil. Dip the scallops in milk, then crumbs. Brush the remaining tablespoon of oil in a shallow 15- by 12-inch baking dish. Lay the scallops in the pan in a single layer, and bake in a preheated 525° F. oven for 10 minutes or until lightly browned. Serve at once.

Spinach and Onion Casserole

1 pound fresh spinach, well washed
1 large onion, sliced and separated into rings
3 tablespoons butter
½ teaspoon dried dill weed
¼ teaspoon salt
Pepper to taste
½ cup water

Combine all ingredients in a 2-quart casserole. Cover and cook in a preheated 525° F. oven for 20 minutes. Stir before serving.

Corn and Tomatoes

10-ounce package frozen corn, thawed enough to separate
   kernels
2 fresh tomatoes, diced
2 tablespoons butter
¼ cup water
¼ teaspoon cumin
¼ teaspoon chili powder
¼ teaspoon salt

Combine all ingredients in a 1½-quart casserole. Cover and cook in a preheated 525° F. oven for 20 minutes.

A BEAUTIFUL BAKED OMELET

This lazy cook's puffy *frittata* doesn't even require separate beating of yolks and whites. Serves four.

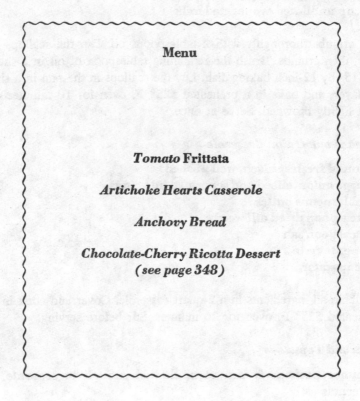

Menu

***Tomato* Frittata**

Artichoke Hearts Casserole

Anchovy Bread

Chocolate-Cherry Ricotta Dessert
(see page 348)

Total Cooking Time: 25 minutes

Plan of Action

Make dessert in advance and chill it. Preheat oven to 350° F. While it is heating, oven-sauté onion and green pepper for *frittata*. Place *frittata* and artichoke casserole on top shelf. Bake 15 minutes. Place bread on lower shelf, and continue baking for 10 minutes. Remove all dishes from the oven, and serve at once.

Tomato Frittata

2 tablespoons olive oil
½ onion, finely chopped
½ green pepper, seeded and chopped
¼ pound cheddar cheese, cut into small dice
1 large (or 2 small) tomato, thinly sliced
8 eggs
½ teaspoon oregano
½ teaspoon salt
Pepper to taste

Preheat oven to 350° F. Pour oil into a 9-inch square or round baking dish (not metal). Brush oil over sides of dish. Sprinkle bottom of dish with onion and green pepper, and oven-sauté for 5 minutes while oven is preheating. Remove dish from oven and cool it slightly. Sprinkle vegetables with cheese cubes, and layer tomato slices on top. In a large bowl, beat eggs well with remaining ingredients. Pour the mixture evenly over the contents of the baking dish, and bake the *frittata* for 25 minutes or until puffy and lightly browned on top. Serve immediately.

Artichoke Hearts Casserole

2 7½-ounce cans artichoke hearts, drained
1½ cups seasoned crumbs (see page 361)
3 tablespoons olive oil
2 tablespoons water
Paprika

Place the artichoke hearts in a 1½-quart casserole. Sprinkle crumbs over the artichoke hearts. Drizzle oil and water over crumbs. Sprinkle with paprika to garnish. Bake, uncovered, in a 350° F. oven for 25 minutes or until crumbs are lightly browned.

Anchovy Bread

1   recipe Anchovy Butter (see page 358)
1   loaf Italian bread

Cut bread into diagonal 1-inch slices, but do not slice all the way through. Spread anchovy butter on each slice. Place loaf on a baking sheet and bake it, uncovered, in a 350° F. oven for 10 minutes.

SATISFYING SOUP AND QUICHE

Sliced cheese melts together to form the easy crust for this quiche.
A hearty supper for four, with some ginger bars left over for another
day.

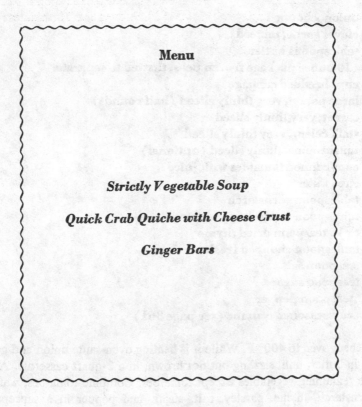

Menu

Strictly Vegetable Soup

Quick Crab Quiche with Cheese Crust

Ginger Bars

Total Cooking Time: 30 minutes

Plan of Action

Preheat oven to 400° F. While it is heating oven-sauté the onion and
garlic for soup. Place soup and quiche on lower shelf, ginger bars on

top shelf. Immediately reduce oven heat to 375° F. Mix frosting for ginger bars. Check ginger bars for doneness at the end of 25 minutes. Everything else cooks for 30 minutes or until vegetables are tender and quiche is set.

Strictly Vegetable Soup

1 onion, chopped
2 cloves garlic, minced
3 tablespoons butter
½ 10-ounce package frozen peas, thawed to separate
1 cup shredded cabbage
1 large potato, very thinly sliced (half rounds)
1 carrot, very thinly sliced
1 stalk celery, very thinly sliced
8 mushrooms, thinly sliced (optional)
2 cups canned tomatoes with juice
2 cups water
1 tablespoon cornstarch
1 tablespoon fresh chopped thyme
    or ½ teaspoon dried thyme
1 tablespoon chopped fresh parsley
1 teaspoon salt
1 teaspoon sugar
½ teaspoon pepper
½ cup seasoned crumbs (see page 361)

Preheat oven to 400° F. While it is heating oven-sauté onion and garlic in butter, until sizzling but not brown, in a 3-quart casserole. Add the remaining vegetables except tomatoes. Combine tomatoes, water, cornstarch, thyme, parsley, salt, sugar, and pepper in a saucepan. Bring the mixture to a boil, stirring constantly. Pour over vegetables in casserole. Cover immediately, reduce oven heat to 375° F., and bake the casserole for 30 minutes or until vegetables are tender. Put a heaping tablespoon of seasoned bread crumbs in the center of each serving.

Quick Crab Quiche with Cheese Crust

1 pound Muenster cheese, sliced
7 to 9 ounces flaked crabmeat
   (tuna can be substituted)
6 eggs
1 cup half-and-half
¼ teaspoon salt
¼ teaspoon cayenne pepper

Line four individual pie pans or casseroles with cheese, or use two 7-inch pie pans. Divide fish between portions. Beat eggs with half-and-half and salt, and divide between baking dishes. Sprinkle each with cayenne pepper. Bake for 20 minutes in a 375° F. oven.

Ginger Cakes

½ cup (1 stick) butter, softened
½ cup sugar
½ cup molasses
2 eggs
2 cups all-purpose flour
2 teaspoons baking powder
¼ teaspoon baking soda
2 teaspoons ground ginger
½ cup raisins
1½ cups sifted confectioners' sugar
1 teaspoon grated lemon rind
Juice of 1 lemon

Using an electric mixer, cream butter. Gradually add sugar, then molasses, then eggs one at a time. Stir flour to lighten it before measuring. Sift flour with baking powder, soda, and ginger. Stir dry ingredients into creamed mixture. Fold in raisins. Spoon the batter into a buttered and floured 13- by 9-inch baking pan and spread it out in an even layer. Bake for 25 minutes in a preheated 375° F. oven, and cool cake in pan on wire rack. Combine confectioners' sugar with grated lemon peel. Add enough lemon juice to make a thin frosting. Brush the frosting over the warm cake. To serve, cut into bars.

Sparing the Ribs: Meatless Meals

Meatless meals are in vogue for many reasons. Some people serve them, on occasion, to cut down on food costs. After all, meat is expensive—probably the most expensive item in our food budgets. Other homemakers are alarmed at the growing number of drugs fed to and injected into meat animals, and they elect to feed their families what they consider a safer menu containing little if any meat. Still others are opposed to the eating of flesh, and stick to a non-meat diet all the time for humane reasons.

Vegetables play an important role in the meatless menu. When you're selecting vegetables for this type of meal be especially choosey, since they will be quite prominent on your dish. Purchase them at the height of freshness—at their succulent best. But bear in mind that fresh vegetables are preferable to frozen only when they are freshly picked. For instance, a slightly wilted head of broccoli or cauliflower is inferior to its frozen counterpart. The more time that elapses between picking a fresh vegetable and eating it, the fewer precious nutrients it has left.

Many an over-zealous novice vegetarian has raced disdainfully past the frozen food section of a market to spend money on lifeless vegetables in the produce section, thinking the choice was nutritionally wise. It wasn't! The technical processes available today make it possible to freeze vegetables close to the height of their nutritional goodness. A freshly picked vegetable *is* superior, but one that's fresh only in the sense that it has not been preserved isn't.

Resist the temptation to wash vegetables before you store them. You will be removing vitamins and minerals along with the dirt, and you also will be reducing the amount of time they'll keep.

Store perishable vegetables either in the vegetable bin of your refrigerator or in air-tight containers in the refrigerator. Vegetables which don't require refrigeration should nonetheless be kept in a dark place to lessen vitamin loss.

You can oven-cook vegetables, conventionally thought of as top-of-the-stove fare, with amazingly pleasant results. And oven-cooking a vegetable is one of the best methods of preserving nutrients. Cut vegetables into uniform-sized pieces so they will cook evenly.

Many ingredients other than vegetables go into meatless menus. Cheese adds zing to some lackluster dishes. Select a nonprocessed variety for maximum nutritional benefits, and for the best taste, also. Just a small amount of cheese can add a large amount of flavor and protein to a dish. Eggs are another staple in the meatless menu. Do be sure that the eggs you use are fresh. And store them in the refrigerator in their cartons.

We don't advocate vegetarianism because of the possible protein problems, and we advise anyone embarking on this regimen to become thoroughly acquainted with the nutritional values of each vegetable and well-versed in the intricacies of balancing protein. But we do appreciate the advantages of a meatless meal from time to time, and we know for sure that meat doesn't necessarily make a meal. Some sumptuous menus can be prepared without it.

MACARONI AND CHEESE FLORENTINE DINNER

This is the first of two variations of this old standby dish that we'd like to share with you. They are so different from each other that chances are you could serve them on consecutive nights without complaints. Serves four.

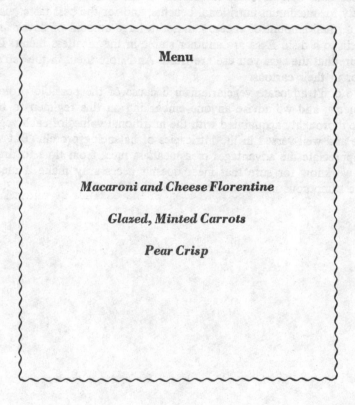

Menu

Macaroni and Cheese Florentine

Glazed, Minted Carrots

Pear Crisp

Total Cooking Time: 1 hour

Plan of Action

Prepare carrots and place on bottom shelf of preheated 375° F. oven.

While carrots are cooking, prepare macaroni and cheese and pear crisp. When carrots have been cooking for 30 minutes, stir them to coat with glaze. Place macaroni dish on bottom shelf and pear crisp on shelf above. Reduce heat and continue to bake another 30 minutes. Pear crisp will cool to just the right temperature while you're eating macaroni and carrots.

Macaroni and Cheese Florentine

1 16-ounce package macaroni elbows
1 16-ounce container smooth cottage cheese
1 10-ounce package chopped spinach, thawed
½ teaspoon salt
⅛ teaspoon white pepper
½ teaspoon crushed dill
¼ cup milk

Cook elbows according to package directions. Drain well and empty into a large, lightly greased casserole. Thoroughly mix cheese, spinach, salt, pepper, and dill into macaroni. Pour milk over. Place on bottom shelf of preheated 350° F. oven and bake for 30 minutes.

Glazed, Minted Carrots

8 large carrots
4 tablespoons butter
2 tablespoons brown sugar, firm packed
2 tablespoons water
1 teaspoon crushed mint

Scrape carrots, cut into pieces about 2 inches long, quarter these lengthwise, and put them into a medium-sized covered casserole. In a small saucepan, melt butter and add brown sugar, continuing to cook stirring constantly until sugar has melted. Add water and pour mixture over carrots. Sprinkle with mint. Cover and place dish on lower shelf of preheated 375° F. oven. When carrots have cooked for 30 minutes, stir them, reduce heat to 350° F. and continue to cook for another 30 minutes.

Pear Crisp

1 17½-ounce can pear halves, drained
½ cup brown sugar, packed
¾ cup all-purpose flour
4 tablespoons butter, softened
1 teaspoon cinnamon
½ teaspoon nutmeg

Grease an 8- by 8-inch square shallow dish. Cut pear halves into chunks and arrange them on bottom of dish. In a medium-sized mixing bowl, thoroughly blend other ingredients using the back of a large spoon. Sprinkle this mixture over pears, and place dish on upper shelf of 350° F. oven. Bake for 30 minutes.

MACARONI AND CHEESE TOMATO DINNER

Another variation of this old favorite.

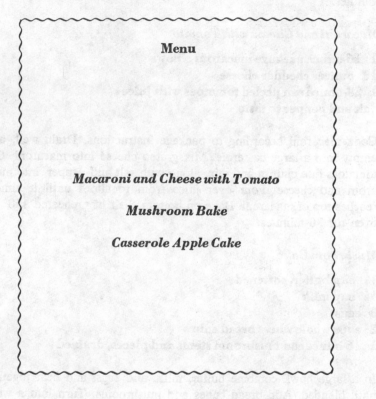

Menu

Macaroni and Cheese with Tomato

Mushroom Bake

Casserole Apple Cake

Total Cooking Time: 1 hour

Plan of Action

Assemble mushroom bake. Preheat oven to 350° F. Prepare apple mixture for cake. Place mushroom bake on bottom shelf, and apple mixture on top shelf of oven. Mix the batter for apple cake. Assemble macaroni and cheese. When apple mixture has been in oven for 15 to 20 minutes, remove it and complete recipe, then return to oven. When mushroom bake has cooked for 30 minutes, add macaroni and cheese to bottom shelf. Cook everything for another 30 minutes.

Macaroni and Cheese with Tomato

1 16-ounce package macaroni elbows
12 ounces cheddar cheese
1 28-ounce can peeled tomatoes with juice
Salt and pepper to taste

Cook macaroni according to package instructions. Drain well, and empty into a large casserole. Mix grated cheese into macaroni. Cut tomatoes into chunks and mix, along with salt and pepper, into macaroni and cheese. Pour over juice from tomatoes until it almost reaches top of macaroni. Bake on bottom shelf of preheated 350° F. oven for 30 minutes.

Mushroom Bake

¼ cup butter, softened
½ cup milk
3 eggs
2 cups whole wheat bread cubes
1 16-ounce can mushroom stems and pieces, drained

In a large bowl, combine butter, milk, and eggs, and beat together until blended. Add bread cubes and mushrooms. Turn into a well-greased, large casserole. Put on bottom shelf of preheated 350° F. oven for 1 hour.

Casserole Apple Cake

½ cup butter
2 eggs, separated
1 cup milk
1½ cups all-purpose flour
2 teaspoons baking powder
¼ teaspoon salt
1 teaspoon vanilla
¾ cup sugar

apple mixture:

4 to 6 apples, peeled and sliced
¼ cup brown sugar
1 teaspoon cinnamon
1 tablespoon butter

Put apples mixed with brown sugar, cinnamon, and dotted with butter in the bottom of a 2-quart casserole. Cook in preheated 350° F. oven for 15 to 20 minutes, or until apples lose their crispness and reduce in size. They should be half-cooked. Stir gently to mix with flavorings. While apples are cooking, allow butter, eggs, and milk to come to room temperature. Sift flour, measure, and sift again with baking powder and salt. Add vanilla to milk. Cream butter until light, gradually adding sugar. Continue to beat until well mixed. Add egg yolks one at a time. Add flour mixture alternately with milk, beginning and ending with flour. Beat egg whites until stiff but not dry. Fold in cake batter. Pour cake batter over apples. Cook 40 minutes longer, until cake is browned on top. A toothpick inserted in the center should come out clean. Serve apple cake warm or at room temperature.

FRUITY PIZZA SUPPER

This new and unusual twist to an old favorite is only faintly reminiscent of Italian pizza. Serves four.

Menu

Fruity Pizza

Meatless Antipasto (see page 335)

Baked Bananas

Total Cooking Time: about 2 hours and 40 minutes

Plan of Action

Prepare pizza dough. While dough is rising, make pizza topping. Preheat oven to 425° F. Assemble pizza. While pizza is cooking, make meatless antipasto. When pizza is done, reduce oven heat to

325 ° F. Remove pizza from oven and let stand 5 minutes before cutting. While pizza is cooling, prepare bananas. Just before serving pizza and antipasto, put bananas in oven and bake for 20 minutes. Put together dessert and serve.

Fruity Pizza

Pizza Dough (see page 359)
¼ **cup olive oil**
1 **small onion, chopped**
½ **teaspoon cinnamon**
¼ **teaspoon garlic powder**
½ **teaspoon salt**
⅛ **teaspoon pepper**
1 **16-ounce can tomatoes in purée**
1 **7-ounce can crushed pineapple**
½ **cup dark raisins**
2 **6-ounce cans tomato paste**
1 **cup grated Parmesan cheese**
½ **pound mozzarella cheese, thinly sliced**

In a large Dutch oven, warm olive oil in 375° F. oven. Add onion and cook until transparent. Remove from oven and add cinnamon, garlic powder, salt, and pepper. Cut up tomatoes and add them, along with purée, to contents of Dutch oven. Drain pineapple well; combine it and raisins with tomatoes. Cover Dutch oven and return it to preheated 375° F. oven for 30 minutes. Stir tomato paste into mixture. Cover and cook at 375° F. for another 90 minutes, removing cover during last 15 minutes.

Let sauce cool slightly. Sprinkle half of Parmesan cheese on each pizza crust. Add sauce, spreading almost to edges. Top with slices of mozzarella. Put one pizza on the middle shelf and one on the bottom shelf of preheated 425° F. oven and bake for 10 minutes. Switch pizza on middle shelf to bottom and pizza on bottom shelf to middle. Continue to cook another 10 minutes, or until sauce is bubbly and crust is golden. If crust browns too soon, cover pizzas with foil and continue to cook.

Baked Bananas (bake while you're eating Pizza)

4 medium-sized firm bananas
2 tablespoons lemon juice
1 cup crushed corn flakes
1 pint vanilla ice cream
½ cup orange liqueur
4 maraschino cherries

Peel bananas and cut them lengthwise. Dip them in lemon juice, then corn flakes, and arrange in a buttered 8-inch square pan. Put on bottom shelf of 325° F. oven for 20 minutes. Remove from oven. Put two banana halves in each of four bowls. Put a scoop of ice cream in each bowl. Pour ⅛ cup of orange liqueur on each ice cream scoop and top with a cherry.

GARBANZO LOAF DINNER

This is the kind of meal that makes people say, "Who needs meat!" Serves four.

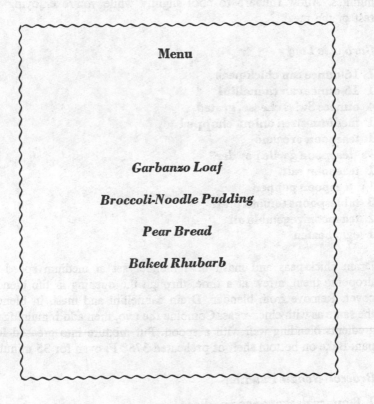

Menu

Garbanzo Loaf

Broccoli-Noodle Pudding

Pear Bread

Baked Rhubarb

Total Cooking Time: 1 hour

Plan of Action

Preheat oven to 375° F. Prepare pear bread and place on top shelf of preheated oven. Cook egg noodles and broccoli according to packages instructions. While noodles and broccoli are cooking, mix ingredients for baked rhubarb, and start preparing garbanzo loaf. When bread has been in oven for 15 minutes, place rhubarb on top shelf of oven and continue cooking. Assemble broccoli-noodle pudding and garbanzo loaf, and place these dishes on bottom shelf when bread has been in oven for 25 minutes. Continue to cook for another 35 minutes. Allow rhubarb to cool slightly while you're enjoying the rest of the meal.

Garbanzo Loaf

1 16-ounce can chick-peas
1 16-ounce can cannellini
4 ounces Swiss cheese, grated
1 medium-sized onion, chopped
1 teaspoon oregano
⅛ teaspoon garlic powder
1 teaspoon salt
⅛ teaspoon pepper
3 tablespoons tomato paste
1 teaspoon vegetable oil
1 egg, beaten

Drain chick-peas and mash in a blender set at medium speed by dropping them, a few at a time, through the opening in the blender cover. Remove from blender. Drain cannellini and mash in blender the same as with chick-peas. Combine the two, then add remaining ingredients blending well with a spoon. Put mixture into greased loaf pan. Bake on bottom shelf of preheated 375° F. oven for 35 minutes.

Broccoli-Noodle Pudding

1 8-ounce package egg noodles
1 10-ounce package frozen broccoli pieces, thawed
3 eggs
1 small onion, finely grated
1 teaspoon salt
⅛ teaspoon white pepper
½ cup raisins

Cook noodles according to package directions. Separate eggs, beating yolks in blender, and add broccoli a little at a time. (Use hole in blender top to do this.) Blend on low speed until broccoli is thoroughly chopped. Drain noodles and mix together noodles, broccoli, onion, salt, pepper, and raisins. Beat egg whites until stiff, and fold them into broccoli-noodle mixture. Put into large greased casserole and bake on bottom shelf of preheated 375° F. oven for 35 minutes, or until center is puffed and looks dry. Serve immediately.

Pear Bread

1   cup all-purpose flour
½   teaspoon cinnamon
½   teaspoon nutmeg
1   teaspoon baking soda
¼   teaspoon salt
¾   cup sugar
⅓   cup vegetable oil
2   eggs, beaten
1   8-ounce can pears

Sift together flour, cinnamon, nutmeg, baking soda, salt, and sugar. Add oil, then eggs, and stir until well mixed. Thoroughly drain and chop pears. Add to batter, folding in. Grease and flour a loaf pan. Pour in batter and bake on top shelf of preheated 375° F. oven for 60 minutes.

Baked Rhubarb

4   cups rhubarb cut into 1-inch long pieces
½   cup water
1   cup sugar

Mix together all ingredients in a casserole. Cover and place on top shelf of preheated 375° F. oven for 45 minutes or until rhubarb is soft. Stir well and serve warm or cold.

MAIN DISH SQUASH PIE DINNER

Zucchini may be substituted if summer squash is not available. But whichever you use, select a firm, unblemished squash for this pie. Serves four.

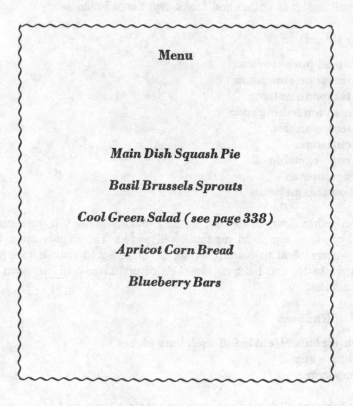

Menu

Main Dish Squash Pie

Basil Brussels Sprouts

Cool Green Salad (see page 338)

Apricot Corn Bread

Blueberry Bars

Total Cooking Time: 35 minutes

Plan of Action

Preheat oven to 400° F. Brown pie crust and remove it from oven. Assemble squash pie and place on cookie sheet on bottom shelf of oven. Make salad and put it in refrigerator to chill. When pie has been in oven for 10 minutes, place Brussels sprouts on bottom shelf; put corn bread and blueberry bars on top shelf and continue cooking for another 25 minutes.

Main Dish Squash Pie

1 9-inch pie crust
1 medium-sized onion
1 tablespoon oil
1 medium-sized summer squash
1 teaspoon Italian seasoning
Garlic powder
2 eggs
1 cup milk
Salt and pepper to taste

Prick pie shell and bake it on cookie sheet in preheated 400° F. oven for about 5 minutes, until lightly browned. Peel, slice, and ring onions. In a small casserole, oven-sauté onion rings in oil until they are transparent but not browned. Wash squash and slice it in very thin circles. Put layer of squash slices in pie crust, add a third of the onions, and sprinkle with a third of the Italian seasoning. Make 2 more layers of squash, onion, and seasoning, topping final layer with a sprinkling of garlic powder. Beat eggs, add milk, salt, and pepper and pour mixture over squash. Place on cookie sheet on bottom shelf of preheated 400° F. oven for 35 to 40 minutes, or until knife inserted in center comes out clean.

Basil Brussels Sprouts

2 10-ounce packages frozen Brussels sprouts, thawed
½ cup water
2 teaspoons crushed basil
Salt and pepper to taste
1 tablespoon butter

Place Brussels sprouts in medium-sized casserole. Add water and sprinkle on basil, salt, and pepper to taste. Cover and cook on bottom shelf of preheated 400° F. oven for 25 minutes. Drain and add butter before serving.

Apricot Corn Bread

1 8-ounce can apricots
1 cup yellow cornmeal
1 cup all-purpose flour
⅓ cup sugar
1 tablespoon baking powder
½ teaspoon salt
1 egg, beaten
⅓ cup salad oil
1 cup milk

Drain apricots well and dice them. In a large bowl, combine next five ingredients. Combine remaining ingredients and stir into dry ingredients until just blended. Fold in apricots. Grease 8-inch square glass baking dish. Pour in mixture and bake on middle shelf of preheated 400° F. oven for 25 minutes.

Blueberry Bars

¾ cup butter, softened
1 cup brown sugar, packed
1⅓ cups all-purpose flour
½ teaspoon baking soda
1⅓ cups raw quick oats
1 teaspoon salt
1 10-ounce jar blueberry preserves

Grease 10-inch by 13-inch glass pan. With the back of a spoon, cream butter, and slowly mix in sugar until well blended. Mix together all dry ingredients and blend into creamed butter and sugar. Sprinkle half of this mixture in bottom of greased pan. Press down firmly with the back of a spoon. Spread blueberry preserves over this and sprinkle remaining mixture on top of blueberries. Bake on middle shelf of preheated 400° F. oven for 25 minutes. This will be just eating temperature by the time you've finished your meal. Cut in squares and serve.

SPANISH RICE DINNER

Be sure you use long grain converted rice for best results. Serves four.

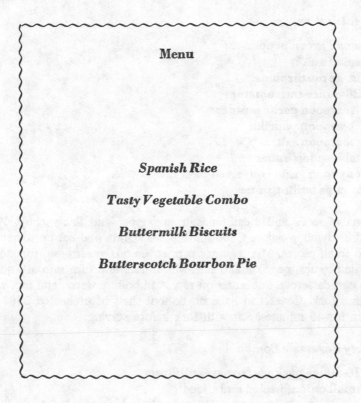

Menu

Spanish Rice

Tasty Vegetable Combo

Buttermilk Biscuits

Butterscotch Bourbon Pie

Total Cooking Time: 45 minutes

Plan of Action

Preheat oven to 350° F. Put pie on top shelf and rice on bottom shelf of preheated oven. Put vegetable combo together, and when pie and rice have been cooking for 15 minutes, place it on bottom shelf of oven. Mix buttermilk biscuit dough. Drop it by spoonfuls onto cookie sheet, and place on top shelf of oven after pie and rice have been cooking for 35 minutes. Continue baking everything for another 10 minutes. Vanilla ice cream will enhance the flavor and richness of the pie.

Spanish Rice

1 small green pepper
1 small onion
3 large mushrooms
1 28-ounce can tomatoes
⅛ teaspoon garlic powder
½ teaspoon paprika
½ teaspoon salt
1 tablespoon butter
1 cup long grain converted rice, raw
2½ cups boiling water

Remove seeds and membranes from pepper and finely chop. Peel and finely chop onion. Chop mushrooms. Drain and cut up tomatoes into small pieces. Mix together pepper, onion, mushroom, tomatoes, garlic powder, paprika, and salt. Mix in rice and turn into a 2-quart greased casserole. Put butter on top. Add boiling water, and mix well with a fork. Cover and bake on bottom shelf of preheated 350° F. oven for 45 minutes. Stir with fork before serving.

Tasty Vegetable Combo

1 10-ounce package frozen cauliflower
1 small onion, peeled and sliced
   (separate the rings and slice them in halves, also)
1 small zucchini squash, scrubbed and thinly sliced
1 teaspoon celery salt
⅛ teaspoon pepper
⅛ teaspoon garlic powder
3 tablespoons butter
¼ cup freshly grated Parmesan cheese

Put frozen cauliflower, onion, and zucchini in medium-sized casserole. Add ¼ cup water. Cover and cook on bottom shelf of pre-heated 350° F. oven for 30 minutes, or until vegetables are fork tender. Drain vegetables well. Add celery salt, pepper, garlic powder, and butter, and toss gently until butter is melted. Add cheese and toss again to coat vegetables.

Buttermilk Biscuits

2 cups all-purpose flour
2 teaspoons baking powder
¼ teaspoon baking soda
½ teaspoon salt
¼ cup butter
1 cup buttermilk

Mix together dry ingredients, and cut in butter with two knives until mixture is crumbly in texture. Stir in buttermilk. Drop batter by spoonfuls (about 12) onto ungreased cookie sheet. Cook on middle shelf of preheated 350° F. oven until golden brown—about 10 minutes.

Butterscotch Bourbon Pie

¼ cup melted butter
1 cup sugar
½ cup light corn syrup
2 eggs, beaten
¼ teaspoon salt
½ teaspoon vanilla extract
½ cup butterscotch chips
¼ cup walnut pieces
⅓ cup bourbon
1 9-inch pie crust, unbaked

Mix butter and sugar. Add corn syrup, eggs, salt, and vanilla. Mix in butterscotch chips, nuts, and bourbon, stirring to distribute pieces evenly. Pour into pie shell and bake on top shelf of preheated 350° F. oven for 40 minutes, or until knife inserted in center comes out clean. Serve topped with vanilla ice cream.

ZIPPY EGGPLANT-ZUCCHINI CASSEROLE DINNER

A marvelous menu when you have a bumper crop of eggplant and zucchini. Serves four.

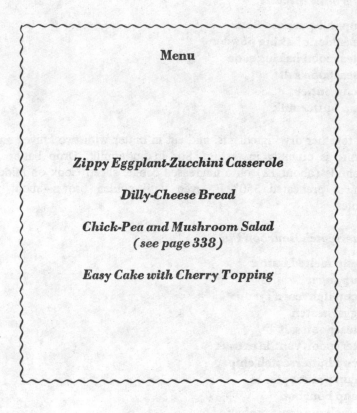

Menu

Zippy Eggplant-Zucchini Casserole

Dilly-Cheese Bread

Chick-Pea and Mushroom Salad
(see page 338)

Easy Cake with Cherry Topping

Total Cooking Time: 1 hour

Plan of Action

About 3 hours before dinner time, prepare dough for bread. Put it in a warm place to rise for 1 hour. Punch down, divide in half, place in loaf pans, and put in warm place to rise for another hour. While bread is rising second time, put eggplant casserole together. After bread has risen second time, put it on middle shelf of preheated 350° F. oven. Place casserole on bottom shelf. Mix cake ingredients. When bread and casserole have been in oven about 30 minutes, remove bread and set aside to cool slightly. Put cake on middle shelf and continue to cook for another 25 to 30 minutes, or until cake top springs back when pressed. Assemble salad while cake and casserole are cooking. Add yogurt to cake just prior to serving.

Zippy Eggplant-Zucchini Casserole

1   medium-sized eggplant
2   small zucchini
Salt
3   tablespoons vegetable oil
1   medium-sized onion, sliced and ringed
1   8-ounce can tomatoes
1   teaspoon salt
½   teaspoon oregano
½   teaspoon basil
⅛   teaspoon pepper
1   cup grated Romano cheese

Peel and slice eggplant. Salt each slice lightly and set in colander to drain for about 20 minutes. (This should eliminate the bitter taste so often associated with eggplant.) Scrub zucchini with a vegetable brush before slicing it. In a large skillet, heat oil and sauté onions until transparent but not brown. Brush salt from eggplant slices, cut them in halves, and sauté them and zucchini slices in the same skillet used for onion, adding more butter if necessary. Preheat oven to 350° F. Cut up tomatoes. Put thin layer of tomatoes on bottom of large casserole. Add a layer of eggplant and sprinkle it with cheese. Add a layer of onion, then a layer of zucchini. Sprinkle these with cheese, some salt, oregano, basil, and pepper. Add some tomatoes. Continue to make layers until all ingredients are used. Cover casserole and put it on bottom shelf of 350° F. oven for 60 minutes.

Dilly-Cheese Bread

4 cups all-purpose flour
2½ tablespoons sugar
2 packages active dry yeast
1 teaspoon salt
2 teaspoons crushed dill
½ cup water
1 cup milk
2½ tablespoons butter
1 egg
⅓ cup grated Parmesan cheese
1 tablespoon butter, softened

Combine flour, sugar, yeast, salt, and dill in large mixing bowl. Heat milk and butter over low heat until butter melts and milk is warm but not hot. Stir milk slowly into flour. Mix in egg. With an electric beater on medium speed, beat for 4 minutes, gradually adding cheese during this time. With a spoon, mix in enough of the remaining flour a little at a time so that dough becomes firm and pulls away from sides of bowl.

On a well-floured board, knead dough for about 10 minutes, until it's elastic in texture. Grease a bowl. Make a ball of dough and turn it in bowl until all surfaces are greased. Cover lightly and put in a warm place to rise for about 1 hour. Dough should double in size. Punch down dough and divide in half. Put each half into a greased loaf pan. Cover pans lightly, and put them in a warm place to rise again for another hour. Brush softened butter on tops of loaves, and place them on middle shelf of preheated 350° F. oven for 25 to 30 minutes or until loaves are golden. Remove loaves from pans, cool slightly, and serve warm.

Easy Cake with Cherry Topping

1 cup all-purpose flour
½ cup sugar
2 teaspoons baking powder
½ teaspoon salt
½ cup milk

1 egg, beaten
¼ cup butter, softened
1 teaspoon vanilla
1 container of cherry yogurt, stirred

Sift dry ingredients together. Mix milk and egg and add it gradually to flour, beating with an electric beater on low for 2 minutes. Add butter and continue to beat for another 2 minutes. Mix in vanilla and turn into greased, 8-inch square pan. Bake on middle shelf of 350° F. oven for 25 to 30 minutes or until top springs back when pressed. Cool 30 minutes. Cut and serve warm with topping of cherry yogurt.

PUFFY OMELET DINNER

If you want to make a no-fail puffy omelet, the easy way to do it is in the oven. Really, it is a miniature soufflé. This menu is perfectly suitable for special occasions that happen to arrive when the budget is lean. Serves four.

Menu

Puffy Omelet with Mushroom Filling

Tomatoes Stuffed with Rice

Individual Herbed Loaves

Cheese and Fresh Fruit in Season

Total Cooking Time: 1 hour, 10 minutes

Plan of Action

Preheat oven to 375° F. Prepare tomatoes and place them on bottom shelf of oven. Remove herbed loaves from refrigerator. Prepare mushrooms, and when tomatoes have been in oven for 30 minutes, place mushrooms on bottom shelf next to them. Ten minutes before tomatoes and mushrooms are done, assemble omelet. Remove tomatoes and mushrooms from oven. Place omelet on top shelf and herbed loaves on bottom shelf. In 10 minutes, peek at omelet. It should be puffy, "set," and lightly browned. Remove pans from oven. Turn omelet onto serving plate and top with mushrooms. Serve tomatoes in their casserole dish and loaves in the foil boats.

Puffy Omelet

Any round ovenproof dish will do, but we like a cast iron frying pan best for this omelet.

1 tablespoon butter
1 tablespoon Parmesan cheese, grated
5 eggs, separated, room temperature
Salt and pepper, to taste

Generously butter a round ovenproof dish. Cut a round of waxed paper to fit the dish, lay it on the bottom and butter that, too. Sprinkle buttered paper with Parmesan cheese. Beat egg yolks in a large bowl until light. Add salt and pepper. Beat egg whites until they stand in stiff peaks. Fold them into the egg yolk mixture until just blended. Pour into prepared dish. Bake in preheated 375° F. oven for 10 minutes, or until puffy, "set," and lightly browned. Invert onto plate. Peel off waxed paper. Turn right-side-up onto serving plate. Top with mushroom filling. Cut into wedges and serve immediately.

Oven-Sautéed Mushrooms

1 pound fresh mushrooms, thickly sliced, or left whole if small
1 teaspoon dried parsley
2 tablespoons butter
2 tablespoons olive oil
Salt and pepper to taste

Put the mushrooms in an oblong baking dish, sprinkle with parsley, dot with butter, and drizzle on oil. Stir to mix ingredients. Cook uncovered on bottom shelf of preheated 375° F. oven for 30 minutes. Remove from oven, and add salt and pepper to taste.

Tomatoes Stuffed with Rice

4 large tomatoes
⅓ cup raw rice
½ teaspoon salt
½ teaspoon sugar
⅛ teaspoon cinnamon
⅛ teaspoon garlic powder
2 tablespoons fresh parsley, chopped, or 1 teaspoon dried parsley
6 tablespoons olive oil, divided
Juice from tomato pulp
4 fresh basil leaves (optional)

Cut off the tomato tops and reserve them. Scoop out the pulp into a close-meshed strainer. Set the strainer in a bowl, and work the pulp with the back of a wooden spoon to extract all the juice. Set the tomato shells on a rack upside down until you're ready to stuff them. Mix together rice, salt, sugar, cinnamon, garlic powder, parsley, and 2 tablespoons of the oil. Spoon into shells, dividing rice evenly among them. Pour the pulp juice over the rice, drizzle 2 tablespoons of oil over that, lay a basil leaf on each shell, and put the tomato tops back on. Set the tomatoes in a baking dish that will just hold them upright. Pour the remaining oil over the tomatoes to coat. Bake on bottom shelf of preheated 375° F. oven for 1 hour, or until rice is tender.

Individual Herbed Loaves

These can be prepared in advance and refrigerated until one hour before dinner.

½ cup (1 stick) butter
1 teaspoon dried oregano
4 Italian sandwich loaves, small size
Paprika

Melt butter with the herbs in the top of a double boiler. Cut the loaves into diagonal slices, but not all the way through. Brush the loaf slices with herbed butter using a pastry brush. Sprinkle tops with paprika. Wrap loaves in aluminum foil, shaping it like boats, leaving top half of each loaf exposed. Bake for 10 minutes at 375° F. Serve loaves in their foil boats.

MOCK MEAT LOAF SUPREME DINNER

This delicious and filling vegetarian fare isn't hard on the pocketbook. Serves four.

Menu

Mock Meat Loaf Supreme

Rice with Mushrooms

Green Peas à la Paris

Orange Delight

Total Cooking Time: about 55 minutes

Plan of Action

Cover soybeans with water and soak overnight. To prepare dinner, turn oven to 350° F. and melt butter in casserole in oven. Add onion, mushrooms, and garlic to melted butter (for rice with mushrooms) and leave in oven. While these are cooking assemble Green Peas à la Paris. When onion and mushrooms are done, assemble rice with mushrooms. Mix batter for orange cake, and pour it into pan. Put cake on top shelf of oven, rice and peas on bottom shelf. Mix ingredients for Mock Meat Loaf Supreme. When other dishes have been in oven 10 minutes, place Mock Meat Loaf on top shelf of oven and continue to cook for 35 minutes or until cake is browned. Let cake cook slightly while you eat dinner.

Rice with Mushrooms

If fresh mushrooms are unavailable substitute canned. The dish will still be flavorful, but the fresh mushrooms are ever so much tastier.

¼ cup butter
1 small onion, chopped
6 ounces mushrooms, thinly sliced
⅛ teaspoon garlic powder
1 cup long grain converted rice
1 beef bouillon cube
2½ cups boiling water

In a medium-sized casserole, melt butter in 350° F. oven. Add onion, mushrooms, and garlic and cook for 10 minutes. Remove casserole from oven. Add rice and stir. Dissolve bouillon cube in boiling water, and pour over rice, mixing well with a fork. Cover casserole and return it to bottom shelf of oven for 45 minutes. Fluff rice with fork before serving.

Mock Meat Loaf Supreme

2 cups soybeans, soaked overnight and parboiled for 5 minutes
½ cup chopped green pepper
1 small onion, finely chopped
1 stalk celery, chopped
1 cup tomato purée
¼ teaspoon garlic powder
½ teaspoon chili powder
½ teaspoon powdered mustard

½ teaspoon cumin
1 tablespoon soy sauce
⅛ teaspoon pepper
Wheatgerm to bind mixture

In a blender purée soybeans a half-cup at a time. In a large bowl, mix soybeans, green pepper, onion, celery, tomato purée, and seasonings. Add enough wheatgerm to bind the ingredients together and give a stiff consistency. Put mixture into greased loaf pan and cook for 35 minutes on top shelf of preheated 350° F. oven. If you like, add tomato slices to top of loaf during last 10 minutes of cooking.

Green Peas à la Paris

6 large lettuce leaves
1 10-ounce package small frozen peas, thawed to separate
½ teaspoon salt
¼ teaspoon sugar
3 tablespoons white wine

Put two lettuce leaves on bottom of 1-quart casserole. Add half the peas. Sprinkle with ¼ teaspoon salt, ⅛ teaspoon sugar, and 1½ tablespoons wine. Cover with two more lettuce leaves. Add another layer using remaining peas, salt, sugar, and wine. Top with remaining two lettuce leaves, cover, and put on bottom shelf of 350° F. oven for 45 minutes. Discard lettuce leaves before serving.

Orange Delight

¾ cup all-purpose flour
¼ teaspoon salt
½ teaspoon baking powder
5 eggs
1¼ cups sugar
2 tablespoons butter, melted
½ cup orange juice
1½ cups milk

Grease 8-inch square glass pan. Sift flour, salt, and baking powder together in a large bowl. In another large bowl, beat eggs with an electric beater, gradually adding sugar. Continue beating on high until mixture becomes thick and golden in color. Reduce speed to low and add butter and orange juice. Mix in flour until just blended. Add milk and beat briefly on low. Pour batter into prepared pan. Set in a larger pan of hot water on bottom shelf of preheated 350° F. oven. (Water should come about halfway up sides of glass pan.) Bake 45 to 50 minutes until top is browned.

Easy Breezy Brunches

A late breakfast, an early lunch, or a combination of breakfast and lunch are all loosely referred to as brunch. In order to truly deserve to be called brunch, the meal should be served between 10 A.M. and 1 P.M. The concept of brunch originated in England around the turn of the century. And it was an extremely upper-crust meal—the "in" way of entertaining if you were anyone in English society. Brunches of this era were sumptuous. They were elegant. And the ladies of England competed in an effort to give the poshest brunch.

But over the years the custom of serving brunches has filtered down to the commoners. Brunches no longer have to be exotic, and many families enjoy them even when there's no company to impress. Brunch is still an acceptable way to entertain, but it's also great for those lazy weekend mornings.

The rules for what is proper to serve at brunch are very flexible. We generally (but not always) have a dish using eggs, and we like to use this meal to see that everyone gets his daily ration of fruit. Some of our brunches consist of truly simple fare—menus you may want to repeat fairly often, as we do. While other of our brunches are a bit more complicated, ones we tend to serve only on special occasions, or when we just feel like giving our families a treat. We serve a more breakfast-like brunch when it's early, and add more luncheon-type dishes if the hour is later.

Eggs are one of the best available brunch foods. Not only are they versatile and inexpensive, they also provide a good quality of protein with a full complement of the amino acids so vital to human health. The tiny egg also is rich in vitamins A, B, and D, as well as the minerals iron and phosphorous.

Select the eggs you're going to use carefully. The color of shell is unimportant. It has nothing to do with quality, but is determined by the breed of hen that laid them. But the freshness of an egg does make a difference. When in doubt about this, hold the egg in question to your ear, and shake it. If you can hear it sloshing around, it's not fresh. (As an egg ages, the white evaporates, leaving the air space in which you can hear the egg moving.)

Properly stored eggs can be kept safely for over a month, providing they're fresh when you buy them. Of course, the fresher they are, the better they are for you. But there's no need to throw out eggs because they're a couple of weeks old. Use them in recipes other than egg dishes.

Fruit is another star of the brunch table. A large bowl of fresh fruit is always a welcome addition, regardless of what else is on the menu. When you're serving fresh fruit, be sure it's ripe but still firm. If you're preparing fruit to use in a recipe, bear in mind that certain fruits (such as bananas and apples) will turn dark if peeled or sliced and exposed to the air. You can preslice these fruits and submerge them in acidulated water, but you'll be sacrificing some of the water-soluble vitamins by doing this.

Fresh fruit isn't always best. If it's not in season, it may look tired from its long journey from some warmer clime, and be expensive to boot. Frozen fruit is better than droopy fresh fruit, and even canned fruit is acceptable as a substitute.

Many of the nutrients provided by fresh fruits are to be found in the skins. While it isn't always feasible to use unpeeled fruit in recipes, it does seem needlessly wasteful to peel fruit such as apples if you're going to eat them raw. Over half of the vitamin A in an apple is in the skin, along with about three-fifths of the vitamin C.

Finally, we think that every brunch should be served with plenty of freshly brewed coffee, or tea for those who aren't coffee lovers. If youngsters are among the diners, hot chocolate is a favorite brunch beverage for them. We have not included these beverages in our menus, leaving their selection up to you.

When you've tried these menus, brunch may become as popular a meal with you as it is with us. A two-meal day is so much easier on the cook than a three-meal day.

ARTICHOKE AND CHICKEN FRITTATA

This brunch, built around an unusual *frittata,* is a great way to start the day—even if it's a late start. Serves six.

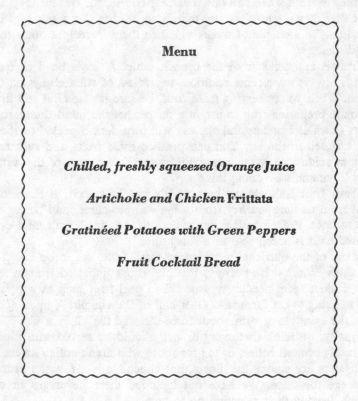

Menu

Chilled, freshly squeezed Orange Juice

Artichoke and Chicken **Frittata**

Gratinéed Potatoes with Green Peppers

Fruit Cocktail Bread

Total Cooking Time: about 1 hour

Plan of Action

Preheat oven to 350° F. Make bread. Assemble potato casserole. Place potatoes on bottom shelf and bread on middle shelf of preheated oven. Slice and chop vegetables and chicken for *frittata.*

When potatoes and bread have been in oven for about 25 minutes, start cooking *frittata*. After potatoes and bread have cooked for 45 minutes, place *frittata* on middle shelf and continue cooking everything for another 15 minutes.

Artichoke and Chicken Frittata

3   tablespoons butter
1   small onion, chopped
1   7½-ounce can artichoke hearts, quartered
¼   teaspoon oregano
¼   teaspoon crushed basil
10 eggs
½   cup half-and-half
1   teaspoon salt
⅛   teaspoon pepper
1   cup cubed cooked chicken
1   large tomato, sliced

In a large skillet, melt butter. Sauté onion, and add artichoke hearts, oregano, and basil to pan. In a large bowl, beat eggs. Add half-and-half, salt and pepper and continue beating until just blended. Pour this into pan over onion and artichokes. Sprinkle cubed chicken on top. Cover, and cook over low heat until eggs are just a little set—about 15 minutes. Place tomato slices on top of *frittata* and bake on middle shelf of preheated 350° F. oven for 10 to 15 minutes or until center is firm.

Gratinéed Potatoes with Peppers

1   pound potatoes, peeled and thinly sliced
2   large green peppers, seeded and cut into thin strips
⅛   teaspoon garlic powder
½   teaspoon salt
¼   teaspoon white pepper
2   cups half-and-half
½   cup grated Romano cheese

Generously butter a shallow glass casserole. Layer half the potatoes on bottom, add a layer of all the pepper strips. Mix together garlic powder, salt, and pepper, and sprinkle half of this on top of pepper strips. Add remaining potato slices. Pour half-and-half over this, and sprinkle Romano cheese on top. Bake on bottom shelf of preheated 350° F. oven for 1 hour and 15 minutes, or until potatoes are fork' tender. Let rest for 5 or 10 minutes before serving.

Note: For a different taste sensation, add anchovies to the top of this dish during the last 10 minutes of cooking.

Fruit Cocktail Bread

1¾ cups flour
2 teaspoons baking soda
1 teaspoon cinnamon
1 teaspoon nutmeg
1 cup sugar
½ teaspoon salt
3 eggs, beaten
¾ cup salad oil
2 cups canned fruit cocktail, drained

Sift together all dry ingredients. Combine eggs and oil, beat well, and add gradually to dry ingredients, mixing thoroughly. Fold in fruit cocktail. Divide between two greased and floured loaf pans, and bake on middle shelf of preheated 350° F. oven for about 1 hour, or until toothpick inserted in the middle comes out clean.

LAMB CROQUETTES WITH POACHED EGGS

Leftover lamb is hard to sell to most people unless it's dressed up. The lamb croquettes in this menu get raves, while getting rid of that leftover lamb. Serves six.

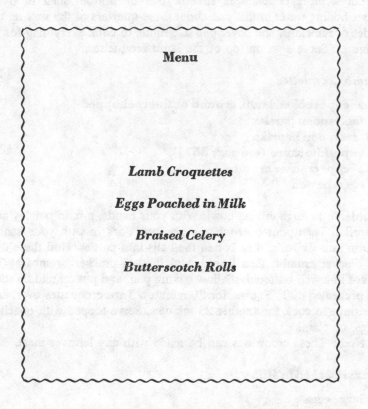

Menu

Lamb Croquettes

Eggs Poached in Milk

Braised Celery

Butterscotch Rolls

Total Cooking Time: 1 hour

Plan of Action

Prepare croquettes, celery, and rolls ahead of time, and keep them, covered, in the refrigerator. One and a half hours before serving time, remove them from refrigerator. Just before cooking time, preheat oven to 400° F. Place celery, covered, on bottom shelf of preheated oven. After celery has cooked for 15 minutes, place croquettes, uncovered, on middle shelf. Cook them for 20 minutes, then turn them, and put rolls next to them, uncovered, on middle shelf. Prepare eggs in ramekins. When rolls have been in the oven for 15 minutes, place ramekins in shallow pan on bottom shelf of oven. Pour boiling water in this pan about three-quarters of the way up the sides of ramekins, and cover pan. Continue to cook everything for 10 minutes. Serve eggs on top of the lamb croquettes.

Lamb Croquettes

2½ cups cooked lamb, ground or finely chopped
1 tablespoon parsley
⅛ teaspoon paprika
1 cup white sauce (see page 357)
1½ cups cracker crumbs
2 eggs, beaten

Put lamb in large mixing bowl. With your hands, mix in parsley and paprika. Then pour over white sauce and work in with your hands. Form into six balls, then flatten the balls into patties. Roll these first in cracker crumbs, then in egg, and then in cracker crumbs again. Place in a well-buttered, shallow baking pan, and put on middle shelf of preheated 400° F. oven for 20 minutes. Turn croquettes over, and continue to cook for another 25 minutes. Serve topped with poached eggs, or plain.

Note: These croquettes can be made with any leftover meat.

Eggs Poached in Milk

6 large eggs
Salt and white pepper to taste
6 tablespoons milk

Break one egg into each of six buttered ramekins. Sprinkle each egg with salt and pepper to taste. Pour 1 tablespoon of milk over each egg. Place ramekins in shallow pan. Put pan on bottom shelf of preheated 400° F. oven, and pour boiling water three-quarters of the way up sides of ramekins. Cover pan and cook for 10 minutes (longer if firmer eggs are desired).

Braised Celery

12 stalks celery
1 chicken bouillon cube
2 tablespoons butter
½ teaspoon salt
1 cup boiling water
½ teaspoon crushed dill

Wash and remove strings from celery. Cut stalks into pieces approximately 2 inches in length. Dissolve bouillon cube, butter, and salt in boiling water. Put celery in large casserole, pour water over it and sprinkle with dill. Cover and place on bottom shelf of preheated 400° F. oven for 1 hour. Serve in small bowls.

Butterscotch Rolls

2 cups flour
4 teaspoons baking powder
1 teaspoon salt
4 tablespoons butter
⅔ cup milk
2 tablespoons butter, melted
1 cup brown sugar, packed

Into a large bowl, sift together flour, baking powder, and salt. With two knives cut in 4 tablespoons butter. Slowly add milk, blending lightly. Roll out dough in a ½-inch-thick rectangle. Mix together 1 tablespoon of melted butter, and ½ cup brown sugar. Spread this on dough and roll up like a jelly roll. Cut into pieces about one-inch thick. Place the pieces touching each other in well-buttered, large, shallow pan. Mix together remaining butter and brown sugar and spread on top of rolls. Bake on middle shelf of preheated 400° F. oven for 25 minutes.

AN OLD-FASHIONED BRUNCH

Good, plain, stick-to-your-ribs fare is the order of the day with this brunch. Easy to prepare, and nutritious to eat, it's guaranteed to be filling. Serves six.

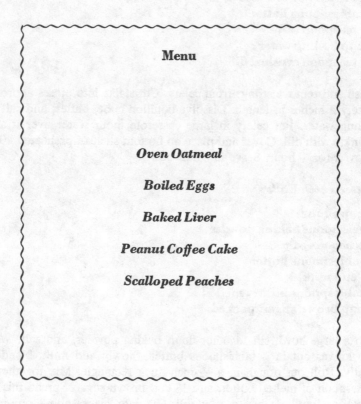

Menu

Oven Oatmeal

Boiled Eggs

Baked Liver

Peanut Coffee Cake

Scalloped Peaches

Total Cooking Time: 35 minutes

Plan of Action

Preheat oven to 400° F. Make coffee cake. Put the oatmeal in double boiler on bottom shelf, and coffee cake on middle shelf of preheated oven. Place liver in a well-buttered, shallow dish. Assemble peaches, and after oatmeal has cooked for 5 minutes, place liver on bottom shelf and peaches on middle shelf of oven. When coffee cake has been in the oven for 20 minutes, remove it and set it aside to cool. Continue cooking other dishes for another 10 minutes, boiling eggs to desired doneness during this time.

Oven Oatmeal

2 cups rolled oats (instant won't work)
4 cups boiling water
1 teaspoon salt

Put oatmeal into the top of a double boiler, add boiling water and salt. Place this over the bottom pan which has been one-third filled with boiling water. Place double boiler on bottom shelf of preheated 400° F. oven and cook for 35 minutes.

Note: These old-fashioned rolled oats are much more nutritious than the popular instant variety of oatmeal.

Baked Liver

2 pounds of calves liver, about ¼-inch thick
Salt and pepper to taste
1 tablespoon butter

In a well-buttered shallow baking dish, place pieces of liver in one layer. Add salt and pepper to taste, and dot with butter. Place dish on bottom shelf of preheated 400° F. oven, and cook for 30 minutes.

Peanut Coffee Cake

This is a plain, basic, no-frills coffee cake. No fancy preparation. But it tastes wonderful.

2 cups all-purpose flour
4 teaspoons baking powder
½ teaspoon salt
1 egg
½ cup sugar

¾ cup milk
3 tablespoons butter, melted
2 tablespoons sugar
½ teaspoon cinnamon
⅓ cup crushed peanuts

Into a large bowl, sift together flour, baking powder, and salt. Beat egg well, and add ½ cup sugar and milk to it, mixing thoroughly. Stir egg mixture into flour. Add butter and beat long enough to blend well. Grease an 8-inch-square shallow pan, and pour batter into it. In a small bowl, mix sugar, cinnamon and peanuts. Sprinkle this on top of batter. Place on middle shelf of preheated 400° F. oven and bake for 20 minutes. Allow to cool slightly before serving.

Scalloped Peaches

6 medium-sized peaches
¼ teaspoon nutmeg
¼ teaspoon salt
1 tablespoon lemon juice
¼ cup water
1 cup brown sugar, packed
¼ cup flour
⅓ cup butter

Pit, peel, and slice peaches into shallow casserole that has been well buttered. Mix together nutmeg, salt, and lemon juice, and pour over peaches. Add water, distributing evenly. With two knives, cut sugar and flour into butter until it is crumblike. Sprinkle this over top of peaches, and place them on the bottom shelf of preheated 400° F. oven for 30 minutes.

A HEARTY SAUSAGE AND MUFFIN BRUNCH WITH A CONTINENTAL FLAVOR

You can prepare each of these dishes in advance, except for beating the eggs, so that when you return home from bird watching, mushroom hunting, beachcombing, or any other early morning activity, everything is just about ready to slide into the oven. Serves six.

Menu

Platter of Peeled, Sliced Melon

Italian-English Muffins

Potato and Sausage Casserole

Total Cooking Time: 35 minutes

Plan of Action

Prepare and refrigerate all dishes. Preheat oven to 350° F. Place potato casserole on the bottom shelf of preheated oven. When casserole has been in oven for 20 minutes, lay sausage links on top of the potatoes, and put muffins on top shelf of oven. Continue to cook both dishes for another 15 minutes. Serve potatoes and sausage right from the casserole, and arrange muffins on a platter.

Italian-English Muffins

6 English muffins, halved
Olive oil
12 slices tomato
Oregano
12 slices mozzarella cheese

Brush the cut side of the muffins lightly with olive oil, place on wire racks in a large shallow roasting pan, and lay a tomato slice on each muffin half. Sprinkle with oregano and top with cheese. Place the pan on the top shelf of a preheated 350° F. oven for 15 minutes, or until cheese is melted and lightly browned and tomatoes are cooked.

Note: The muffins come out crunchy enough for us in the process of baking on wire racks, but, if desired, you can toast them slightly before adding other ingredients. This recipe is also a fine way of using up leftover toasted muffins.

Potato and Sausage Casserole

4 large potatoes, peeled, whole
2 tablespoons butter, melted
1 medium onion, finely chopped or grated
6 eggs
¼ cup milk
1 teaspoon salt
¼ teaspoon nutmeg
White pepper to taste
1 tablespoon fresh parsley, chopped
12 brown and serve sausages

Parboil potatoes in salted water for 10 minutes. They should be quite firm. Allow them to cool. (If you're in a hurry, the cooling can be hastened by running cold water over them.) Butter an 11-inch by 7-inch baking dish. Grate the potatoes coarsely into the dish. Sprinkle onion on top. Beat the eggs with the milk, salt, nutmeg, and pepper until they are light, at least 5 minutes. Stir the parsley into the eggs. Pour the egg mixture over the potato, mixing just enough to smooth the potato into an even layer. Place the baking dish on the bottom shelf of preheated 350° F. oven. Bake for 20 minutes. Then lay the sausages on top of the potato casserole, and continue baking for another 15 minutes, or until a knife inserted in the center comes out clean. Allow the potato casserole to rest for about 5 minutes before serving, so that it may be cut neatly into squares.

OODLES OF NOODLES AND HAM

Good fare for a late brunch that will have to last the diners until supper. Serves six.

Menu

Chilled Vegetable Juice

Ooodles of Noodles

Tutti-Frutti Ham

Sweet Potato Biscuits

Total Cooking Time: 45 minutes

Plan of Action

Preheat oven to 350° F. Prepare ham and place it on bottom shelf of preheated oven. Assemble noodles. When ham has been in oven for

15 minutes, place noodle casserole on bottom shelf of oven. Make biscuit batter and drop by spoonfuls onto greased cookie sheet. When ham has been in oven for 35 minutes, place biscuits on top shelf and continue to bake everything until biscuits are golden, about 10 to 12 minutes.

Oodles of Noodles

1 16-ounce package wide noodles
3 tablespoons butter
12 ounces sour cream
2 egg yolks, beaten
Salt and pepper to taste
1 cup soft bread crumbs

Cook noodles according to package instructions. Drain and mix with 2 tablespoons of butter, tossing until all noodles are coated. Combine sour cream, egg yolks, salt and pepper. Fold sour cream into noodles and turn into a large greased casserole. Top with bread crumbs and dot with remaining butter. Bake on bottom shelf of preheated 350° F. oven for 30 minutes.

Tutti-Frutti Ham

1 slice of precooked ham, about 1½ pounds
1 7-ounce can crushed pineapple
1 7-ounce can peach slices
¼ cup brown sugar, packed

Make slashes 2 inches apart all around slice of ham. This will prevent it from curling, and cause it to lay flat while cooking. Drain pineapple, leaving just a little juice in it. Drain peach slices, leaving a bit of juice. Cut peach slices into chunks. Mix fruit with brown sugar. Put ham in large casserole. Pile fruit on top of ham and place on bottom shelf of preheated 350° F. oven for 45 minutes.

Sweet Potato Biscuits

1   **medium-sized sweet potato, cooked and peeled**
2   **tablespoons butter**
1   **teaspoon baking powder**
⅛   **teaspoon salt**
1   **cup all-purpose flour**
¼   **cup milk**

Mash potato, and mix in butter until it melts. Sift together baking powder, salt, and flour. Gradually add to sweet potato. Mix in milk thoroughly. Drop batter by spoonfuls onto greased cookie sheet. Bake on middle shelf of preheated 375° F. oven for 10 to 12 minutes.

French Toast and Bacon

French toast and bacon, both of which are conventionally cooked on top of a stove, are even more delicious when they're oven-cooked. Serves four.

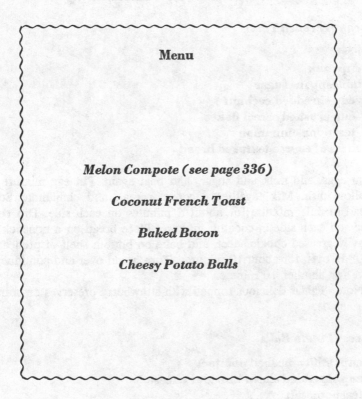

Menu

Melon Compote (see page 336)

Coconut French Toast

Baked Bacon

Cheesy Potato Balls

Total Cooking Time: 20 to 25 minutes

Plan of Action

Make melon compote ahead of time and refrigerate. Potato balls can be made ahead and refrigerated, also. Put bread for French toast to soak in egg mixture. Remove potatoes from refrigerator. Arrange bacon on broiler pan. Preheat oven to 400° F., and when bread has been soaking for 5 minutes, put bacon on top shelf of preheated oven. Finish assembling French toast, and put it on bottom shelf of oven. When toast has been in oven for 5 minutes, put potato balls on bottom shelf. In another 5 minutes, turn French toast. Continue cooking for another 10 minutes. Serve immediately.

Coconut French Toast

6 eggs
1 cup milk
2 tablespoons sugar
½ cup shredded coconut
½ cup crushed cereal flakes
½ teaspoon cinnamon
8 slices of coarse-textured bread

Beat eggs, add milk and sugar, and beat again. Put egg mixture in shallow dish. Mix together coconut, cereal, and cinnamon. Soak bread in milk mixture for about 5 minutes on each side. Dip each piece on each side in coconut mixture. Place bread on a nonstick or heavily greased cookie sheet, and bake on bottom shelf of preheated 400° F. oven for about 10 minutes. Turn bread over and continue to bake for another 10 minutes.

Note: This is delicious topped with strawberry preserves or orange marmalade.

Cheesy Potato Balls

3 cups stiffly mashed potatoes
1 cup shredded sharp Cheddar cheese
1 teaspoon salt
⅛ teaspoon pepper
2 eggs, beaten
1 cup cracker crumbs

Mix together first four ingredients. Form into small balls and roll first in egg, then in crumbs. Place in single layer on nonstick cookie sheet and put on bottom shelf of preheated 400° F. oven for about 15 minutes.

Egg and Salmon Pie

Everything in this brunch-with-a-punch, except the main dish, can be made ahead of time. If fresh salmon isn't available canned may be substituted, but it won't be as tasty. Serves six.

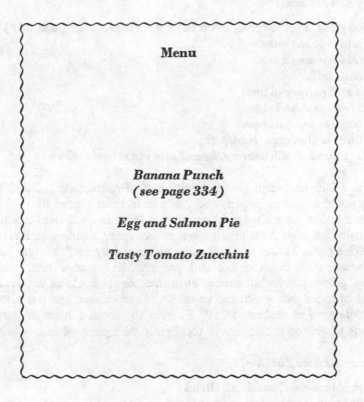

Menu

Banana Punch
(see page 334)

Egg and Salmon Pie

Tasty Tomato Zucchini

Total Cooking Time: 1 hour

Plan of Action

Preheat oven to 350° F. Remove tomato zucchini from refrigerator. Assemble egg and salmon pie. Place pie on middle shelf of preheated oven. When pie has been in oven for 20 minutes, place tomato zucchini, covered, on bottom shelf. When tomato zucchini has been in oven for 30 minutes, take it out, remove cover, sprinkle with cheese, and return to oven, uncovered. Cook both dishes for another 10 minutes.

Egg and Salmon Pie

Pastry for double-crust, deep dish 9-inch pie (see page 359)
5 tablespoons butter
2 tablespoons flour
2 cups milk
Salt and pepper to taste
2½ cups cooked rice
1 large onion, chopped
3 hard boiled eggs, chopped
1½ pounds fresh salmon, boned and cut into chunks

Line 9-inch deep-dish pie plate with half of rolled pastry. Put 2 tablespoons of butter in pan, and put pan in oven turned to 350° F. When butter has melted, add onion, and leave in oven until onion is translucent. Melt remaining butter in saucepan, blending in flour to make a paste. Slowly add milk, stirring constantly until mixture bubbles and thickens. Add salt and pepper. Mix together rice, onion, eggs, salmon, and white sauce. Turn into pie shell. Cover with other half of rolled pastry. Slit top so moisture can escape, and put pie on middle shelf of preheated 350° F. oven for about 1 hour. If pastry starts to get too brown, cover top lightly with piece of foil.

Tasty Tomato Zucchini

2 medium-sized zucchini, sliced
½ pound fresh mushrooms
1 16-ounce can tomatoes
2 pieces of toast, cubed
1 cup freshly grated Parmesan cheese

Scrub and slice zucchini. Wash and slice mushrooms, stems and all. Drain tomatoes, reserving juice, and cut them into chunks. In a 2-quart casserole, make layers using half the zucchini, half the mushrooms, half the toast cubes, half the tomatoes and a little of the juice from the tomatoes. Repeat layers, using remainder of ingredients except cheese. Refrigerate until ready to put into oven. Cook, covered, on bottom shelf of preheated 350° F. oven for 30 minutes. Remove casserole from oven and sprinkle top with cheese. Return to bottom shelf of oven, uncovered, and bake for another 10 minutes.

COD CURRY

Few people are indifferent about curry. They either love it or they hate it. So if you're serving this brunch, check to make sure that the recipients of your efforts are curry lovers. Cod Curry may be made oven-ready ahead of time and refrigerated. Serves four.

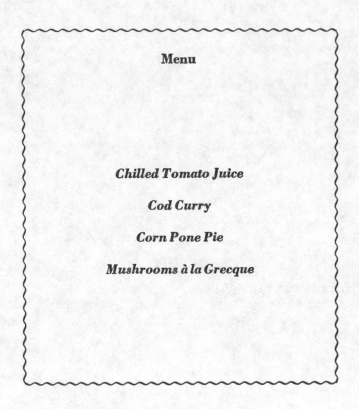

Menu

Chilled Tomato Juice

Cod Curry

Corn Pone Pie

Mushrooms à la Grecque

Total Cooking Time: about 1 hour

Plan of Action

Preheat oven to 350° F. Assemble corn pone pie, and place it on middle shelf of preheated oven. Remove cod curry from refrigerator.

Prepare mushrooms. When corn pone pie has been in oven for 10 minutes, place curry on middle shelf of oven. In another 5 minutes, put mushrooms on bottom shelf. Continue to cook all dishes for another 30 minutes, or until fish flakes and knife inserted in center of pie comes out clean.

Cod Curry

¼ cup butter, melted
1½ teaspoons curry powder
¼ cup raisins
1 teaspoon Worcestershire sauce
¼ teaspoon salt
⅛ teaspoon pepper
1 cup fresh bread crumbs
1½ pounds cod fillets, fresh or frozen, cut in four or more
   pieces
Parsley sprigs for garnish

Mix butter, curry powder, raisins, Worcestershire sauce, salt, and pepper together. Add bread crumbs and blend. If more moisture is desired, add a few drops of water. Grease a large, shallow baking dish. Arrange cod fillets in it. Top each piece of fish with curry stuffing. Bake on middle shelf of preheated 350° F. oven for 30 minutes. Garnish with parsley sprigs.

Note: Some like it hot, and others don't. Adjust the amount of curry you use to the tastes of the people you're cooking for.

Corn Pone Pie

3 eggs, beaten
¼ pound butter, melted
½ cup cornmeal
1 cup sour cream
½ pound Swiss cheese, grated
1 8½-ounce can creamed corn
1 8-ounce can cut corn, drained
4 jumbo-sized black olives, chopped

Mix together all ingredients. Pour into a well-greased 10-inch quiche dish. Bake on middle shelf of preheated 350° F. oven for 1 hour, or until knife put in middle of pie comes out clean.

Note: Bacon bits may be used in place of black olives to give this pie a different flavor.

Mushrooms à la Grecque

1 pound mushrooms
2 tablespoons oil
¼ cup lemon juice
¼ teaspoon salt
1 cup dry white wine

Wash mushrooms, and cut off ends of stems. Mix all the other ingredients and heat to simmer in a small saucepan. Put mushrooms in casserole, pour hot liquid over, cover, and cook for 30 minutes on bottom shelf of preheated 350° F. oven.

SHRIMP AND SOUFFLÉ BRUNCH

Like all soufflés, this one must be whisked out of the oven and onto the table so that everyone can appreciate its puffy beauty before it begins to fall. Serves eight.

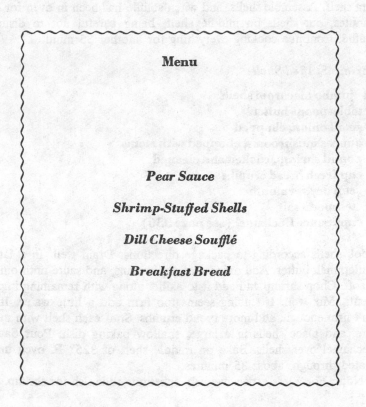

Menu

Pear Sauce

Shrimp-Stuffed Shells

Dill Cheese Soufflé

Breakfast Bread

Total Cooking Time: approximately 2 hours

Plan of Action

About 2 hours and 45 minutes before brunch time, start making bread (or make bread the day before). After it has risen for the second time, bake it on middle shelf of preheated 350° F. oven for about 35 minutes. Reduce heat to 325° F. While bread is cooking, prepare soufflé. Turn bread out of pans and allow to cool while the rest of the meal is cooking. When bread is out of oven and oven has cooled to 325° F., place soufflé on bottom shelf of oven. Prepare pears, and when soufflé has been in oven for 5 minutes, gently add pears to bottom shelf. Assemble shells, and when soufflé has been in oven for 45 minutes, put shells on middle shelf, being careful not to disturb soufflé. Continue cooking everything for another 35 minutes.

Shrimp-Stuffed Shells

24 jumbo macaroni shells
3 tablespoons butter
1 small onion, chopped
4 ounces mushrooms, chopped with stems
1 pound shrimp, cooked and cleaned
1 cup fresh bread crumbs
¼ cup dry vermouth
½ teaspoon salt
3 cups Sauce Béchamel (see page 356)

Cook shells according to package directions. Drain well. In a large skillet, melt butter. Add onion and mushrooms, and sauté until onion is soft. Chop shrimp and add it to skillet along with remaining ingredients. Mix well. If stuffing seems too firm add a little water. If it isn't firm enough, add more bread crumbs. Stuff each shell with mixture, and place shells in a large, shallow baking dish. Pour Sauce Béchamel over shells. Bake on middle shelf of 325° F. oven until heated through, about 35 minutes.

Note: For a less expensive dish, substitute tuna fish for shrimp.

Dill Cheese Soufflé

5 tablespoons butter
⅓ cup flour
½ teaspoon salt
1¼ cups milk
1½ cups shredded Monterey Jack cheese
1 teaspoon dill
5 eggs

In a medium-sized saucepan, melt butter. Sprinkle in flour and salt, mixing with back of wooden spoon to form paste. Gradually add milk, stirring constantly over medium heat until sauce thickens. Add cheese and continue stirring until cheese melts. Remove from heat and stir in dill. Separate eggs, putting whites into chilled medium-sized bowl and yolks into small bowl. Beat egg whites to stiff-peak stage. Beat egg yolks until lemon colored. Mix a little cheese sauce into egg yolks, then put yolks in with cheese sauce, mixing well. Fold cheese sauce into beaten whites. Pour into 2-quart soufflé dish and bake on bottom shelf of preheated 325° F. oven until knife comes out clean when inserted in middle, about 1 hour and 20 minutes.

Pear Sauce

4 pounds pears
1 cup sugar (more or less depending on desired sweetness)
1 teaspoon cinnamon
½ teaspoon nutmeg
4 tablespoons butter
1½ cups cold water

Peel, core, and quarter pears. Combine sugar, cinnamon, and nutmeg. Put layer of pears on bottom of casserole. Sprinkle with part of sugar mixture, and dot with butter. Continue to layer, using all ingredients. Add water, cover, and place on bottom shelf of preheated 325° F. oven for 1 hour and 15 minutes. Stir well before serving.

Breakfast Bread

1 package active dry yeast
¼ cup sugar
1½ cups lukewarm water
1 teaspoon salt
⅓ cup butter, melted
4 cups flour (approximately)

Dissolve yeast and sugar in water. Place in warm place until mixture bubbles. Add salt and butter to yeast. Turn oven to 200° F. Put three cups of flour in large mixing bowl, stirring in yeast mixture. Mix well, adding more flour until dough is fairly stiff and pulls away from sides of bowl. Add more than 4 cups if necessary. Knead dough on a floured surface for about 10 minutes, or until it has an elastic quality. Turn off oven. Roll dough into a ball, and place it in a greased bowl, turning to coat all sides. Cover lightly with a cloth, and put bowl in warmed oven until dough doubles in size, about 1 hour. Punch down dough and divide it in half, placing each half in a greased bread pan. Cover lightly and allow to rise again for about 45 minutes. Preheat oven to 350° F. Bake bread on bottom shelf for about 35 minutes or until golden. Turn out onto rack and allow to cool while remainder of meal is cooking.

ASPARAGUS OMELET ROULADE

This puts the humble egg into the gourmet class. Serves six.

Menu

Stewed Apricots and Cranberry Sauce

Asparagus Omelet Roulade

Mushrooms and Oysters on Toast

Brunch Pie

Total Cooking Time: 1 hour and 30 minutes

Plan of Action

Put apricots to soak the night before brunch. Preheat oven to 400° F. Place apricots with water in which they've been soaking into a casserole. Cover and put on bottom shelf of preheated oven. Assemble brunch pie and place on bottom shelf of oven. Bake for 40 minutes, remove from oven, and set aside to cool. Continue cooking apricots until they've been in oven 1 hour. Remove from oven and complete recipe, returning apricots and cranberries to bottom shelf of oven for another 30 minutes. During this time, prepare mushrooms and oysters, and assemble egg portion of omelet. Remove fruit from oven and set aside to cool. Place mushrooms on middle shelf of oven, and omelet on bottom shelf. When omelet has been cooking for 20 minutes, remove it and complete recipe. Allow oysters and mushrooms to cook another 5 minutes.

Stewed Apricots with Cranberry Sauce

1 16-ounce package dried apricots
4 cups water
1 pound cranberries
1½ cups sugar

Wash apricots and put them to soak in water overnight. Place apricots and water in which they've been soaking into large casserole. Cover, and put on bottom shelf of preheated 400° F. oven for 1 hour. Remove from oven and drain, reserving liquid. Put enough water with this liquid to make 2 cups. Put cranberries and sugar in casserole. Add apricots and pour liquid over this. Return to bottom shelf of oven and continue to cook for another 30 minutes. Serve warm or cold.

Asparagus Omelet Roulade

12 eggs
2 cups white sauce (see page 357)
½ teaspoon salt
⅛ teaspoon white pepper
1¼ cups cooked, chopped asparagus
1¼ cups grated white Cheddar cheese
1 small onion, chopped and sautéed

Separate eggs, beating egg yolks. Add beaten yolks to white sauce by putting a little white sauce in the yolks first, then adding this to sauce. Beat egg whites until peaks form. Fold cooled white sauce into egg whites. Line 13-inch by 10-inch shallow pan with waxed paper, lightly grease paper, and pour in omelet mixture. Bake on bottom shelf of preheated 400° F. oven for 20 minutes. Turn out on tea towel or waxed paper. Combine asparagus, cheese, and onion, and spread over omelet. Roll up as you would a jelly roll using waxed paper or towel as a guide to keep omelet from breaking. Place seam side down on platter and slice as you would a jelly roll.

Mushrooms and Oysters on Toast

3 tablespoons butter
6 slices of bread
12 large mushrooms
12 large oysters, drained
3 slices of bacon, halved

Butter bread and arrange in single layer on nonstick cookie sheet or shallow pan. Slice mushrooms, and make a layer of them on each piece of bread, top with two oysters, and then with bacon. Place on middle shelf of preheated 400° F. oven for 20 to 25 minutes, or until bacon is browned.

Brunch Pie

1¾ cups flour
¾ cup sugar
½ cup butter
1 egg
½ cup dark molasses
¼ cup boiling water
¼ teaspoon baking soda

In a large bowl mix together flour, sugar, and butter by cutting with two knives. Beat egg and add molasses. Mix water and soda until soda has dissolved, and add this to egg and molasses. Set aside ½ cup of flour mixture, and add egg to the remaining portion. Pour into well-buttered 9-inch pie plate. Sprinkle remaining flour mixture on top, and put on bottom shelf of preheated 400° F. oven for 40 minutes. Set aside to cool.

PANCAKES AND EGGS

If you don't have powdered sugar to complete the pancake recipe, you can make it by blending granulated sugar in your blender for a few minutes. Serves six.

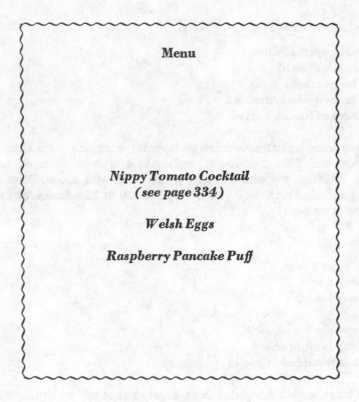

Menu

Nippy Tomato Cocktail
(see page 334)

Welsh Eggs

Raspberry Pancake Puff

Total Cooking Time: about 30 minutes

Plan of Action

Prepare tomato cocktail in advance, and chill it well in the refrigerator. Make pancake batter ahead of time and put in refrigerator, stirring well just before cooking. Preheat oven to 350° F. Melt butter in skillet and put pancake batter into it, placing on middle shelf of preheated oven. Prepare eggs, and when pancake has been cooking for 15 minutes, place eggs on bottom shelf of oven. Continue cooking for another 15 minutes or until pancake is golden brown. Remove both eggs and pancake from oven, and top pancake with berries and powdered sugar.

Welsh Eggs

6 ounces longhorn cheese, grated
12 eggs
Seasoned salt to taste
6 slices of bread

Lightly sprinkle six well-buttered ramekins with cheese. Break 2 eggs into each one. Sprinkle with seasoned salt, and top with remaining cheese. Place ramekins on bottom shelf of preheated 350° F. oven for 15 minutes. Toast bread. Butter toast and cut it in halves from corner to corner to form triangles. Slide two halves into opposite sides of ramekins (beside eggs) being careful not to break egg yolks.

Raspberry Pancake Puff

3 tablespoons sugar
1 cup flour
½ teaspoon salt
4 eggs
3 cups half-and-half
2 tablespoons butter
1 10-ounce package frozen raspberries, thawed,
   or fresh berries if in season
¼ cup confectioners' sugar

Combine sugar, flour, and salt in a large bowl. In a medium-sized bowl, lightly beat eggs. Mix half-and-half into eggs and add to flour, mixing well. Heat butter in large skillet until it's sizzling but not brown. Quickly remove from heat and pour batter into pan. Place on middle shelf of preheated 350° F. oven until golden brown, about 30 minutes. Top with berries. Sprinkle on powdered sugar. And serve immediately.

Party Time

A party can be anything from a coffee klatch to a full-scale dinner party with all the trimmings. It may be just your weekly bridge game, or it may be a gala New Year's Eve fête that's scheduled for your home this year. The party you're giving may be a simple slumber party for a group of fidgety teenagers, or a buffet for people you'd like to impress—favorably. Maybe you're just having a few intimate friends in for cocktails, or you may be planning a tea in honor of Great Aunt Harriet.

Everybody loves a party! But, too often, the one who misses out on the fun and hears about the festivities second-hand is the hostess. In an effort to put her best culinary foot forward, she often foregoes the pleasures of entertaining, making a wilted appearance from time to time. But an impressive menu doesn't have to mean slaving in the kitchen while your guests are enjoying themselves. Whatever type of party you're having, the oven is your ally. Properly used, it will enable you to present a cool front while serving your guests hot, delicious food. That's not to say you won't have to spend some time in the kitchen, but it will be a minimum of time. Most of your work will be done in advance, and the oven will take care of the last minute details.

Parties are easier on those who give them if preparations are made ahead. We don't mean just fussing with food. Select the dishes, glasses, silverware, and table linens that you want to use, and be sure they're shiny clean. If it's to be a sit-down affair, have your table set well in advance. Get out the serving dishes you plan to use, and don't forget about serving pieces—the spoons and forks, the sugar spoons and butter knives. A last-minute search for the right spoon to use with a certain food can cause chaos in the best-planned schedule.

If the party is to be one with a complicated menu featuring many recipes, a small label placed beside each serving dish with the name of the food to be served in it comes in handy at that rushing time when you're trying to get everything on the table at once. This method is especially useful if guests help with last minute serving. They don't have to keep asking you where you want what. If the menu is exotic, it may be difficult to identify foods. We leave the labels on the table so that guests know what each dish contains.

Proper party preparation—the kind that a busy oven facilitates—makes these functions run so smoothly that you'll find you really can have fun at your own parties. We've been doing it for years!

THE COCKTAIL PARTY

These dishes are a tight fit in the average-sized oven, but it can be done, and it is a delicious assortment for a cocktail party. Serves about 12.

Menu

Olive Canapés

Moira's Artichoke Dip

Caraway Chunks

Sausage-Stuffed Mushrooms

Assorted Cheeses and Crackers

Cocktails

Total Cooking Time: 30 minutes

Plan of Action

Prepare ahead, cover, and refrigerate artichoke dip, caraway chunks, stuffed mushrooms, and olive canapé mixture. Make toast for olive canapé mixture just prior to oven time. One hour before party remove everything from refrigerator. Thirty minutes before serving time, put artichoke dip on bottom shelf of preheated 375° F. oven. In 10 minutes, add stuffed mushrooms to top shelf. Make toast and spread olive mixture on it. When artichoke dip has been in oven 20 minutes, put caraway chunks on top shelf and olive canapés on bottom shelf. Continue to cook everything for another 10 to 12 minutes.

Olive Canapés

1½ cups minced green olives
3 tablespoons minced onion
½ cup mayonnaise
¼ teaspoon curry powder
1 cup grated Swiss cheese
10 pieces of white bread lightly toasted

Combine first four ingredients in a bowl, mixing thoroughly. Add Swiss cheese and stir to blend. Spread mixture on toast. Put on cookie sheet, and place on bottom shelf of preheated 375° F. oven for 10 minutes, or until cheese is melted and bubbly. Cut toast into quarters and serve hot.

Moira's Artichoke Dip

1 7½-ounce can artichoke hearts, chopped
1 4-ounce can green chilies (Mexican), chopped
½ cup mayonnaise
½ cup grated Parmesan cheese

Mix together all ingredients in a casserole, and bake on the bottom shelf of a preheated 375° F. oven for 30 minutes.

Note: Serve this as a spread with an assortment of crackers.

Caraway Chunks

½ cup mayonnaise
1 tablespoon finely grated onion
1 teaspoon dry mustard
½ cup dry bread crumbs

¼ cup caraway seeds
2 cups cubed cooked ham
1 cup mayonnaise
2 tablespoons grated Parmesan cheese

In a small bowl, thoroughly mix ½ cup mayonnaise, onion, and dry mustard. In another small bowl, mix bread crumbs and caraway seeds. Roll each piece of ham first in mayonnaise mixture, then in bread crumbs. Place pieces on a lightly greased cookie sheet. Bake on top shelf of a 375° F. oven for 10 to 12 minutes, or until ham pieces are lightly browned. While ham is cooking, blend together mayonnaise and Parmesan cheese. Serve this mixture as a dip for the piping hot ham pieces.

Sausage-Stuffed Mushrooms

1 pound medium-sized mushrooms
¼ pound sweet Italian sausage
¼ cup olive oil
1 large onion, finely chopped
¼ teaspoon garlic powder
½ teaspoon salt
⅛ teaspoon pepper
½ teaspoon oregano
½ teaspoon basil
1 cup bread crumbs

Wash mushrooms and carefully remove stems without tearing caps. Chop stems into small pieces. Remove sausage from casing. In a skillet, heat oil and sauté onion in it. Add sausage meat, garlic powder, salt, pepper, oregano, basil and mushroom stems. Cook until sausage is well-browned. Add bread crumbs, stirring well, and remove from heat. Drain off any excess oil. Stuff mushroom caps with this mixture. Place them in a rectangular pan with a nonstick surface, and bake on top shelf of preheated 375° F. oven for 20 minutes.

BUFFET FOR TEN

Buffets are a relaxed way of entertaining, allowing guests to eat at their leisure. This buffet offers something for everyone, and since much of it is make-ahead fare, it's easy on the hostess.

Menu

Super-Spread Aubergines with Crackers

Stuffed Sardines

Orange Ham Rolls

Avocado Potato

Brussels Sprouts Pie

Mushroom-Watercress Salad (see page 340)

Caraway Cheese Sticks

Party Gingerbread

Total Cooking Time: about 2 hours and 25 minutes

Plan of Action

Day before buffet: Preheat oven to 350° F. Place eggplant for super spread and gingerbread on bottom shelf of oven. Make cheese sticks.

When eggplant and gingerbread have been cooking for 30 minutes, add cheese sticks to top shelf of oven, continue cooking another 15 minutes. Finish making super spread. When everything has cooled, store super spread, covered, in refrigerator, wrap cheese sticks in foil, and cover gingerbread with plastic wrap.

Day of Buffet: In the morning, make ham rolls except for sauce, cover, and refrigerate. Stuff sardines, cover, and refrigerate. (Don't drizzle on oil until oven time.) Wash and oil potatoes. Assemble salad and refrigerate. One hour and forty minutes before serving time, prick potatoes and put on bottom shelf of preheated 350° F. oven. Assemble Brussels sprouts pie, and when potatoes have been cooking for about 1 hour, place pie on middle shelf of oven. Make sauce for ham rolls. Coat rolls with sauce and, when pie has been in oven for 15 minutes, place ham rolls on bottom shelf of oven. In another 5 minutes, remove potatoes from oven and stuff them. Return stuffed potatoes to bottom shelf. Drizzle oil on sardines, and place them on middle shelf of oven. Continue cooking everything for another 20 minutes, and during this time, toss salad.

Super-Spread Aubergines

1 **large eggplant**
2 **tablespoons butter**
1 **medium-sized onion**
2 **large tomatoes**
⅛ **teaspoon garlic powder**
1 **teaspoon salt**
⅛ **teaspoon white pepper**
¼ **cup olive oil**
1 **teaspoon lemon juice**

Prick eggplant skin in two or three places. Bake whole eggplant in casserole placed on bottom shelf in preheated 350° F. oven for 45 minutes or until soft to the touch. While eggplant is cooking, melt butter in oven in another casserole. Grate onion very finely. Peel and seed tomatoes, and cut them into small pieces. Add onion, tomato, garlic powder, salt, and pepper to butter in oven, and cook until onion is transparent and tomato is mushy. Remove eggplant from oven and, when it's sufficiently cool to handle, peel and cut it into very small pieces. Add onion-tomato mixture and mash with a fork. Mix in olive oil well. Chill thoroughly and serve with crackers.

Note: The tomatoes you use in this make-ahead, bake-ahead treat should be extremely ripe.

Stuffed Sardines

20 large sardines
¼ teaspoon garlic powder
¼ cup green olives, pitted and finely chopped
¼ cup parsley, finely chopped
¾ cup fresh bread crumbs
2 teaspoons finely chopped onion
Olive oil

Wash and drain sardines. Split them in halves lengthwise leaving back skin in one piece. Remove backbone. Mix garlic powder, olives, parsley, bread crumbs, and onion. Moisten this with olive oil until desired consistency is achieved. Stuff sardines. Place them in greased shallow pan. Drizzle a bit of olive oil over them, and bake on the middle shelf of a preheated 350° F. oven for about 20 minutes.

Orange Ham Rolls

4 cups cooked rice
¼ cup chopped peanuts
2 tablespoons chopped chives
⅔ cup mayonnaise
20 slices boiled ham, very thin
½ cup orange marmalade
¼ cup peanut butter
1 large seedless orange
3 tablespoons orange juice
½ teaspoon cinnamon

Peel and chop orange, reserving 3 tablespoons of juice. Mix orange, rice, peanuts, chives, and mayonnaise. Divide mixture and spread it evenly on slices of ham. Roll ham slices and place them seam side down in a shallow baking dish. In a small saucepan, combine marmalade, peanut butter, orange juice, and cinnamon. Warm over low heat until ingredients are blended. Coat ham rolls with sauce, pouring remaining sauce over them. Cook on bottom shelf of preheated 350° F. oven until warmed through, about 30 minutes.

Avocado Potato

12 medium-sized potatoes
Oil
3 large ripe avocados
3 tablespoons butter
1½ teaspoons salt
¼ teaspoon white pepper
3 cups sour cream

Wash and oil potatoes. Prick each one with a fork and place them on the bottom shelf of a preheated 350° F. oven for 1 hour and 20 minutes or until soft. Remove potatoes from oven. Peel and mash avocados. Cut potatoes in halves lengthwise. Scoop out pulp, reserving skins, and mash butter into the pulp. Mix salt, pepper, and sour cream into avocado. Add avocado to potato and mix together well. Fill potato skins and put them on cookie sheet. Return to oven until heated through—about 20 minutes.

Brussels Sprouts Pie

3 10-ounce packages frozen Brussels sprouts, cooked and drained
1 medium onion, chopped
2 tablespoons butter
3 eggs, beaten
1½ cups milk
3 cups soft bread crumbs
¼ teaspoon garlic powder
1 teaspoon salt
3 hard-boiled eggs
2 cups Cheese Sauce Suprême (see page 357)

Chop Brussels sprouts. Turn oven to 350° F. Put butter in pan into oven until butter melts. Add onion and continue to cook until onion is transparent. Mix together eggs and milk. Combine sprouts, onion, bread crumbs, garlic, and salt. Stir in milk and egg, and turn into a

greased large rectangular baking dish. Bake on middle shelf of preheated 350° F. oven for 45 minutes. Cut into squares. Slice hard-
boiled eggs and put one slice in center of each square. Serve with
warm cheese sauce.

Caraway Cheese Sticks

2 cups all-purpose flour
½ teaspoon salt
¼ teaspoon white pepper
¼ pound butter, softened
1 pound sharp cheese, grated
¼ cup caraway seeds

Sift together flour, salt, and white pepper. With the back of a wooden
spoon, cream butter and cheese together, and then blend into flour
mixture to form a stiff dough. With your hands, roll the dough into
individual pieces about 2 inches long and ¾ inch in diameter. Dip
one side of these pieces in caraway seeds, pressing them into dough
so they'll stick. Place pieces on well-greased cookie sheet with about
an inch between each piece. Place cookie sheet on middle shelf of
preheated 350° F. oven and bake for about 15 minutes. These cheese
sticks should not become browned. Cool them on a wire rack and
wrap in foil until ready to serve.

Party Gingerbread

½ cup butter, softened
½ cup sugar
2 eggs, beaten
2½ cups flour
1½ teaspoons baking powder
½ teaspoon baking soda
½ teaspoon salt
1 teaspoon ginger
1 teaspoon cinnamon
¼ teaspoon powdered cloves
1 cup dark molasses
1 cup boiling water

Cream together butter and sugar until light. Beat in eggs. Sift together flour, baking powder, baking soda, salt, ginger, cinnamon, and cloves. Add the flour mixture to the butter, sugar, and eggs, blending well. Beat until thoroughly mixed. Turn into a well-greased 12- by 8-inch shallow pan and bake on bottom shelf of preheated 350° F. oven for 45 minutes, or until top springs back when touched.

Note: This can be dressed up with the addition of whipped cream and a cherry, or simply by topping with vanilla ice cream.

TEEN SLUMBER PARTY

At a teen party, food is important. This menu for six features the types of food most teens enjoy.

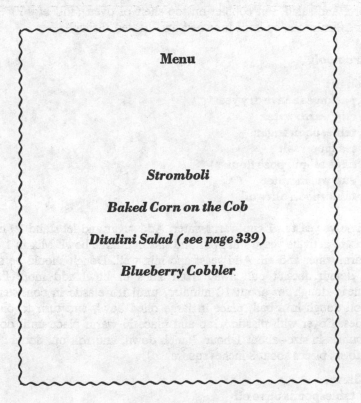

Menu

Stromboli

Baked Corn on the Cob

Ditalini Salad (see page 339)

Blueberry Cobbler

Total Cooking Time: about 1 hour and 5 minutes

Plan of Action

Assemble *stromboli* a few hours ahead and refrigerate it, covered, on a lightly greased cookie sheet until ready to bake. Make *ditalini* salad and refrigerate. Prepare corn, except for water, and set aside. Forty-five minutes before serving time, add water to corn and place it on bottom shelf of preheated 400° F. oven. Remove *stromboli* from refrigerator. When corn has been cooking for 15 minutes, place *stromboli* on top shelf of oven, and continue cooking for another 30 minutes, assembling blueberry cobbler during this time. Serve *stromboli*, corn, and salad. Put cobbler on top shelf of oven (still at 400° F.) for 20 minutes, or until browned and heated through.

Stromboli

Dough:
2 packages active dry yeast
1 cup warm water
1 tablespoon sugar
1 teaspoon salt
5 cups all-purpose flour
1 cup warm water
1 tablespoon olive oil

Dissolve yeast in 1 cup warm water. Add sugar and let stand 10 minutes to activate yeast. Put flour and salt in a large bowl. Mix in 1 cup warm water and oil. Add yeast and mix well. Dough should be stiff. If dough doesn't pull away from sides of bowl add more flour. Knead dough for about 10 minutes, until it's elastic in consistency. Roll dough in a ball, place in large oiled bowl, and turn to oil all sides. Cover with plastic wrap and place in warm place until dough doubles in size—about 1 hour. Punch down, and roll out dough. Cut into six pieces about 8 inches square.

Filling:
2 tablespoons olive oil
2 green peppers, seeded, and sliced
1 large onion, peeled, sliced and ringed
18 slices of salami
18 slices of boiled ham
12 slices of mozzarella cheese

Heat olive oil in a skillet with an oven-proof handle in oven set at 400° F. Oven-sauté peppers and onion rings in hot oil until they are soft. Arrange 3 slices of salami and 3 slices of ham on one-half of each piece of dough, leaving about 1 inch on edges. Divide peppers and onion rings in 6 equal parts, placing them on top of salami and ham. Top with 2 pieces of mozzarella for each piece of dough. Fold dough over filling and pinch edges tightly together to seal. Brush tops with oil and place on lightly greased cookie sheet. Put on top shelf of preheated 400° F. oven for 30 minutes.

Baked Corn on the Cob

6 ears of corn
1 cup hot water

Husk corn, reserving the husks but removing the corn silk. Rinse husks in water, and put 2 on bottom of Dutch oven. Add 3 ears of corn, another 2 husks, 3 remaining ears of corn, and top with layer of 2 remaining husks. Add water. Cover and bake on bottom shelf of preheated 400° F. oven for 45 minutes, less time if corn is very fresh.

Blueberry Cobbler

1 cup all-purpose flour
1 tablespoon sugar
½ teaspoon salt
1½ teaspoons baking powder
½ cup butter
1 egg, beaten
⅓ cup milk
1 16-ounce can blueberry pie filling

Sift together flour, sugar, salt, and baking powder. Cut in butter to make crumbly mixture. Stir in egg and then milk, until dry ingredients are moistened. Butter 8-inch square pan. Pour in blueberry pie filling. Drop dough on top of this in 6 equal portions. Bake on top shelf of preheated 400° F. oven for 20 minutes, or until top is brown and blueberry filling is heated through. Serve topped with vanilla ice cream.

MAD HATTER TEA PARTY

This tea-time cuisine is the make-ahead kind that leaves you free to pour. The tart tray looks impressive and tastes delightful, and your guests may find they aren't too hungry when dinner comes around. Serves six.

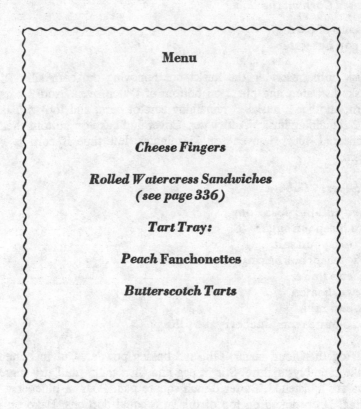

Menu

Cheese Fingers

Rolled Watercress Sandwiches
(see page 336)

Tart Tray:

Peach Fanchonettes

Butterscotch Tarts

Total Cooking Time: 45 minutes

Plan of Action

Well in advance of the tea party, preheat oven to 425° F., and fill cupcake tins with pastry for both tart recipes. Put shells for butter-scotch tarts on middle shelf of oven, and bake about 10 minutes. While these shells are baking, finish preparing *fanchonettes*. Remove shells from oven, and place *fanchonettes* on bottom shelf of oven. Finish assembling butterscotch tarts and when *fanchonettes* have been in the oven for 25 minutes, place butterscotch tarts on middle shelf. Remove both from oven when meringue has browned. Cool before serving. Cheese fingers and watercress sandwiches can be made ahead of time and refrigerated. Just before tea time, pop cheese fingers onto top shelf of preheated 400° F. oven for about 5 minutes.

Cheese Fingers

1½ cups grated Cheddar cheese
¼ cup chopped pimento
¼ cup half-and-half
1 egg, beaten
12 slices of white bread

Mix together cheese, half-and-half, and egg. Remove crusts from bread, lightly toast, and spread each piece with cheese mixture. Cut into long narrow pieces, four from each piece of toast. Place on cookie sheet with nonstick surface, and bake on top shelf of pre-heated 400° F. oven for about 5 minutes or until cheese is puffy. Serve immediately.

Peach Fanchonettes

Pastry for double pie crust (see page 359)
6 peach halves, canned or fresh
2 egg yolks
½ cup half-and-half
½ cup sugar
¼ teaspoon salt
Cinnamon

Line 6 muffin cups with pastry. Place a peach half, cut side down, in each one. Beat egg yolks until they're lemon-colored and frothy.

Mix in half-and-half, sugar, and salt. Divide this equally, pouring over peach halves. Sprinkle tops with cinnamon, and bake on bottom shelf of preheated 425° F. oven for 30 minutes.

Butterscotch Tarts

Pastry for double pie crust (see page 359)
1½ cups brown sugar, packed
¼ cup water
3 cups milk, divided
6 tablespoons flour (approximately)
3 egg yolks
4 tablespoons butter
1 teaspoon vanilla
3 egg whites
¼ teaspoon salt
5 tablespoons sugar
½ teaspoon almond extract

Line 6 muffin cups with pastry. Prick sides and bottoms with fork and bake on middle shelf of preheated 425° F. oven until browned, about 10 minutes. While shells are browning, heat brown sugar and water in the top of double boiler placed *directly* over medium heat until mixture forms syrup, then place this over boiling water in bottom of double boiler. Combine 1½ cups of milk with flour to form thin, runny paste. Beat egg yolks and add them to remaining milk, mixing well. Add flour-milk mixture gradually to syrup in top of double boiler, stirring constantly. When this is well blended, add a little to the egg yolks, and then add egg yolks to top of double boiler. Let this cook, stirring constantly until mixture is thick and smooth. Add butter and vanilla, and cook until butter has melted and blended in. Let cool a bit while making meringue. To make meringue beat egg whites and salt until stiff, fold in granulated sugar, and add almond extract. Divide butterscotch among 6 prebaked shells. Add meringue, and bake on middle shelf of preheated 425° F. oven for 5 to 10 minutes, or until meringue is nicely browned.

Note: The secret of a good meringue that doesn't separate is to spread it thick, and be sure it seals the edges of whatever it tops.

BRIDGE PARTY

Nibble food is the order of the evening (or afternoon) for most bridge parties. These tidbits, while served hot, are equally good as they cool. There's no need to worry about them as the game progresses. But the *pièce de résistance* in this menu is the impressive dessert. You don't have to tell anyone how easy it is to make. Just stand up and take your bows. Serves eight.

Menu

Zucchini Snacks

Garlic Cheese Balls Surprise

Hot Shrimp Rounds

Peppers Stuffed with Anchovy

Baked Alaska Hawaiian

Total Cooking Time: 35 minutes

Plan of Action

Prepare cheese balls in advance, cover, and refrigerate. Assemble and freeze the Alaska, leaving meringue to make just before oven-time. Stuff peppers and refrigerate, but don't drizzle on oil and sprinkle with black pepper until just before baking. Make zucchini snacks about 1 hour before guests arrive. A half-hour before bridge time, add oil and black pepper to peppers. Place them on bottom shelf of preheated 375° F. oven. Start assembling shrimp rounds. When peppers have been cooking for 5 minutes, put zucchini snacks on middle shelf of oven. Continue preparing shrimp rounds. When peppers have been cooking 20 minutes, put cheese balls on middle shelf and shrimp rounds on bottom shelf. Continue to cook for another 10 minutes. When you've played your last hand of bridge, make meringue. Frost frozen cake with it and put on bottom shelf of preheated 500° F. oven for about 5 minutes.

Zucchini Snacks

3 cups thinly sliced zucchini
½ cup finely chopped onion
1 teaspoon parsley flakes
½ teaspoon salt
½ teaspoon oregano
⅛ teaspoon pepper
¼ teaspoon garlic powder
½ cup grated Parmesan cheese
1 cup prepared biscuit mix
½ cup oil
4 eggs, beaten

In a medium-sized bowl, combine all ingredients. Grease large rectangular pan. Spread zucchini mixture in pan and bake on middle shelf of preheated 375° F. oven for 25 minutes. Allow to cool slightly and cut into bite-sized pieces.

Garlic Cheese Balls Surprise

1   cup grated Cheddar cheese
4   tablespoons butter, softened
¼   teaspoon salt
⅛   teaspoon garlic powder
¼   cup all-purpose flour
24 cocktail onions

Put cheese and butter in bowl and cream together with back of a wooden spoon. Mix in salt and garlic powder. Add flour gradually, blending well. Wrap a ball of dough around each onion. Place cheese balls in ungreased rectangular pan, and bake on middle shelf of preheated 375° F. oven for 15 minutes. Serve either hot or cold.

Note: You can use your imagination and vary the surprise. Olives make a tasty center, and peanuts work well, too.

Hot Shrimp Rounds

½   pound shrimp, cooked and cleaned
2   tablespoons butter
1   small onion, finely chopped
½   teaspoon curry powder
Salt and pepper to taste
2   tablespoons sour cream
12 pieces of toast, cut in rounds and buttered
12 slices of tomato (use firm tomatoes)

Finely chop shrimp. Turn oven to 375° F. and put casserole containing butter into oven. When butter has melted, add onion and continue to cook until onion has softened. Remove from oven, and mix in curry powder, salt and pepper to taste, and shrimp. Cover and return to bottom shelf of preheated 375° F. oven for about 15 minutes, or until heated through. Remove from oven and stir in sour cream. Line up toast rounds on cookie sheet. Put a tomato slice on each one and top with shrimp mixture, evenly divided between toast rounds. Pop into oven for about 10 minutes to heat through. Serve hot.

Peppers Stuffed with Anchovy

1 28-ounce can Italian plum tomatoes, drained and chopped
⅔ cup bread crumbs
1 can flat anchovy fillets, drained and chopped
1 clove garlic, finely chopped
2 tablespoons olive oil
6 medium-sized sweet green peppers, seeded and quartered

Combine first five ingredients. Divide this mixture between the quartered peppers. Bake stuffed peppers in a well-oiled oblong pan on bottom shelf of preheated 375° F. oven for 30 minutes. Serve at room temperature.

Baked Alaska Hawaiian

1 angel food cake (that has been baked in a tube pan)
1 quart vanilla ice cream, softened
1 7-ounce can crushed pineapple, well drained
6 egg whites
½ teaspoon cream of tartar
1 cup sugar

Cut cake in half horizontally to form two layers. Make a hollow in each layer (on the cut side). Mix pineapple into softened ice cream, and mound it into hollow in bottom layer of cake. Add top layer. It's all right if ice cream peeks out of sides. Place cake on foil-lined cookie sheet, and put it in freezer until ice cream is *very* hard. Preheat oven to 500° F. Beat egg whites and cream of tartar until foamy. Slowly add sugar, beating constantly until whites are stiff and shiny. Remove cake from freezer and frost it with meringue, completely covering cake surfaces and sealing it right to the foil with meringue. Bake on bottom shelf of oven for about 5 minutes or until meringue is lightly browned. Let stand 10 minutes before cutting.

HAPPY NEW YEAR PARTY

A gala New Year's Eve menu that will fill up ten to twelve cele-brants may result in a vote to have next year's party at your place, too!

Menu

Strawberry Champagne Punch
(see page 334)

Hors d'Oeuvre Squares

Gobble Bits

Hot Crab Spread

Happy Clam Dip

Festive Chicken with Rice

Peanut Slaw (see page 341)

Chocolate Nut Meringues

Orange Cheesecake

Total Cooking Time: about 3 hours and 35 minutes

Plan of Action

On December 30th: Assemble cheesecake and place it on middle shelf of preheated 275° F. oven. When cheesecake has baked for about 1 hour, mix meringues. (This should take about 10 minutes.) Place meringues on bottom shelf of oven, and continue to cook both items for another 50 minutes (a total of 2 hours for the cheesecake). Remove both from oven, and increase heat to 425° F. While meringues and cheesecake are baking, prepare crust for hors d'oeuvre squares. Bake crust on middle shelf of preheated 425° F. oven for 8 to 10 minutes. Remove from oven and finish recipe. When cooled, cover cheesecake and squares and store in refrigerator. Put cooled meringues in air-tight cannister. Assemble gobble bits, crab spread, and clam dip. Cover and refrigerate.

On December 31st: A few hours before party time, brown chicken on middle shelf of preheated 400° F. oven. Chop pepper and onion for chicken recipe. Just before party time, preheat oven to 375° F. Place clam dip and crab spread on bottom shelf. After they've been cooking for 10 minutes, add gobble bits to top shelf and continue cooking another 15 minutes. During this time put punch in bowl.

About 50 minutes before you want to serve the chicken, assemble it and put on middle shelf of preheated 400° F. oven for 40 minutes. Toss slaw with mayonnaise.

Hors d'Oeuvre Squares

Pastry for double pie crust (see page 359)
4 3-ounce packages cream cheese, softened
¼ cup grated onion
2 tablespoons sherry
6 small or medium-sized firm tomatoes, sliced (about 25 slices)
25 mushroom caps
25 flat anchovy fillets (caviar may be used instead)
Watercress for garnish

Roll out pie crust into two rectangles, about 12- by 14-inches. Put on two nonstick baking sheets, prick well with a fork, and bake on middle shelf of preheated 425° F. oven for 8 to 10 minutes or until lightly browned. Remove from oven and set aside to cool. Mix together cream cheese, onion, and sherry, adding more sherry if needed to make cheese spreadable. When pie crusts have cooled, spread them with cream cheese mixture. Cover lightly and chill. A few hours before serving, decorate as follows: Place tomato slices in a layer on top of cheese, leaving room in between to cut pastry. Put a mushroom cap on top of each tomato slice, and an anchovy fillet on top of each mushroom cap. Garnish with sprigs of watercress. Cut into squares between the tomato slices. Cover and chill until ready to serve.

Gobble Bits

1½ cups dry bread crumbs
¼ cup sesame seeds
3 tablespoons oil
½ teaspoon dry mustard
⅓ cup peach preserves
⅛ teaspoon garlic powder
1 chicken bouillon cube
½ cup hot water
3 cups cooked turkey, cubed

In a medium-sized bowl, mix together bread crumbs, sesame seeds, and oil. In another bowl, mix peach preserves, mustard, and garlic. Dissolve bouillon cube in hot water and add to peach preserves, blending well. Dip cubed turkey first in preserves and then in bread crumbs. Place in single layer on large nonstick baking sheet. Bake on top shelf of preheated 375° F. oven for about 15 minutes, or until lightly browned.

Hot Crab Spread

2 8-ounce packages cream cheese, softened
2 tablespoons half-and-half
1 tablespoon Worcestershire sauce
1 small onion, minced
Several dashes hot pepper sauce
1 pound frozen crabmeat, thawed, cleaned, and shredded

Mix all ingredients together, blending well. Turn into a buttered 1½-quart casserole and bake on bottom shelf of 375° F. oven for about 15 minutes (longer if made ahead and refrigerated). Serve with small bread rounds.

Happy Clam Dip

½ pound butter, softened
1½ cups bread crumbs
¼ teaspoon salt
1 teaspoon oregano
⅛ teaspoon garlic powder
2 7-ounce cans minced clams, drained, juice reserved

Cream together butter and bread crumbs, softening with a little reserved clam juice. Add remaining ingredients and mix well. Turn into
a 1½-quart casserole and bake on bottom shelf of preheated 375° F.
oven for 15 minutes, longer if made ahead and refrigerated. Serve
with assorted crackers.

Festive Chicken with Rice

Chicken is light enough to make it a good choice for a New
Year's Eve party, when the main dish is served late in the evening.

½ cup butter
6 chicken breasts, halved
1 cup all-purpose flour
1 teaspoon salt
⅛ teaspoon pepper
1 teaspoon poultry seasoning
⅛ teaspoon garlic powder
2 cups long grain converted rice, divided
1 large green pepper, seeded and chopped, divided
1 large onion, chopped, divided
3 cups chicken stock (or 3 bouillon cubes dissolved in 3 cups
     boiling water)
1 28-ounce can crushed tomatoes
Salt and pepper to taste

Divide butter, and melt in two large shallow baking pans while oven
is heating to 400° F. In a bag, shake together flour, salt, pepper,
poultry seasoning, and garlic powder. Shake each piece of chicken in
this mixture to coat. Divide chicken and place skin side up in pans
with butter. Put on middle shelf of preheated 400° F. oven, and bake

30 to 35 minutes or until lightly browned. Remove chicken from pans. Divide rice, green pepper, and onion between pans. In a large saucepan, combine remaining ingredients and bring to a boil. Divide this mixture in half and pour over rice in pans, stirring with a fork to mix. Return chicken to pans, cover with foil, and place on middle shelf of preheated 400° F. oven for 40 minutes. Remove foil for last 10 minutes of cooking time.

Chocolate Nut Meringues

Egg whites beat best when they're at room temperature.

3 egg whites
¼ teaspoon cream of tartar
¾ cup sugar
⅓ cup cocoa
1 teaspoon almond extract
1 cup unsalted peanuts, finely chopped

Beat together egg whites and cream of tartar until foamy. Add sugar gradually, beating until peaks form. Fold in remaining ingredients. Line baking sheet with brown paper, and drop meringue, a teaspoonful at a time, onto lined baking sheet. Put on bottom shelf of preheated 275° F. oven for 50 minutes or until meringues are set. Remove from oven and cool before storing in air-tight cannister.

Orange Cheesecake

1¼ cups vanilla wafer crumbs
2 tablespoons sugar
4 tablespoons butter, melted
1 pint creamed cottage cheese
1 8-ounce package cream cheese
4 eggs
1 cup sugar
Juice of 1 orange
Grated zest of 1 orange
½ cup half-and-half

Heat oven to 350° F. Stir together crumbs, 2 tablespoons of sugar, and butter. Press onto bottom of 9-inch springform pan. Bake on middle shelf of oven for 10 minutes. Set aside to cool. Reduce heat to 275° F. With an electric mixer, beat together cottage cheese, cream cheese, and eggs. Add 1 cup sugar, orange juice, zest, and half-and-half. Turn into springform pan on top of crust, and return to middle shelf of 275° F. oven for 2 hours or until a knife inserted in middle comes out clean. Cool, remove sides of pan, and refrigerate until ready to serve.

Note: For an even richer dessert, top with whipped cream.

KOFFEE KLATCH

This is a good menu to serve when friends are coming over for a chat, some coffee, and a bit of deliciously fattening food. Serves 12.

Menu

Peach Quiche

Sunshine Coffee Cake

Apple Surprise Muffins

Total Cooking Time: 45 minutes

Plan of Action

Preheat oven to 375° F. Assemble sunshine coffee cake and put it on bottom shelf of oven. Prepare quiche and muffins. When coffee cake has been cooking for 20 minutes, put muffins on middle shelf of oven. In another 5 minutes, add quiche to bottom shelf, and continue cooking everything for another 20 minutes.

Peach Quiche

Try saying it fast ten times!

Pastry for double pie crust (see page 359)
¾ cup chopped peaches
4 ounces mild Cheddar cheese, shredded
3 eggs
½ cup mayonnaise
⅓ cup half-and-half
½ teaspoon cinnamon

Line 12 cupcake or muffin-pan cups with rolled-out pastry. Divide peaches and cheese between 12 pastry cups. Beat eggs and mix with mayonnaise, half-and-half, and cinnamon. Pour into pastry cups. Bake on middle shelf of preheated 375° F. oven for 20 minutes or until browned. Let rest at least 10 minutes before serving.

Note: These are delicious cold, too.

Sunshine Coffee Cake

Be sure and buy the prehulled sunflower seeds for this. Hulling them is a miserable job.

½ cup (1 stick) butter
1½ cups sugar
4 eggs, separated
1 cup sour cream
2 cups all-purpose flour
2 teaspoons baking powder
1 teaspoon baking soda
¼ cup sunflower seeds, hulled
1 teaspoon vanilla extract

Cream together butter and sugar. Beat egg yolks and add. Mix in sour cream. Sift together flour, baking powder, and baking soda, and mix into butter. Add sunflower seeds and vanilla. Beat egg whites, and fold them into batter. Pour into greased and floured tube pan, and bake on bottom shelf of preheated 375° F. oven for 45 minutes, or until food pick inserted in middle comes out clean.

Apple Surprise Muffins

2 cups all-purpose flour
3 teaspoons baking powder
¼ teaspoon salt
¼ cup butter, softened
⅓ cup sugar
1 egg, beaten
1 cup milk
1 large apple (or 2 small apples)
1 teaspoon cinnamon
2 tablespoons sugar

Sift together flour, baking powder, and salt. Cream butter and sugar. Beat egg into butter. Alternately add some of the dry ingredients and some of the milk, stirring to blend until all of the flour and milk have been used. Grease 12 large muffin-pan cups. Pour in batter to about half-fill each cup. Peel, core, and divide apple into 12 pieces. Push a piece down into the middle of the batter in each muffin cup. Mix cinnamon and 2 tablespoons sugar. Sprinkle on top of muffins. Place on middle shelf of preheated 375° F. oven for about 25 minutes, or until browned.

In the Good Old Summertime

Beautiful deep summer, the longest days of the year, yet the season itself always seems far too short. We want to pack so much into it—carefree picnics, lots of company, the satisfactions of gardening. How can we accomplish it all and still have time to relax on the porch swing with a tall, cool lemonade?

Oven-cooking can help in three ways, as we illustrate in this chapter, to make summer slower-paced and more enjoyable for the cook. First, because oven-cooked foods require so much less pot-watching than top-of-the-range fare, you'll find you can assemble menus in the cool of the morning or late evening and, when you put them into the oven, stay out of the kitchen except for an occasional peek or stir while the hot work is going on. Not only that, you can turn out some fantastic feasts for those ravenous folk who have been surfing, sailing, swimming, and otherwise making hay while the sun shines. Whoever came up with the notion that in summer appetites wane must never have returned home after a day at the beach with family or friends whose thoughts have turned to food. The truth is, summer appetites are very keen—it is cooks who grow faint. That's why we've designed stay-out-of-the-kitchen menus for "remote cooking" and postponed-dining.

Another virtue of summer oven-cooking is in providing festive dishes for weekend guests without spending all your playtime in the kitchen. The secret, of course, is to get all the major dishes prepared in advance and stashed away in the refrigerator to be unveiled at the appropriate hour. For this purpose, we've created two-day menus that can be oven-cooked the day before company arrives. All that is then required is a few last-minute touches and, in some cases, a little reheating.

Third, there's that little garden you may have flourishing away in the backyard sun. It is a sad reality that seeds put in the soil at the same time in spring tend to produce ripe and ready vegetables in a sudden end-of-summer bonanza. After all the tender loving care you gave those plants, you'll want to take advantage of the results, but how many ripe zucchini and tomatoes can one family consume? Our answer is to prepare relishes, sauces, baked goods and the like that don't have to be eaten right away and yet don't require days over a hot canning kettle. For these we turn to oven-cooking coupled with refrigerator or freezer storage. Some of our favorite harvest-time recipes are included in this chapter. You'll find them easy to make and delightful to have on hand when you can put them to good use, such as after a full day of summer fun.

Glorious summer—make the most of every moment!

STAY OUT OF THE KITCHEN I— HEARTY BEEF AND LENTILS

Cook this menu in the cool of the evening—you won't even need to be in the kitchen while it is baking. The dishes need no reheating and may be served whenever needed to satisfy six hungry beachcombers.

Menu

French Beef Salad

Lentils with Red Garlic Sauce
(sauce recipe on page 355)

Celery, Carrot, and Green Pepper Sticks

Italian Bread (bakery bought)

"Peach of a Pear" Crisp

Total Cooking Time: 2 hours

Plan of Action

Oven-sauté onions for beef and garlic for lentils while oven is heating to 325° F. Cook potted beef for salad and lentil casserole on lower shelf of oven for 1 hour. Place fruit casserole on top shelf, and continue cooking for 1 hour more. Drain and cool beef slightly. Finish salad and make sauce. Refrigerate everything until needed.

French Beef Salad

2   tablespoons olive oil
2   onions, chopped, divided
3   pounds boneless chuck steak or roast, trimmed of fat and
    gristle
2   cups well-seasoned beef broth or stock
1   cup vinaigrette (see page 344)
¼   cup minced fresh flat parsley
Pepperoncini, about 8, chopped
    (or use any favorite pickle)
Salt and pepper to taste
Lettuce leaves

Combine oil and half the chopped onions in a 3-quart casserole. Oven-sauté the onions until they are sizzling while the oven heats to 325° F. Add beef and broth or stock. Cover and cook for 2 hours or until the meat is tender. Drain the beef, reserving stock. (Part of it can be used in the red garlic sauce, the rest saved for a later use.) Cool the meat about 15 minutes in the refrigerator, then dice it. Toss the beef with the remaining raw chopped onion, vinaigrette, parsley, pepperoncini or pickles, and salt and pepper to taste. Marinate the salad in the refrigerator overnight or for several hours. Serve on crisp lettuce leaves.

Note: You may wish to add a little extra wine vinegar or Dijon mustard to the salad. It is definitely a matter of "taste and see."

Lentils with Red Garlic Sauce

¼ cup olive oil
2 cloves garlic, minced
2 cups dried lentils, picked over and washed
1 quart (4 cups) water or stock
½ cup tomato sauce or stewed tomatoes
1 teaspoon salt
½ teaspoon basil
½ teaspoon oregano
Pepper to taste
Red Garlic Sauce (see page 355)

Combine oil and garlic in a 3-quart casserole that will double as a server. Oven-sauté garlic until sizzling while the oven heats to 325° F. Add all the remaining ingredients except garlic sauce. Cover tightly and bake the casserole for 2 hours, or until the lentils are tender. Refrigerate until needed. Allow the lentils to become room temperature, and serve them with garlic sauce on the side.

"Peach of a Pear" Crisp

6 to 8 fresh peaches
6 to 8 fresh pears
1 cup all-purpose flour
1 cup light brown sugar
½ teaspoon cinnamon
½ cup (1 stick) butter

Peel, core, and slice fruit into sixths. Lay them in a buttered 11-inch by 8-inch baking dish. In a bowl, mix together flour, sugar, and cinnamon. With a pastry blender or two knives, cut in butter to make a crumbly mixture and sprinkle this on top of fruit. Bake 1 hour at 325° F. Refrigerate until needed. Serve at room temperature.

STAY OUT OF THE KITCHEN II– PATIO CHICKEN DINNER

Just reheat the main dish in the oven for 30 minutes while you sip a beverage on the patio! Serves four.

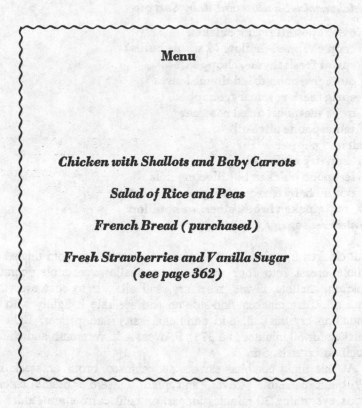

Menu

Chicken with Shallots and Baby Carrots

Salad of Rice and Peas

French Bread (purchased)

*Fresh Strawberries and Vanilla Sugar
(see page 362)*

Total Cooking Time: to cook—1 hour
to reheat—30 minutes

Plan of Action

Heat oven to 375° F. Bake chicken for 30 minutes on top shelf. Add vermouth and chicken bouillon crystals to chicken. Place carrots on top shelf, rice and peas on lower shelf. Cook everything 30 minutes longer. Fluff rice and peas; add vinaigrette. Refrigerate food until dinner time.

Reheat chicken and carrots in a 300° F. oven for 30 minutes.

Chicken with Shallots and Baby Carrots

3 to 3½ pound frying chicken
¼ cup chopped shallots (2 whole bulbs)
3 sprigs fresh thyme, chopped,
 or ½ teaspoon dried thyme leaves
1 sprig fresh rosemary, chopped,
 or ¼ teaspoon dried rosemary
3 tablespoons olive oil
Salt and pepper
½ cup dry vermouth
1 teaspoon chicken bouillon crystals
1 pound baby carrots, scraped
½ cup chicken broth, stock, or bouillon
Watercress sprigs (optional)

Cut chicken into small serving pieces. Separate legs from thighs. Cut whole breast into four pieces. In a shallow casserole, combine chicken, shallots, thyme, rosemary, and oil. Stir to coat everything with oil. Turn chicken skin-side-up and sprinkle it lightly with salt (bouillon crystals will add additional salt) and pepper. Bake the chicken for 30 minutes in a 375° F. oven. Add vermouth and chicken bouillon crystals. Stir.

At this time, combine carrots and chicken broth or stock in a 1½-quart casserole. Cover, and place casserole beside chicken. Cook everything 30 minutes longer, or until carrots are tender and chicken is done. Cool 20 minutes. Refrigerate until needed.

Reheat dishes in a 300° F. oven for 30 minutes, or until hot throughout. Remove chicken to a warm platter. Garnish with carrots and watercress sprigs, if desired.

Salad of Rice and Peas

1 cup rice
2 cups fresh peas
1 tablespoon butter
½ teaspoon salt
2 cups boiling water
½ cup vinaigrette (see page 344) or more, to taste

Combine all ingredients, except vinaigrette, in a 2-quart casserole. Cover and cook at 375° F. for 30 minutes or until all water is absorbed. Fluff rice and peas gently with a fork. Stir in vinaigrette. Refrigerate until serving time.

STAY OUT OF THE KITCHEN III—
HAM AND ZUCCHINI TEMPTER FOR A HOT
NIGHT

Bake this easy menu the night before or early in the day. No need to heat up anything at dinner time. Just slice Italian bread and serve to four.

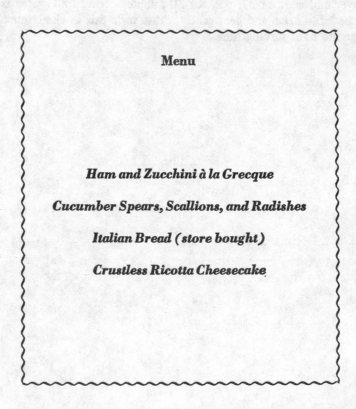

Menu

Ham and Zucchini à la Grecque

Cucumber Spears, Scallions, and Radishes

Italian Bread (store bought)

Crustless Ricotta Cheesecake

Total Cooking Time: about 50 minutes

Plan of Action

Assemble ham and zucchini casserole and cheesecake. Heat oven to 375° F. Place cheesecake on top shelf, ham and zucchini casserole on lower shelf. Bake for 40 minutes. Remove cheesecake if it is puffed and golden on top. Cook ham and zucchini 10 minutes longer, or until zucchini is just tender. Cool casserole 20 minutes; refrigerate. Cool cheesecake completely; refrigerate.

Ham and Zucchini à la Grecque

1½ pound ham slice
2½ to 3 pounds zucchini
½ pound mushrooms
1 onion, chopped
1 green pepper, seeded and chopped
¼ teaspoon ground coriander
¼ teaspoon pepper
Salt, optional
¼ cup olive oil
Juice of ½ lemon
2 tablespoons chopped fresh parsley

Trim ham slice of fat, and cube ham. Scrub zucchini well, and slice into quarters lengthwise, then across into ¾-inch chunks. Wash and trim mushrooms; leave them whole. Combine ham, zucchini, mushrooms, onion, green pepper, coriander, pepper, and salt (if using any —the ham is salty), in a shallow baking dish, approximately 12-inch by 9-inch, and drizzle oil over all. Bake for 50 minutes or until zucchini is tender, stirring once. Cool 20 minutes; refrigerate. Sprinkle with parsley before serving.

Crustless Ricotta Cheesecake

1½ pounds (3 cups) ricotta cheese
2 cups confectioners' sugar
3 eggs
1½ teaspoons vanilla extract
½ teaspoon almond extract
1 teaspoon grated orange rind
1 tablespoon candied citron, finely chopped
2 ounces dark, sweet chocolate, coarsely chopped
2 tablespoons toasted slivered almonds

Combine first six ingredients and blend well by hand, in an electric mixer or a processor fitted with the steel blade. Fold in remaining ingredients. Pour the mixture into a buttered and floured 9-inch square pan, and bake the cheesecake at 375° F. for 40 minutes or until it is slightly puffed and golden on top. Cool completely in pan on wire rack. (The cheesecake will fall a bit, which is normal.) Refrigerate until needed.

STAY OUT OF THE KITCHEN IV—
WOULD YOU BELIEVE OVEN-BAKED CHOWDER?

And it's just about the easiest and coolest way to deal with a batch of fresh fish. Serves four.

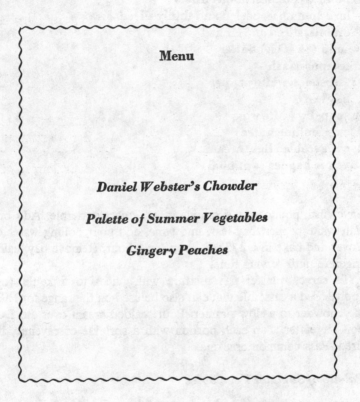

Menu

Daniel Webster's Chowder

Palette of Summer Vegetables

Gingery Peaches

Total Cooking Time: 1 hour

Plan of Action

Heat oven to 375° F. Place chowder on lower shelf, vegetables and peaches on top shelf. Cook for 30 minutes. Remove vegetables and peaches. Continue cooking chowder for 30 minutes. Finish vegetable platter. Refrigerate everything. When ready to serve, bring chowder to a simmer in a kettle, and pour scalded cream over. Do not boil.

Daniel Webster's Chowder

2 pounds cod or haddock fillets
4 large potatoes, peeled and thinly sliced
2 onions, sliced and ringed
¼ cup (½ stick) butter
2 teaspoons salt
½ teaspoon white pepper
1 bay leaf
½ cup dry white wine
2 cups boiling water
2 cups scalded light cream
Cayenne pepper (optional)
Crackers

Layer fish, potatoes, and onions in a 3-quart casserole. Add butter, salt, white pepper, bay leaf, and wine, and pour boiling water over. Cover and bake in a 375° F. oven for 1 hour. Remove bay leaf. Refrigerate until serving time.

To serve, transfer fish mixture with juices to a kettle (unless you've used a casserole that can also be used on the range top). Bring the chowder to a slow simmer. Pour scalded cream over all. Do not boil thereafter. Top each portion with a sprinkle of cayenne, if desired. Pass common crackers.

Palette of Summer Vegetables

1 summer squash, sliced ½-inch thick on the diagonal
½ pound green beans, trimmed and left whole
1 cup baby carrots, scraped
¾ cup chicken broth or prepared bouillon
4 sprigs parsley and/or celery leaves
1 clove garlic
1 bay leaf
6 peppercorns

2 sweet red peppers, seeded and cut into strips
Salt to taste
3 tablespoons salad oil
1½ tablespoons wine vinegar
2 tablespoons minced fresh coriander or parsley
¼ cup sunflower seeds

Place squash, beans, and carrots in separate bundles in a 3-quart casserole. Add broth or bouillon, parsley or celery, garlic, bay leaf, and peppercorns. Cover and cook at 375° F. for 30 minutes. Remove and discard garlic, bay leaf, and peppercorns. Drain the vegetables and arrange them on a platter with pepper strips. Sprinkle them with salt to taste, salad oil, vinegar, coriander or parsley, and sunflower seeds. Cover the dish with plastic wrap and refrigerate until needed.

Gingery Peaches

4 ripe but firm peaches, peeled
1 cup water
½ cup sugar
1 teaspoon ground ginger
2 tablespoons brandy
8 whole cloves

Place the peaches in a casserole that will just hold them. In a small saucepan, combine water, sugar, and ginger. Bring the mixture to a boil, stirring until sugar is dissolved. Then boil for 5 minutes without stirring. Remove from heat and stir in brandy. Place 2 cloves in each peach, and pour the syrup over them. Bake them, covered, in a 375° F. oven for 30 minutes. Cool slightly, then refrigerate, covered, until needed.

COOK EARLY FOR WEEKEND GUESTS I—SUMMERHOUSE DINING

Every dish on these two menus can be served to eight guests without reheating. Cook everything early on Friday, finish aspic and green bean salad that evening, and "cook" meringues. (Actually, all you do is leave them in the oven overnight.)

Menus

Liptauer Cheese and Crackers (see page 335)

Seasoned Beef and Vegetables in Aspic

Rye Bread, Flavored Butters (see page 358)

Tossed Green Salad

Fruit and Cream-Filled Meringues

Mushroom Caviar, Crackers

Chicken in Cointreau

Green Bean Salad

French Rolls, Butter

Blue Cheese Pears (see page 347)

Total Cooking Time: 3 hours

Plan of Action

Place chicken breasts skin side up in a shallow roasting pan. Brush them with melted butter, and put them under a hot broiler until golden brown. Remove chicken; turn off broiler.

Heat oven to 500° F. Sear beef for 30 minutes on lower shelf. Add chopped vegetables to pan, reducing heat to 350° F. Oven-sauté the vegetables for 10 minutes. Add braising ingredients to beef and cover it. At the same time, place mushrooms in the oven to sauté on top shelf. Remove mushrooms when brown and somewhat dry, 20 to 30 minutes.

Place sauced chicken in the oven on top shelf to cook for 40 minutes. Baste at least once. Remove chicken.

Cook green bean casserole on the top shelf, or on the lower shelf next to beef, for 30 minutes or until tender-crisp.

When beef has braised for 2½ hours, add whole carrots, cover, and continue braising for 30 minutes or until carrots are tender.

Later, finish aspic, green bean salad, and cook meringues. Preheat oven to 400° F. Place meringues in oven, on top shelf, and turn off heat. Leave them there overnight (or longer) without opening the oven door.

Seasoned Beef and Vegetables in Aspic

2 tablespoons vegetable oil
4 to 5 pound bottom round roast
1 green pepper, seeded and chopped
1 carrot, chopped
1 stalk celery, chopped
1 large onion, chopped
1 clove garlic, minced
2½ cups water
2 teaspoons salt
¼ teaspoon whole peppercorns
4 whole cloves
2 bay leaves
½ teaspoon dried thyme leaves
4 whole carrots, scraped
1 package frozen snowpeas, thawed to separate

1 **envelope unflavored gelatin**
¼ **cup dry sherry or vermouth**
2 **tablespoons minced fresh flat parsley**

Preheat oven to 500° F. Pour oil into a Dutch oven, place beef in it, and sear for 20 minutes in the hot oven. Sprinkle chopped green pepper, carrot, celery, onion, and garlic around roast, and lower heat to 350° F. Oven-sauté vegetables with the beef for 10 minutes. Add water, salt, peppercorns, cloves, bay leaves, and thyme. Cover and simmer the roast in the oven for 2½ hours. Add whole carrots, cover, and cook 30 minutes longer, or until meat and carrots are tender. Strain pan juices into a bowl through a colander lined with rinsed cheesecloth. Chill beef, carrots, and strained juices.

Trim fat from beef, slice it thinly, and arrange in overlapping rows on a large platter. Slice carrots and place them around meat, alternating carrots with thawed snowpeas. Remove congealed fat from broth and measure broth; you should have 1¾ cups. If not, add tinned beef broth to make up the difference. Taste to correct seasoning. It should be quite flavorful, since it will be served cold. In a small saucepan, sprinkle gelatin over ½ cup broth, and stir the mixture over low heat until the gelatin is completely dissolved. Combine gelatin mixture with the remaining broth and the sherry or vermouth. Chill until it is thick but not set. Spoon the gelled broth over meat and vegetables, completely covering them. (A brush can be used if needed.) Sprinkle with parsley as a garnish. Refrigerate until serving time.

Meringue Shells

4 **egg whites**
½ **teaspoon cream of tartar**
1 **cup sugar**
½ **teaspoon almond extract**
1 **quart (4 cups) drained fresh fruit**
   or frozen fruit, thawed
1 **pint heavy cream, whipped and sweetened with 2 tablespoons**
   sugar

Preheat the oven to 400° F. Combine egg whites and cream of tartar. Beat until foamy. Gradually beat in sugar until meringue forms stiff peaks. Beat in almond extract. Divide the meringue between two well-buttered 8-inch or 9-inch pie pans, and spread it with a table knife into a thick pie-shell shape. Place the pie pans in the hot oven, and turn off heat. Leave the meringues there overnight without opening the oven door.

To serve, fill the meringues with drained fruit and top with sweetened whipped cream. Cut into wedges.

Mushroom Caviar

12-ounce package fresh mushrooms
1 tablespoon dry vermouth or white wine
3 tablespoons butter
2 shallots or 1 clove garlic, minced
2 tablespoons creamed cottage cheese
¼ cup chopped black olives
¼ cup chopped toasted almonds
Juice of ½ lemon (or more, to taste)
1 teaspoon minced fresh parsley
¼ teaspoon salt
¼ teaspoon pepper
4 hard-boiled eggs
1 bunch scallions, peeled and coarsely chopped
Crackers or melba rounds

Wash mushrooms, towel them dry, and chop them. Place them in a baking dish with vermouth or wine, butter, and shallots or garlic. Bake them in a 350° F. oven for 30 minutes or until the liquid has evaporated and mushrooms are brown and somewhat dry. Cool mushrooms. Blend in cheese, olives, almonds, lemon juice, parsley, salt, and pepper. Chill the mixture. Mound the caviar in a serving dish and garnish it with sliced eggs, scallions, and crackers or melba rounds.

Chicken in Cointreau

4 to 5 whole chicken breasts
6 tablespoons butter, melted
1½ cups cold chicken broth
3 tablespoons cornstarch
2 cups orange juice

½ cup dry vermouth or white wine
2 teaspoons salt
¼ teaspoon white pepper
½ cup orange marmalade
⅓ cup Cointreau
½ cup whole almonds
1 small cantaloupe cut into melon balls (optional)
Sprigs of watercress (optional)

Cut whole chicken breasts in half. Place them, skin side up, in a shallow roasting pan, and brush them with some of the melted butter. Broil until golden brown on skin side.

In a saucepan, mix broth and cornstarch until smooth. Add orange juice, vermouth or wine, salt, pepper, and the remaining butter. Bring the mixture to a boil, stirring constantly. Turn off heat. Stir in marmalade and Cointreau. Spoon the sauce evenly over the chicken, and bake the dish in a 350° F. oven for 40 minutes or until cooked through, basting at least once. Remove chicken to a serving dish. Stir almonds into sauce remaining in baking pan, and spoon that over the chicken. Refrigerate until serving time. Garnish, if desired, with melon balls and watercress.

Green Bean Salad

3 pounds fresh green beans
1 cup water
Salt
1 cup sweet vinaigrette (see page 345)
1 cup chopped onion
2 tablespoons minced fresh basil
   or 1 teaspoon dried basil

Wash and trim off the ends of green beans. Cut them into 1-inch lengths, and place them in a 3-quart casserole with water. Salt them lightly. Cover the casserole, and bake the beans in a 350° F. oven for 30 minutes or until they are tender-crisp. Drain and refresh beans under running cold water. Toss the drained beans with sweet vinaigrette, onion, and basil. Let the salad marinate in the refrigerator until serving time.

COOK EARLY FOR WEEKEND GUESTS II—
PICNICKING IN STYLE

A portable chicken picnic to pack and take to parts unknown—but keep perishable foods well chilled!—and an oven-barbecued spareribs dinner to serve on the patio. Cook everything on Friday, then just relax with your guests. The recipes serve six.

Menu

Picnic Oven-Fried Chicken

*Creamy Cornloaf with Sliced
Muenster Cheese*

*Crunchy Vegetables Vinaigrette
(see page 338)*

Mandarin Orange Cake

Super Spareribs

Salad of Chick-Peas and Black Olives

Assorted Rolls (bakery bought)

Layered Fruit Compote (see page 349)

Total Cooking Time: 3 hours and 45 minutes

Plan of Action

Heat oven to 350° F. While it is heating, oven-sauté onion and garlic for chick-peas and onion in butter for cornloaf. Then remove these baking dishes from the oven.

Bake orange cake for 30 minutes on a shelf in the middle of the oven. While it is baking prepare chicken for oven and prepare cornloaf except for final mixing of wet and dry ingredients.

After removing cake, raise oven heat to 375° F. Place chicken on top shelf of oven and bake for 15 minutes. Meanwhile finish preparing cornloaf and chick-peas.

When chicken has cooked for 15 minutes, place cornloaf and chick-peas on lower shelf. Bake for 45 minutes. During this time, prepare spareribs. Remove chicken and cornloaf.

Reduce heat to 325° F. Place spareribs on top shelf. Bake spareribs and continue cooking chick-peas for 2 hours. Remove spareribs. Add salt and oregano to chick-peas and cook them 15 minutes more.

Prepare layered fruit compote. Prepare frosting and mandarin oranges for cake; frost cake. Finish salad of chick-peas and black olives, but don't spoon it onto lettuce until ready to serve.

Store all dishes in the refrigerator until needed.

Picnic Oven-Fried Chicken

2 small frying chickens
2 cups toasted seasoned crumbs (see page 361)
⅓ cup toasted wheat germ
2 teaspoons chicken bouillon crystals
  or 1 teaspoon salt
2 teaspoons paprika
½ teaspoon ground thyme
½ teaspoon pepper
3 tablespoons vegetable oil

Cut chickens into serving pieces. Separate legs from thighs. In a large plastic bag, mix all the remaining ingredients. Shake the bag to blend oil thoroughly with dry mixture. Coat 2 or 3 chicken pieces at a time by shaking them in the bag; chicken should be damp when coated.

Place the pieces on an oiled baking sheet. Bake 1 hour at 375° F. Cool slightly. Refrigerate until needed. Serve at room temperature, but do not allow leftover chicken to remain at room temperature after serving.

Creamy Cornloaf with Sliced Muenster Cheese

A moist loaf that keeps well and is flavorful even when served cold.

1 onion, finely chopped
½ cup (1 stick) butter
½ pound cottage cheese or ricotta
16-ounce can creamed corn
3 eggs, separated
1 cup all-purpose flour
1 tablespoon baking powder
1 teaspoon salt
1 cup cornmeal
2 tablespoons sugar
Scant ¼ teaspoon crushed anise (optional)
½ pound sliced Muenster cheese

Preheat oven to 375° F. While it is heating, oven-sauté onion in butter in a loaf pan until butter is melted and sizzling but not brown. Pour butter and onion into a large mixing bowl and let it cool slightly. Use the butter remaining in loaf pan to grease it on all sides. Line the bottom of the pan with thin, plain white paper, also buttered. Thoroughly blend the cooled butter with onion, cheese, creamed corn, and egg yolks. Stir all-purpose flour to lighten it before measuring. Sift flour with baking powder and salt. Stir in cornmeal. In a third bowl, beat egg whites until they form stiff peaks. Gradually beat in sugar. When ready to bake, add dry ingredients all at once to cheese-corn mixture. Blend well. Fold in egg whites and anise, if using. Spoon the batter into prepared pan, and bake for 45 minutes or until a cake tester inserted in the center comes out clean. Cool 10 minutes in pan on wire rack, then remove from pan to cool completely. Serve with sliced Muenster cheese on the side.

Mandarin Orange Cake

¾ cup soft butter
1½ cups sugar
3 eggs
2 teaspoons grated orange rind
3 cups sifted cake flour
3 teaspoons baking powder
½ teaspoon salt
½ cup orange juice
⅔ cup milk
Curacao glaze (recipe follows)
11-ounce can mandarin oranges, drained (reserve juice for
  glaze)

In the large bowl of an electric mixer, combine butter, sugar, eggs, and orange rind. Beat until light and fluffy. Sift together flour, baking powder, and salt. Combine orange juice and milk. Add the flour mixture alternately with the juice-milk to the creamed mixture, beginning and ending with flour. Pour the batter into a buttered and floured 2-inch by 9-inch baking pan. Bake on the top shelf of a preheated 350° F. oven for 30 minutes, or until a cake tester inserted in the center comes out dry. Cool cake in pan on wire rack. Prick the top of the cake lightly with a fork. Pour the glaze over the cake, a little at a time, until it is all absorbed. Arrange the orange slices in an attractive pattern on top. Serve from pan.

Curacao Glaze: In a saucepan, combine ¼ cup juice from oranges, ½ cup (1 stick) butter, and 1 cup sugar. Stir over low heat until butter melts. Bring to a boil over medium heat, and cook for 5 minutes, stirring constantly. Remove from heat. Stir in ½ cup orange liqueur and oranges.

Super Spareribs

3 pounds spareribs
1 cup chili sauce
1 cup water
1 green pepper, seeded and finely chopped

1 large onion, finely chopped
1 clove garlic, minced
⅓ cup vinegar
¼ cup dark brown sugar
1 tablespoon Worcestershire sauce
1 teaspoon salt
½ teaspoon dry mustard
½ teaspoon basil
¼ teaspoon pepper
⅛ teaspoon turmeric
⅛ teaspoon Tabasco

Cut spareribs into serving pieces, and lay them in one layer in a shallow roasting pan. Mix all the remaining ingredients, blending well. Pour the barbecue sauce over the ribs. Bake for 2 hours in a 325° F. oven, basting every 30 minutes. Turn ribs once.

Salad of Chick-Peas and Black Olives

¼ cup olive oil
1 onion, chopped
1 clove garlic, minced
1½ cups dried chick-peas, picked over and rinsed
1½ quarts boiling water
½ teaspoon oregano
1 teaspoon salt
¼ teaspoon pepper
8-ounce can pitted black olives
4 to 6 scallions with green tops, chopped
½ cup sweet vinaigrette (see page 345)
1 small head romaine lettuce
4 hard-boiled eggs

In a heavy 3-quart casserole, oven-sauté onion and garlic in oil while oven is heating. When sizzling, remove from the oven, and cool slightly. Add chick-peas and boiling water. Cover and bake for 1 hour at 375° F. Reduce heat to 325° F. and cook 2 hours longer or until tender, adding more hot water if and when needed. When peas are tender, add oregano, salt, and pepper. Cook 15 minutes longer.

Drain only if there is too much liquid for salad; that is, if the peas are soupy. Mix the chick-peas with olives, scallions, and vinaigrette. Refrigerate, covered. Wash lettuce leaves, shake them dry, and wrap them loosely in a towel. Chill the lettuce. When ready to serve, make a bed of lettuce and spoon chick-peas into the center. Garnish with quartered eggs.

COOK EARLY FOR WEEKEND GUESTS III—DINING ALFRESCO

A candlelit table with fine linens under the stars—what could be more pleasant on a moonlit July evening! This calls for a touch of elegance. . . . Serves four.

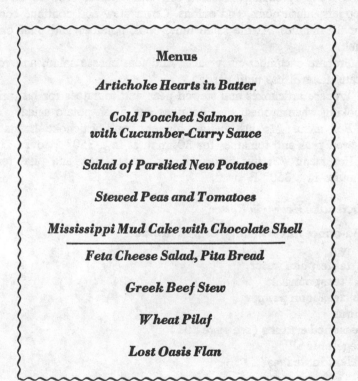

Menus

Artichoke Hearts in Batter

*Cold Poached Salmon
with Cucumber-Curry Sauce*

Salad of Parslied New Potatoes

Stewed Peas and Tomatoes

Mississippi Mud Cake with Chocolate Shell

Feta Cheese Salad, Pita Bread

Greek Beef Stew

Wheat Pilaf

Lost Oasis Flan

Total Cooking Time: earlier in day—about 2½ hours
to reheat—30 minutes just before dinners

Plan of Action

Preheat oven to 325° F. Place salmon on top shelf, flan on lower shelf. Cook salmon for 30 minutes, flan for 50 to 60 minutes. Meanwhile, assemble cake. Raise heat to 350° F. when flan is removed. Oven-sauté beef and garlic for 15 minutes. Add liquids, and place stew on lower shelf, cake on top shelf. Cook 40 to 45 minutes or until cake is done. Remove cake. Continue cooking stew for 15 minutes while spreading chocolate on warm cake. Add to stew the peppers, mushrooms, and onions. Cover stew and continue cooking for 30 minutes. At the same time, cook potatoes and pilaf on top shelf.

Prepare cucumber-curry sauce and feta cheese salad, and refrigerate these dishes until needed.

Prepare artichokes and stewed peas and tomatoes for last minute cooking when needed. Peel potatoes and finish potato salad.

For menu #1: just before dinner, cook artichoke hearts and stewed peas and tomatoes for 30 minutes in a 350° F. oven.

For menu #2: just before dinner, reheat stew and pilaf for 30 minutes in a 350° F. oven.

Artichoke Hearts in Batter

7½-ounce can artichoke hearts, drained
1 egg
1 tablespoon water
¼ teaspoon salt
⅛ teaspoon pepper
Flour
Seasoned crumbs (see page 361)
Vegetable oil
4 lemon wedges

Cut artichoke hearts in half. Beat egg with water, salt, and pepper. Dip artichoke halves in flour, then egg mixture, then crumbs to coat them completely. Chill them until ready to cook. Lay them in an oiled pan, and drizzle a few drops of oil on each. Bake in a 350° F. oven for 30 minutes or until golden. Serve with lemon wedges as a first course.

Cold Poached Salmon with Cucumber-Curry Sauce

3 pounds salmon steaks (at least 1-inch thick)
½ cup dry white wine
½ cup water
1 small onion, sliced
2 slices lemon
2 sprigs fresh parsley
1 bay leaf
1 teaspoon salt
6 peppercorns
Cucumber-Curry Sauce (recipe follows)

Lay the salmon steaks in one layer in a buttered shallow casserole. In a small saucepan, combine the remaining ingredients, except sauce, and bring the mixture to a boil. Pour the poaching liquid over the fish. Cover loosely with a tent of foil. Bake at 325° F. for 30 minutes, or until fish flakes apart easily when tested with a fork. Carefully lift salmon steaks out of poaching liquid, and lay them on a platter. Refrigerate, covered. When ready to serve, garnish platter with sauce.

Cucumber-Curry Sauce: Peel, seed, and finely chop 1 cucumber. Mix it with ½ cup mayonnaise, ½ cup sour cream, 2 tablespoons fresh lemon juice, 1 teaspoon curry powder, and 1 teaspoon sugar. Refrigerate until needed.

Salad of Parslied New Potatoes

2 pounds new potatoes, scrubbed
1 cup water
1 tablespoon vinegar
1 teaspoon salt
2 tablespoons minced fresh parsley
¼ cup minced onion
¾ cup sweet vinaigrette (see page 345)

Combine the first four ingredients in a 2-quart casserole. Cover and bake at 350° F. for 35 to 45 minutes or until potatoes are tender. (Timing depends on how small the potatoes are.) Drain immediately. When cool enough to handle, peel the potatoes and cut them in halves or quarters, depending on size. Combine them with parsley, onion, and sweet vinaigrette. Refrigerate, covered, until well chilled.

Stewed Peas and Tomatoes

10-ounce package frozen peas, thawed to separate
3 tomatoes, peeled, seeded, and chopped
1 teaspoon cornstarch
1 teaspoon sugar
¼ teaspoon salt
½ cup water
2 tablespoons butter
¼ teaspoon dried basil
Dash of pepper
4 slices French bread, toasted and buttered

Combine peas and tomatoes in a 2-quart casserole. Stir cornstarch, sugar, and salt into water until they are dissolved. Pour this mixture over the vegetables. Dot them with butter; sprinkle with basil and pepper. Cover and bake at 350° F. for 25 minutes.

To serve, reheat at 350° F. for 20 minutes or until heated through, and top with toasted French bread.

Mississippi Mud Cake with Chocolate Shell

1 cup boiling coffee
1 ounce bourbon
⅔ cup unsweetened cocoa
2 eggs
1½ cups sugar
¾ cup vegetable oil
2 teaspoons vanilla extract
1 teaspoon baking soda
1 teaspoon baking powder
½ teaspoon salt
2 cups all-purpose flour
1 cup chocolate chips

Remove boiling coffee from heat, and stir in bourbon. Add cocoa, and stir until it is dissolved and smooth. In the large bowl of an electric mixer, beat eggs with sugar until thick and light in color. Beat in oil and vanilla. Add chocolate mixture. Blend in soda, baking powder, and salt. Then stir in flour until well-blended. Pour the batter into a buttered tube pan with removable ring, and bake the cake in a preheated 350° F. oven for 40 to 45 minutes or until a cake tester inserted in the center comes out dry. Meanwhile, melt chocolate chips over hot water. When cake is done, put the pan on a wire rack over waxed paper. Remove outer ring. With spatula, spread melted chocolate over the top and sides of the warm cake. Cool completely. Remove the rest of pan.

Greek Beef Stew

3 tablespoons flour
1 teaspoon paprika
1 teaspoon salt
¼ teaspoon pepper
2½ pounds lean beef, cut into strips
¼ cup (½ stick) butter
2 cloves garlic, minced
2 cups beef broth
1 cup dry white wine
2 teaspoons tomato paste
1 teaspoon brown sugar
¼ teaspoon allspice
Dash of cayenne pepper
2 green peppers, seeded and cut into strips
6-ounce can mushrooms, drained
8-ounce jar small white onions, drained

In a plastic bag, combine flour, paprika, salt, and pepper. Shake beef strips in this mixture until they are evenly coated. In a Dutch oven, melt butter in oven while heating it to 350° F. Stir beef and garlic into the butter, and oven-sauté the mixture for 15 minutes. Add broth, wine, tomato paste, brown sugar, allspice, and cayenne. Cover and cook for 1 hour. Add green peppers, mushrooms, and onions. If liquid has reduced below 2 cups, add more broth or wine. Cover and continue to cook for 20 to 30 minutes, until meat and peppers are tender. Cool 20 minutes. Refrigerate. Remove congealed fat when cold.

Reheat, covered, in a 350° F. oven for 30 minutes.

Wheat Pilaf

1 small onion, chopped
2 tablespoons olive oil
1 cup cracked wheat
½ teaspoon salt
¼ teaspoon pepper
¼ teaspoon ground thyme
¼ teaspoon turmeric
2½ . cups boiling beef or chicken broth, or prepared bouillon
2 tablespoons melted butter

In a 2-quart casserole, oven-sauté onion in oil until it is sizzling. Stir in wheat, salt, pepper, thyme, and turmeric. Add 2 cups boiling broth or bouillon. Cover and bake for 30 minutes in a 350° F. oven.

To reheat: fluff well with a fork, pour remaining ½ cup broth over, drizzle on melted butter, and bake, uncovered, for 20 minutes at 350° F. Fluff again before serving.

Lost Oasis Flan

⅔ cup sugar
⅛ teaspoon cream of tartar
2 tablespoons water
6 egg yolks
8-ounce can crushed pineapple, well-drained
¼ teaspoon cinnamon
2 cups heavy cream
⅓ cup vanilla sugar (see page 362)
   or ⅓ cup sugar and ½ teaspoon vanilla extract
¼ cup finely chopped dates
1 pomegranate

In a small heavy saucepan, combine ⅔ cup sugar, cream of tartar, and water. Stir over low heat until sugar is dissolved. Raise the heat to medium and continue cooking, not stirring but continually watching, until sugar turns a golden caramel color. Quickly pour the caramel over the bottom of an oven-warmed 1½-quart baking dish. Tilt and turn the dish to coat sides and bottom, and keep turning as the mixture cools until it has all adhered to the dish. Chill the dish while making the custard.

In a bowl, whisk together egg yolks, pineapple, and cinnamon. Scald cream with ⅓ cup vanilla sugar, stirring to dissolve sugar. (If using vanilla extract, add that to the egg yolk mixture.) Pour scalded cream in a slow stream into the egg yolk mixture, whisking constantly. Add dates. Pour the custard into the prepared baking dish, and place it in a larger pan of hot water so that the water comes two-thirds of the way up the sides of the mold. Bake 50 to 60 minutes in a 325° F. oven or until the custard is set. Test by inserting a table knife 1 inch from the center. It should come out clean. Cool. Cover with plastic wrap and refrigerate 6 hours or longer. Unmold just before serving. Place empty mold in hot water to loosen caramel remaining in it, and pour the caramel over the custard.

Peel pomegranate, and use the seeds to garnish each portion of flan.

ASSORTED VEGETABLE HARVEST

Especially for gardeners, the end of summer yields a wealth of vegetables—just as appetite and inspiration falter. Here's an oven-full of good things to bake on a rainy day, using up the harvest-time odds and ends. All these delightful side dishes will keep for a week or more in the refrigerator.

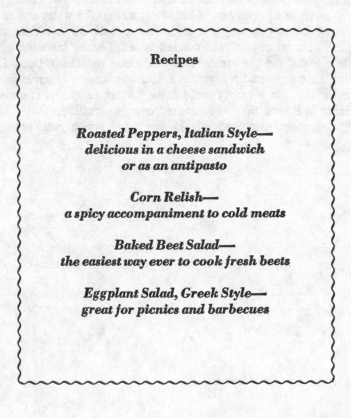

Recipes

Roasted Peppers, Italian Style—
delicious in a cheese sandwich
or as an antipasto

Corn Relish—
a spicy accompaniment to cold meats

Baked Beet Salad—
the easiest way ever to cook fresh beets

Eggplant Salad, Greek Style—
great for picnics and barbecues

Total Cooking Time: about 2 hours

Plan of Action

Heat oven to 450° F. Roast peppers on top shelf for 30 minutes or until quite brown. Remove peppers, cool, and put into plastic bags. Reduce heat to 350° F. Place corn relish on lower shelf, beets and eggplants on top shelf. Remove beets and eggplants when tender, about 1 hour. Cook corn relish until quite thick, approximately 30 minutes longer. When peppers, beets, and eggplants are cool, finish assembling these dishes.

Roasted Peppers, Italian Style

12 green peppers, whole
2 cloves garlic, finely minced
½ teaspoon dried basil
½ teaspoon salt
Freshly ground black pepper to taste
About ½ cup olive oil

Place the whole peppers on the oiled rack of a broiler pan on the top shelf of a 450° F. oven. Roast them until the thin outer skins are quite brown, about 30 minutes, turning frequently during cooking. Cool slightly, and put the peppers into two or three plastic bags. (Their steam will then make them easier to peel.) Peel off the browned skin when peppers are cool enough to handle, seed them, and cut them into strips. Add the remaining ingredients and enough olive oil to cover generously. Refrigerate in a covered container. The flavor improves after they have marinated for a day or two.

Yield: 1 to 1½ quarts.

Corn Relish

5 cups raw fresh corn cut from cobs
2 sweet red and 4 green peppers, chopped about the size of corn kernels
4 onions, chopped
1 stalk celery, with leaves, chopped
1½ cups cider vinegar
1½ cups light brown sugar

1 tablespoon salt
1½ teaspoons dry mustard (more, if you like it hot)
1 teaspoon turmeric
½ teaspoon pepper

Combine the vegetables in a Dutch oven or casserole of 4-quart capacity. In a saucepan, combine the remaining ingredients, and stir them over low heat until sugar is dissolved. Pour mixture over the vegetables. Bake at 350° F. for 1 hour and 30 minutes or until quite thick, stirring often during the last 20 minutes of cooking. Cool and chill. Keeps well under refrigeration for three weeks or more.
    Yield: 2 quarts.

Baked Beet Salad

6 large beets
1 small onion, finely chopped
½ teaspoon salt
1 teaspoon capers
½ cup sweet vinaigrette (see page 345)

Wash beets and trim off ends. Wrap them in foil, and place in a baking pan. Roast them in a 350° F. oven for 1 hour or until they are tender when pierced with a knife point. Unwrap and cool beets. Peel and cut them into julienne strips. Combine beets with the remaining ingredients. Refrigerate in a covered container.
    Serves six.

Eggplant Salad, Greek Style

3 large eggplants
3 tomatoes, peeled, seeded, and chopped
1 large onion, finely chopped
⅓ cup lemon juice
½ cup olive oil
1 teaspoon salt
Freshly ground black pepper to taste
1 teaspoon oregano
¼ cup pine nuts

Prick eggplant skin in two or three places. Place whole eggplants on the top oven rack, and roast them for about 1 hour at 350° F. They are done when the skin is wrinkled and they are soft to the touch. Cool, then peel eggplants. Chop the flesh, discarding seeds. Toss the eggplant with the remaining ingredients. Store the salad in a covered container in the refrigerator.

Yield: about 2 quarts.

THE GREAT ZUCCHINI HARVEST

It happens to every vegetable farmer sometimes—a superabundant zucchini harvest! Here's an ovenful of recipes to make the most of the season's bounty, whether you want to use up your own crop or simply take advantage of seasonal low prices. Remember that these foods can be frozen for later use!

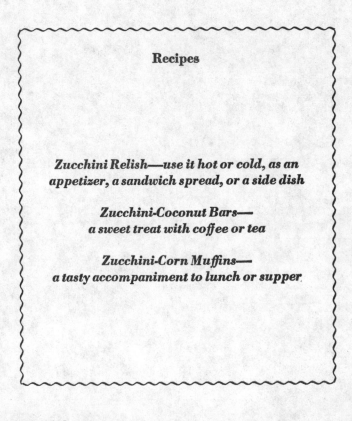

Recipes

Zucchini Relish—use it hot or cold, as an appetizer, a sandwich spread, or a side dish

Zucchini-Coconut Bars— a sweet treat with coffee or tea

Zucchini-Corn Muffins— a tasty accompaniment to lunch or supper.

Total Cooking Time: 2 hours

Plan of Action

Preheat oven to 400° F. While it is heating, oven-sauté onions, peppers, and garlic for relish. Finish assembling relish, and place it on lower shelf. Place muffins on top shelf and bake 20 minutes, or until they are golden brown and dry when tested with a cake tester. Remove muffins and reduce heat to 350° F. Place zucchini-coconut bars on top shelf and bake them for 30 to 35 minutes. Remove bars. Continue cooking relish for 1 hour and 10 minutes (a total of 2 hours for the relish).

Zucchini Relish

½ cup olive oil
2 large onions, chopped
4 green peppers, seeded and cut in chunks
4 cloves garlic, minced
3 large zucchini, cut into half-rounds, ¼ inch thick
    (scrub zucchini well before cutting)
2 28-ounce cans tomatoes with juice,
    or 1½ quarts (6 cups) fresh tomatoes, peeled and chopped
¼ cup chopped fresh parsley
¼ cup chopped fresh basil
    or 1½ tablespoons dried basil
¼ cup wine vinegar
¼ cup sugar
2 teaspoons dried oregano
2 teaspoons salt
1 teaspoon pepper
1 cup pitted black olives (optional)
6 anchovy fillets (optional)

Preheat oven to 400° F. Combine oil, onions, green peppers, and garlic in a Dutch oven. While oven is heating, oven-sauté these vegetables for 10 minutes. Remove pan from oven. Add all the remaining ingredients. Bake, uncovered, on lower shelf of oven for 2 hours, stirring two or three times. After 20 minutes, reduce heat to 350° F.

   Yield: 2½ to 3 quarts.

Zucchini-Coconut Bars

¾ cup (1½ sticks) butter, softened
1 cup light brown sugar, firmly packed
2 eggs
1 teaspoon vanilla extract
1¾ cups all-purpose flour
1½ teaspoons baking powder
½ teaspoon salt
2 cups coarsely grated zucchini, loosely packed
1 cup shredded coconut
1 cup chopped walnuts
1 tablespoon cinnamon sugar (see page 361)

Cream butter until light. Gradually add sugar. Beat in eggs, one at a time, then vanilla. Stir flour to lighten it before measuring. Sift together flour, baking powder, and salt. Blend the dry ingredients into the creamed butter mixture, but do not overbeat. Fold in zucchini, coconut, and walnuts. Spoon the batter into a buttered and floured 12-inch by 8-inch baking pan, and sprinkle the top with cinnamon sugar. Bake in a 350° F. oven for 30 to 35 minutes or until a cake tester inserted in the center comes out dry. Cool in pan on wire rack. Cut into 24 bars.

Zucchini-Corn Muffins

1 cup all-purpose flour
1 cup cornmeal
1 tablespoon baking powder
½ teaspoon salt
½ teaspoon cinnamon
1 cup soured milk (see page 362) or buttermilk
¼ cup honey
1 egg, beaten
¼ cup (½ stick) butter, melted and cooled slightly
1 cup coarsely grated zucchini, loosely packed

Stir flour to lighten it before measuring. Combine the dry ingredients in a large bowl, and stir them until they are very well blended. In another bowl, combine milk, honey, egg, and melted butter. Pour the mixture all at once into dry ingredients, and stir until just combined. Fold in zucchini. Spoon the batter into a 12-cup muffin pan which has been buttered and floured (paper liners may be used instead), filling each cup about three-quarters full. Bake for 20 minutes in a preheated 400° F. oven or until muffins are risen, golden brown, and a cake tester inserted in the center of a muffin comes out dry. Cool in pan on a wire rack for 5 minutes. Remove muffins from pan to cool completely, unless, of course, you wish to serve them warm immediately!

THE GREAT TOMATO HARVEST

With just a few tomato plants, you can find yourself with unexpected red and green riches on your hands, just about the time the weatherman announces the first killing frost. Here's how you can put your oven to work providing tasty tomato treats for the weeks ahead.

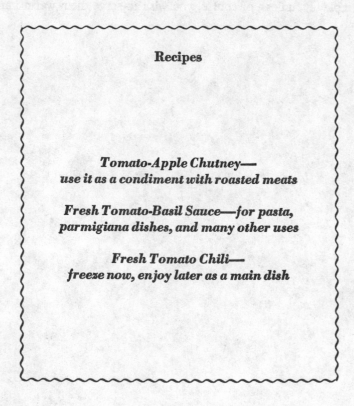

Recipes

Tomato-Apple Chutney—
use it as a condiment with roasted meats

Fresh Tomato-Basil Sauce—for pasta,
parmigiana dishes, and many other uses

Fresh Tomato Chili—
freeze now, enjoy later as a main dish

Total Cooking Time: about 3 hours

Plan of Action

Preheat oven to 375° F. Oven-sauté meats for chili on top shelf for 30 minutes. Add green pepper, onion, celery, and garlic, and continue cooking for 20 minutes. At the same time, place tomato sauce and chutney on lower shelf. When sautéing is completed, add remaining ingredients to chili. Tomato sauce cooks in approximately 1½ hours; chutney, 2 hours and 45 minutes; and chili (after tomatoes are added), 1 hour and 45 minutes.

Tomato-Apple Chutney

4 cups tomatoes, peeled and cut in half-slices (green, half-green, or a combination of green and ripe tomatoes)
3 cups apples, sliced
1 large onion, chopped
1 cup raisins
Peel of 1 lemon, chopped
Juice of 1 lemon
1 clove garlic, minced
3 dried whole hot red peppers
1 cinnamon stick
1 teaspoon salt
½ teaspoon ground ginger
¼ teaspoon cayenne pepper
¼ teaspoon ground cloves
1 cup cider vinegar
1½ cups brown sugar, firmly packed
1 cup coarsely chopped walnuts

In a Dutch oven, combine tomatoes, apples, onion, raisins, lemon peel and juice, garlic, red peppers, cinnamon, salt, ginger, cayenne, and cloves. In a saucepan, mix vinegar with sugar, and stir the mixture over low heat until the sugar is dissolved. Pour this liquid over the tomato-apple mixture, and bake the chutney on the lower shelf of a 375° F. oven, stirring occasionally, for about 2½ hours or until it is reduced and thickened. Remove cinnamon stick and red pepper pods. Stir in walnuts. Continue to cook for 15 minutes. Cool and refrigerate the chutney, covered (keeps 3 weeks or more), or freeze it in ½-pint containers.

Yield: 5 cups.

Fresh Tomato-Basil Sauce

This simplest of sauces holds the taste of summer.

⅓ cup olive oil
3 cloves garlic, minced
18 peeled ripe tomatoes, coarsely chopped
2 teaspoons salt
½ teaspoon pepper
3 tablespoons minced fresh basil
3 tablespoons minced fresh parsley

In a large shallow roasting pan or casserole (not aluminum) combine oil and garlic, and oven-sauté them on the lower shelf of a 375° F. oven until the oil is sizzling but the garlic is not browned. Add tomatoes, salt, and pepper, and bake, uncovered, stirring occasionally about 1 hour and 15 minutes or until the sauce thickens to the desired consistency. Add basil and parsley, and cook 15 minutes longer. Sieve or not, as you wish. Keeps well for over a week in a covered container in the refrigerator, or freeze it in pint containers.

Yield: about 1 quart.

Fresh Tomato Chili

2 pounds lean pork, cubed
2 pounds lean beef, cubed
2 tablespoons vegetable oil
1½ cups chopped onion
1 cup chopped green pepper
1 stalk celery, chopped
1 clove garlic, minced
3½ cups peeled and chopped ripe tomatoes
2 cups beef broth or stock
4-ounce can Mexican green chilies, chopped
2½ tablespoons chili powder
2 teaspoons salt
1 teaspoon oregano
1 teaspoon sugar
½ teaspoon ground cumin
½ teaspoon dried coriander
½ teaspoon dried thyme leaves

In a large shallow baking pan or casserole (not aluminum) combine pork, beef, and oil. Oven-sauté the meats on the top shelf of a 375° F. oven for 30 minutes. Add onion, green pepper, celery, and garlic, and continue to cook for 20 minutes. Add all the remaining ingredients and cook for 1 hour and 45 minutes, or until chili reaches the desired consistency. Cool completely, and freeze in serving-sized containers whatever portion will not be used immediately. If you wish, to serve, combine with cooked, drained kidney beans, or grated Monterey Jack cheese, or both.

Yield: about 2 quarts.

The Big Baking Day

The pleasures of cooking are more apparent when you indulge in a big baking day. Stocking up the larder with homemade food holds a certain basic satisfaction that is part of our heritage—and it's a tangible accomplishment that pays future dividends. In earlier times, every family had a big baking day, of necessity, since getting a wood-oven up to the right heat and maintaining it long enough to cook unprocessed foods was not possible on an everyday basis. Saturday was the day of choice to bake the week's breads, beans, and pies, and they frequently had to last for the week ahead.

For our generation, any day or evening that you're in the mood to cook and have the time can be a big baking day. We believe in making the most efficient use of time spent in the kitchen, and this chapter especially reflects that philosophy. It could be summed up in the adage, "if a little is good, a lot is better," or, if you're going to throw yourself into cooking, why not bake a few extras for the days when you're working or playing elsewhere?

Cook-now, eat-later recipes in this chapter are built around what will fit into one average-sized oven at one time. Three casseroles instead of one are not only a practical use of oven heat and a boon for busy days ahead, but they are much easier to assemble at one time than on three different occasions. Similar ingredients need only be taken out once, vegetables can be chopped in one process for more than one dish, and utensils washed up in one batch.

When engaged in a big baking day, it goes smoother if you do as much of the assembly work in advance as possible, turning on the oven when you have the ingredients prepared and the dishes fairly well put together.

If you're subject to occasional yens to immerse yourself in cooking, it's a good idea to keep enough staples on hand to avoid frustration: the standard baking ingredients like flour, sugar, salt, eggs, chocolate, shortening, and leavening; the flavor vegetables like garlic, onions or shallots, carrots, celery, and green pepper; fats, oils, and a full complement of herbs and spices; cans of tomatoes and chicken or beef broth. With these ingredients dependably available, you can prepare an infinite variety of dishes from whatever meats and seasonal vegetables you happen to have on hand that week.

When following recipes, if you've run out of one ingredient, consider whether a substitution is possible. Frequently, it *is* possible, and some of the happiest discoveries are made by taking a chance on a change. All recipes are really patterns. You must stay within the formula, but you can often use different materials than specified. Of course, the more you learn about the chemistry of foods, the more successfully you can take those creative risks.

FAST FOOD FROM YOUR OWN FREEZER

Make ahead and freeze these fast food favorites, and you'll be ready to whip up some super snacks and quick suppers. One word of warning: the aroma of oven-cooked tomato sauce is so inviting that you may find yourself or others dipping into it even before it's completely cooked. But if you do manage to get these foods safely into the freezer, you'll have the makings of spaghetti and meatballs, or meatball sandwiches, pizzas, plus a basic tomato sauce (total yield 8 to 9 cups) of infinite usefulness.

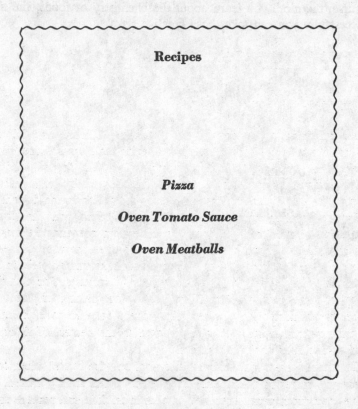

Recipes

Pizza

Oven Tomato Sauce

Oven Meatballs

Total Cooking Time: about 2 hours and 30 minutes

Plan of Action

Prepare pizza dough and let it rise. Prepare and cook tomato sauce in a 325° F. oven for 2 hours, lower shelf. Prepare meatballs and bake for 30 minutes, on top shelf, anytime during the cooking of the tomato sauce. When meatballs and tomato sauce are cooked, raise the oven heat to 425° F. Finish pizzas and bake them for 20 minutes if they are to be frozen, 25 to 30 minutes if they are to be served.

Pizza

Pizza dough (see page 359)
2½ to 3 cups thick tomato sauce
1 teaspoon oregano
¼ cup grated Parmesan cheese
½ pound mozzarella cheese, coarsely shredded
Optional toppings: mushrooms, pepperoni slices, green
  pepper slices, or flat anchovies

After punching down dough, divide it into 2 portions. Oil two 12-inch round pizza pans. Flatten the dough, and press it into place in each pan, making a slightly thicker rim around the edge of the "pie." If dough is too elastic to spread in pans easily, let it rest for 10 minutes and try again. Resting relaxes the gluten in the dough.

Spread half the tomato sauce (1 to 1½ cups) on the dough rounds to 1 inch from the edge. Sprinkle with oregano, Parmesan, and mozzarella. Spoon the remaining sauce over the top; it doesn't have to be perfectly even. For a crisp crust, bake immediately in the lower half of a preheated 425° F. oven for 20 minutes. For a thicker crust, let pizzas rest for 15 to 20 minutes before baking. If pizzas are to be served immediately rather than frozen, bake 25 to 30 minutes or until bottom crusts are golden brown to the center. (Lift crusts with a spatula to look underneath.)

To freeze pizzas, loosen crusts and cool on wire racks. When cold, freeze the pizzas in their pans, uncovered. When solidly frozen, remove them from pans, wrap well in aluminum foil, and replace them in the freezer.

To cook frozen pizzas, unwrap them, place them in pans in the lower portion of a cold oven. Set the heat at 425° F., and bake for 25 minutes.

Optional toppings may be added during the last 15 minutes of baking. Sprinkle the toppings with 1 teaspoon olive oil for each pizza.

Oven Tomato Sauce

¾ cups olive oil
3 teaspoons minced garlic (about 5 cloves)
4 chicken wings or the equivalent in other chicken parts
2 pork chops or ½-pound piece of boiling beef
3 35-ounce (2-pound, 3-ounce) cans Italian-style tomatoes
2 6-ounce cans tomato paste
⅓ cup chopped fresh parsley
1½ tablespoons dried basil
1 teaspoon oregano
1 tablespoon salt
1 tablespoon sugar
¾ teaspoon black pepper
1 whole dried red pepper (optional)

Heat oven to 325° F. While it is heating, put oil, garlic, and meat into a large oven pan (not aluminum) or casserole. If shallow, 16- by 11- by 3-inch is about the right size; if deep, 5-quart capacity. When garlic and meat are sizzling (do not let the garlic brown), remove pan from oven and add all the remaining ingredients. Bake for 2 hours, stirring occasionally. Break up tomatoes, turn meat, and scrape sides of pan as you stir. If the sauce seems to be simmering too fast, reduce oven heat to 300° F. When the sauce is cooked, remove the meat and red pepper. Cool and freeze any sauce you will not use within a week—½ pint and 1 pint containers are convenient sizes for storing sauce in the freezer.

The meat cooked in the sauce can be used for lunches or with macaroni. We separate meat and sauce so that the sauce will keep longer.

Yield: 8 to 9 cups.

Oven Meatballs

3 pounds lean ground beef
1½ cups fresh bread crumbs
3 eggs
½ cup beef stock or prepared beef bouillon
1 large onion, finely chopped
1 clove garlic, minced (optional)
⅓ cup grated Parmesan cheese
¼ cup chopped fresh parsley
2 teaspoons salt
½ teaspoon pepper

Combine all ingredients in a large bowl and blend well. Shape into 24 round meatballs, 2 to 2½ inches in diameter. Bake them on oiled baking sheets in a preheated 325° F. oven for 30 minutes or until just cooked through.

To freeze, cool the meatballs completely. Wash and re-oil baking sheets. Freeze the meatballs on the baking sheets until they are solidly frozen, then place in double plastic bags and return to freezer. You will be able to take out as many as are needed at any time, since they will not stick together.

The meatballs may be thawed and reheated in simmering tomato sauce. This takes about 15 to 20 minutes. Stir occasionally to prevent sticking.

SLOW AMERICANA

Here are some old-timers (slightly updated) to conjure up memories of a black woodstove with banked fires that couldn't be turned off with the flick of a switch—so the cook's bonus was the special flavor that slow, low-heat cooking imparts.

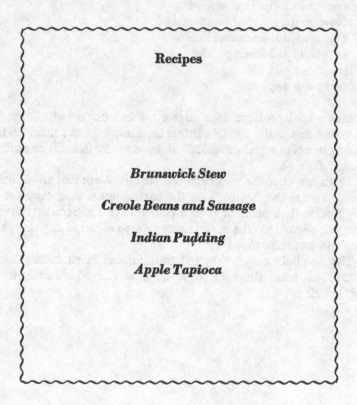

Recipes

Brunswick Stew

Creole Beans and Sausage

Indian Pudding

Apple Tapioca

Total Cooking Time: about 3 hours

Plan of Action

Soak beans for 2 hours before beginning. (If it is more convenient, they can be soaked overnight.) Prepare pudding recipe.

Heat oven to 300° F., and oven-sauté bacon and vegetables for Creole beans while it is heating. Place stew and tapioca on the lower shelf, beans and pudding on the middle shelf. Bake everything for 1 hour. Remove apples, add cold milk to pudding, and check to see if beans need more water. Continue cooking stew, beans, and pudding for another hour and 15 minutes. Add vegetables to stew; add seasonings and sausage to beans. Cook everything 45 minutes longer.

Brunswick Stew

3 pounds lean beef, cubed
1 pound veal or lamb, cubed
1 large onion, chopped
2 green peppers, seeded and chopped
1 1-pound can tomatoes with juice
Water
2 teaspoons salt
½ teaspoon pepper
1 teaspoon Gravy Master
1 whole dried hot red pepper pod
1 bay leaf
1 pound potatoes, cubed
1 cup corn kernels
1 cup lima beans or green beans

Combine the first five ingredients in a large shallow baking dish (not aluminum), and add enough water to come almost up to the top of the meat. Add salt, pepper, Gravy Master, red pepper, and bay leaf. Cover with foil, and bake the dish for 2 hours and 15 minutes in a 300° F. oven. (The meat is supposed to be so tender as to be falling apart.) Remove red pepper and bay leaf. Add potatoes, corn, and beans. If too dry, add a little water. Re-cover and cook for 45 minutes. Taste to correct seasoning, adding more salt or pepper if desired.

Serves six to eight.

Creole Beans and Sausage

2 cups kidney beans
2 quarts boiling water
4 slices bacon, chopped
1 large onion, chopped
1 stalk celery, chopped
2 cloves garlic, minced
1 quart boiling water or more
1 teaspoon salt
½ teaspoon pepper
1 pound fully cooked, smoked sausage

Wash and pick over beans. Soak them in 2 quarts of boiling water for 2 hours, allowing them to cool. Drain beans. Combine bacon, onion, celery, and garlic in a heavy 3-quart casserole or bean pot, and let this mixture oven-sauté for 15 minutes in a 300° F. oven. Add beans and enough boiling water to just cover them. Bake for 2 hours and 15 minutes, checking once in a while to see if more boiling water is needed. At the end of this time, add salt, pepper, and sausage cut into 1-inch slices. Cook 45 minutes longer or until beans are quite tender. To thicken juices, remove ½ cup beans, mash them, and return them to pot.

Serves six to eight.

Indian Pudding

5 cups milk, divided
⅔ cup molasses
⅓ cup sugar
½ teaspoon cinnamon
¼ teaspoon nutmeg
¼ teaspoon ginger
1 teaspoon salt
¼ cup (½ stick) butter
½ cup cornmeal

Combine 4 cups milk with molasses, sugar, cinnamon, nutmeg, ginger, salt, and butter in a saucepan, and bring the mixture to a boil, stirring. Slowly add cornmeal while continuing to stir, and cook until the mixture is thick. Pour it into a buttered 2-quart casserole. Bake for 1 hour in a 300° F. oven. Pour the remaining cup of cold milk over the top, and *don't* stir. Continue baking pudding for 2 hours longer. Serve warm or at room temperature with ice cream as a topping.

Serves four to six.

Apple Tapioca

4 cups apples, peeled and sliced (about 6 large)
½ cup brown sugar, firmly packed
¾ teaspoon cinnamon
½ teaspoon salt
2 tablespoons minute tapioca
Juice of 1 lemon
1 cup boiling water

Toss apples with sugar, cinnamon, salt, and tapioca until the coating is evenly blended. Put them into a 2-quart casserole. Pour the lemon juice over the apples, then add the boiling water. Cover and cook for 1 hour in a 300° F. oven.

Serves four.

MAIN DISHES FOR THE WEEK I— BASICALLY STEWED

Here are three easy and different, basically stewed, meat dishes to bake, freeze, reheat and serve on some busy evening with rice or noodles. Stews improve with reheating, a nice bonus.

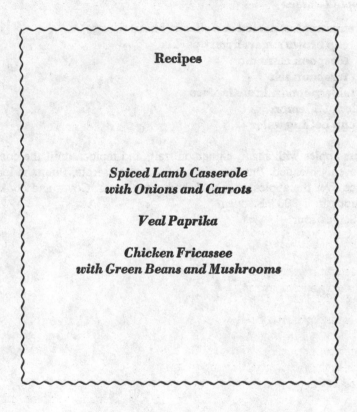

Recipes

Spiced Lamb Casserole with Onions and Carrots

Veal Paprika

Chicken Fricassee with Green Beans and Mushrooms

Total Cooking Time: 1½ hours

Plan of Action

Preheat oven to 375° F. While it is heating, oven-sauté vegetables for veal, and set them aside until needed. Bake lamb, uncovered, for 30 minutes on lower shelf. Bake chicken, uncovered, also on lower shelf, for the same amount of time, adding butter, onion, and mushrooms during the last 10 minutes. Reduce oven to 350° F. Add remaining ingredients to lamb; cover. Add remaining ingredients except green beans to chicken; cover. Bake them both for 1 hour; add green beans to chicken during last 30 minutes of this time. At the same time, complete veal dish and bake that, covered, on the top shelf for 1 hour.

Spiced Lamb Casserole with Onions and Carrots

⅓ cup flour
½ teaspoon salt
½ teaspoon pepper
3 pounds boneless stewing lamb, trimmed of fat and cubed
3 tablespoons vegetable oil
4 cups chicken broth or stock
¼ cup soy sauce
2 tablespoons tomato paste
2 tablespoons lemon juice
1 tablespoon honey
1 tablespoon Worcestershire sauce
1 teaspoon chili powder
1 teaspoon paprika
½ teaspoon dry mustard
6 large carrots, cut into 3-inch chunks
24 small onions, peeled

Combine flour, salt, and pepper in a plastic bag. Shake lamb pieces in the mixture, about 1 pound at a time, to coat them. Place the lamb in a Dutch oven, drizzle oil over, and brown the meat in a 375° F. oven for 30 minutes. Meanwhile, in a saucepan, combine all the remaining ingredients, except vegetables, and bring the mixture to a simmer. When lamb is browned, add vegetables, pour broth over, and continue to cook, reducing heat to 350° F., for 1 hour, or until meat and vegetables are tender. Cool completely, remove any fat that rises to the top, and freeze the stew in serving-size containers.

Serves six.

Veal Paprika

1 onion, finely chopped
1 green pepper, seeded and finely chopped
2 tablespoons butter
3 pounds stewing veal, trimmed and cubed
4 teaspoons Hungarian sweet paprika
1 teaspoon salt
¼ teaspoon pepper
1½ cups hot chicken broth or stock
Sour cream

Oven-sauté onion and green pepper in butter in a 3-quart casserole until the vegetables are sizzling and transparent. Add veal, paprika, salt, pepper, and broth or stock. Cover and bake at 350° F. for 1 hour or until the meat is quite tender. Cool completely. Freeze in serving-size containers.

When reheated, stir sour cream into pan juices. Do not boil afterward. The entire recipe reheated would take 2 cups sour cream. If you use less of the casserole at a meal, reduce sour cream accordingly.

Serves six.

Chicken Fricassee with Green Beans and Mushrooms

½ cup flour
1 teaspoon salt
½ teaspoon pepper
3½ to 4 pound frying chicken, cut into small serving pieces
2 tablespoons vegetable oil
1 tablespoon butter
1 large onion, finely chopped
12 ounces fresh mushrooms, washed and trimmed
2 cups hot chicken broth or stock
½ cup dry white wine
½ teaspoon dried thyme
½ teaspoon dried marjoram
½ teaspoon salt
1 pound green beans, trimmed and cut into 2-inch lengths

In a plastic bag, combine flour, salt, and pepper. Toss chicken pieces in the mixture, a few at a time, to coat them. Shake the pieces to remove excess flour. Place them, skin side up, in an oiled roasting pan, drizzle with oil, and bake them for 20 minutes in a 375° F. oven. Add butter to pan along with onion and mushroom slices, around but not on chicken pieces. Bake 10 minutes longer. Add broth or stock, wine, thyme, marjoram, and salt. Cover pan with foil and bake for 30 minutes. Uncover and add green beans. Re-cover and bake 30 minutes longer or until beans are barely tender and chicken is done. Cool completely. Freeze in serving-size containers. If any fat rises to the top, remove that before reheating.

Serves four.

MAIN DISHES FOR THE WEEK II— ODDS AND ENDS

Use up a few odds and ends of cooked meat to put together these tasty main dishes that use fresh vegetables as extenders. The cooking time for these dishes is scant, in anticipation of reheating, so if any one is to be served immediately, it may need a little longer cooking time.

Recipes

Zucchini Fans

Cabbage Rolls with Raisin Sauce

Pepper Hash

Total Cooking Time: 1 hour

Plan of Action

Assemble dishes. Preheat oven to 350° F. Place cabbage rolls on top shelf, zucchini and hash on lower shelf. Cook zucchini for 20 minutes, hash for 30 minutes, and cabbage rolls for 1 hour, basting once or twice.

Zucchini Fans

2 large zucchini
1 teaspoon dried oregano
Salt and pepper to taste
½ to ¾ pound fully cooked ham, thinly sliced
1 large onion, thinly sliced
2 large tomatoes, thinly sliced
⅓ cup olive oil, or any vegetable oil
¼ pound cheddar cheese, coarsely grated

Scrub the zucchini well. Cut off stems and a bit more if they curve sharply. Slice each zucchini lengthwise several times toward the thick end, *but stop about 2 inches before the end so the slices are attached.* Spread the slices slightly apart, like a fan. Place zucchini in a large, shallow casserole that will just fit them, and sprinkle the cut sides with oregano, salt, and pepper to taste. Place slices of ham, onion, and tomato between zucchini slices. Drizzle oil over all. Cover with foil and bake for 20 minutes in a preheated 350-degree oven or until zucchinis are barely tender. Uncover and cool for 20 minutes. Cover and refrigerate. Freeze, if desired.

Before reheating, sprinkle with cheese. Bake, uncovered, in a 350° F. oven for 20 minutes.

Serves two as main course, four as side dish.

Cabbage Rolls with Raisin Sauce

12 outer leaves of cabbage
2 cups leftover cooked meat (beef, chicken, lamb, or pork),
     ground or finely chopped
1 cup leftover cooked rice

1 cup seasoned bread crumbs (see page 361)
  (2 cups cooked rice or crumbs can be used in place of 1 cup of
  each)
1 egg
1 small onion, finely chopped
½ teaspoon salt
¼ teaspoon pepper
¼ teaspoon ground thyme
2 cups tomato purée or tomato sauce
1½ cups prepared bouillon or stock
2 tablespoons brown sugar
2 tablespoons vinegar
1 teaspoon salt
¼ teaspoon pepper
½ teaspoon dried basil
½ cup raisins

Parboil cabbage leaves for 3 minutes in a large pan of boiling salted water; drain them. Mix together meat, rice, crumbs, egg, onion, ½ teaspoon salt, ¼ teaspoon pepper, and thyme, blending well. Divide the stuffing between the leaves (about 2 full tablespoons each). Starting at the thick end, roll them up, tucking ends in to form neat "packages." Place them seam side down in a large shallow casserole, about 12- by 8-inches. Mix together all the remaining ingredients, and pour the sauce over the rolls. Bake, uncovered, at 350° F. for 1 hour, basting once or twice. If they seem too dry, add more bouillon or stock during cooking. When done, cool 20 minutes. Cover and refrigerate rolls. If desired, freeze them in serving-size containers when they are completely cold.

Reheat at 350° F. for 25 to 30 minutes.

Serves four to six.

Pepper Hash

End of cooked roast beef, ¾ to 1 pound
2 large raw potatoes
1 small onion
2 tablespoons steak sauce
1 tablespoon Worcestershire sauce

½ teaspoon salt
Scant ½ teaspoon pepper
1 green pepper, chopped
2 tablespoons vegetable oil
Garlic salt

Grind beef, potatoes, and onion, or chop them in a food processor. Mix them with steak sauce, Worcestershire, salt, and pepper. Pack the mixture lightly into a greased 2-quart casserole or loaf pan. Top with green pepper. Pour oil over all, and sprinkle the green pepper with garlic salt. Bake, uncovered, for 30 minutes in a 350° F. oven. Cool for 20 minutes. Cover and refrigerate. If desired, freeze when completely cold.

Reheat for about 20 minutes in a preheated 350° F. oven. If you wish, serve with poached eggs.

Serves two.

MAIN DISHES FOR THE WEEK III— THINGS YOUR MOTHER TAUGHT YOU NEVER TO DO

There are a few oven-cooking surprises in these main dishes. Trust us; they work.

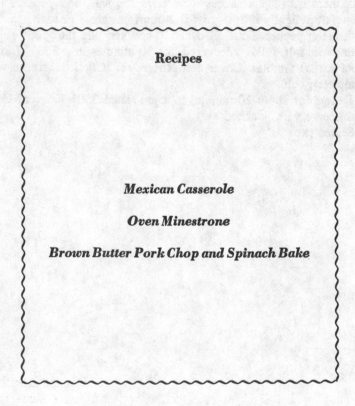

Recipes

Mexican Casserole

Oven Minestrone

Brown Butter Pork Chop and Spinach Bake

Total Cooking Time: 1 hour

Plan of Action

Heat oven to 350° F. and, while it is heating, oven-sauté onion for pork chop dish and garlic and onion for soup. Assemble dishes. Place pork chop casserole on top shelf, and the other two on lower shelf. Bake 35 minutes. Stir soup and Mexican casserole, adding peas to soup and corn to Mexican dish. Cook them 10 minutes longer, and remove them from the oven. At the same time, add apple rings to pork chops, and cook them 15 minutes more.

Mexican Casserole

1 pound lean ground beef
¼ pound sausage meat
Vegetable oil (optional)
2 green peppers, seeded and chopped
1 large onion, chopped
28-ounce can tomatoes (with juice), chopped
1 cup water
1 cup elbow macaroni, uncooked
4-ounce can green chilies, chopped
2 teaspoons chili powder
2 tablespoons chopped fresh parsley
2 tablespoons cornstarch
1 teaspoon salt
¼ teaspoon pepper
½ teaspoon dried oregano
¼ teaspoon ground cumin
Hot pepper sauce to taste (try ⅛ teaspoon)
1½ cups fresh or canned corn kernels
¼ pound Monterey Jack cheese, coarsely grated

In a large skillet, quickly brown meat over high heat. (If you sprinkle a little salt in the skillet, you will not have to use oil.) Add green peppers and onion, and sauté until they are limp. Add all the remaining ingredients except corn and cheese, and bring the mixture to a full rolling boil. Pour the contents of the skillet into a 3-quart casserole, cover, and bake in a preheated 350° F. oven for 35 minutes. Add corn, stir, cover, and continue to cook for 10 minutes. Cool 30 minutes, uncovered, before storing in the refrigerator, covered. Sprinkle with cheese before reheating.

Note: If you want to freeze this dish, omit macaroni and water.
Serves four to six.

Oven Minestrone

As a base for soup, homemade stock is the best, tinned broth is second best, and bouillon cubes are lowest on the totem pole. There are times in the lives of many of us, however, when the first two choices simply aren't available. Here is a soup you can make (in the oven, at that!) which will not suffer from its bouillon base, because the mingling flavors of several vegetables create the equal of homemade stock.

2 tablespoons olive oil
1 clove garlic, minced
1 small onion, chopped
¼ head of a small cabbage, shredded
1 small zucchini, sliced into half rounds
1 carrot, thinly sliced
1 stalk celery, with leaves, sliced
½ cup small shell macaroni, uncooked
4 beef bouillon cubes
½ teaspoon dried basil
¾ teaspoon salt
¼ teaspoon pepper
3½ to 4 cups boiling water
2 tablespoons tomato paste
½ 10-ounce package frozen peas, thawed to separate only

In a 3-quart casserole, combine oil, garlic, and onion, and oven-sauté these vegetables until they are sizzling, while heating oven to 350° F. Remove from oven, and add the remaining vegetables, macaroni, bouillon cubes, basil, salt, and pepper. Pour in boiling water to within 1 inch of the top of the casserole, no more than 4 cups. Add tomato paste and stir. Cover and bake for 35 minutes, then stir and add peas. Cover and cook 10 minutes longer. Cool 30 minutes, uncovered, before storing in the refrigerator, covered.

Note: If you want to freeze this soup, omit macaroni.

Yield: about 2 quarts.

Brown Butter Pork Chop and Spinach Bake

Brown butter and fennel add an interesting flavor to this risotto-style rice.

1 large onion, sliced and separated into rings
2 tablespoons butter
¾ cup brown rice, uncooked
10-ounce package frozen leaf spinach, thawed
2 tablespoons grated Parmesan cheese
6 medium-thick pork chops
½ teaspoon salt
¼ teaspoon pepper
¼ teaspoon crushed fennel seeds
1½ cups boiling beef broth
1 cup seasoned bread crumbs (see page 361)
6 cored apple rings, raw, unpeeled, ½-inch thick

In a shallow 12-inch by 8-inch casserole, oven-sauté onion rings in butter while oven is heating to 350° F., cooking until butter is brown but not burned. Remove from oven, and sprinkle uncooked rice over onions. Spread a layer of thawed spinach on top. Sprinkle spinach with grated cheese. Lay pork chops over the other ingredients so as to cover them as completely as possible. Stir salt, pepper, and fennel seeds into boiling broth, and pour the broth between the chops so that it goes to the bottom of the casserole. Sprinkle chops with crumbs. Bake, uncovered, for 45 minutes; place an apple ring on each pork chop, and bake 15 minutes longer.

Serves three to six.

MAIN DISHES FOR THE WEEK IV—
MEAT AND FRUIT

Perfect companions, meat-and-fruit main dishes create dinners of easy elegance. Keep it simple with a green vegetable or salad, hot rolls, and a cool, creamy dessert.

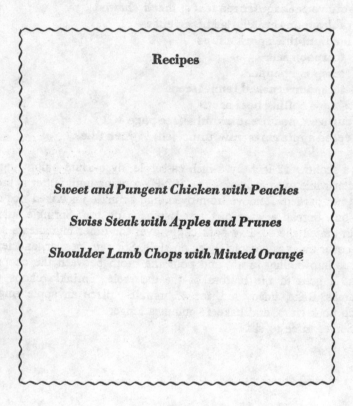

Recipes

Sweet and Pungent Chicken with Peaches

Swiss Steak with Apples and Prunes

Shoulder Lamb Chops with Minted Orange

Total Cooking Time: 1 hour

Plan of Action

Assemble dishes and place them in a preheated 350° F. oven, chicken on top shelf, and the 2 other dishes on lower shelf. Cook them for 30 minutes. Add honey to chicken. Cook 10 minutes longer. Add apples to Swiss steak. Remove chicken. Continue cooking chops and steak for 20 minutes, a total of 1 hour.

Sweet and Pungent Chicken with Peaches

6 chicken breasts, boned and skinned
Dijon mustard
1 cup butter cracker crumbs
3 tablespoons butter, melted
3 large fresh peaches
3 tablespoons honey

Brush chicken breasts with mustard. Dip them in cracker crumbs to coat, and lay them in a buttered shallow baking dish. Drizzle butter evenly over chicken. Peel, halve, and stone peaches. Stick 2 whole cloves into each peach half. Place the peaches around chicken. Bake, uncovered, for 30 minutes in a 350° F. oven. Spoon ½ tablespoon honey over each chicken breast. Bake 10 minutes longer. Cool 20 minutes, cover, and refrigerate. If desired, cover with foil and freeze when dish is completely cold. Reheat in a 300° F. oven for 30 minutes.

Note: Whole cloves are not to be eaten. If you wish, you may remove them before serving.

Serves three to six.

Swiss Steak with Apples and Prunes

Tea is an effective tenderizer for braised meats. In this dish, dried apples can be used in place of fresh, in which case they are added with the prunes.

6 pieces boneless chuck steak, about 3 pounds
Flour
1 tablespoon vegetable oil
1 small onion, finely chopped
½ stalk celery with leaves, finely chopped
1 cup beef broth
½ cup strong tea
½ teaspoon salt
¼ teaspoon pepper

¼ teaspoon allspice
¼ teaspoon ground thyme
12 prunes, pitted
3 large apples, peeled, cored, and quartered

Dip steaks in flour. In a skillet, quickly sear steaks in vegetable oil over high heat, adding onion and celery to pan as you turn steaks. Remove steaks and vegetables to a shallow baking dish. In the same skillet, bring broth and tea to a boil, scraping brown bits from the pan, and pour the mixture over steaks. Add remaining ingredients except apples, cover, and bake at 350° F. for 40 minutes. Add apples, re-cover, and cook 20 minutes longer. Cool, uncovered, for 20 minutes, then cover and refrigerate. If desired, cover with foil and freeze when dish is completely cold. Reheat in a 300° F. oven for 30 minutes.

Serves six.

Shoulder Lamb Chops with Minted Orange

6 large shoulder lamb chops
Flour
1 tablespoon butter
½ cup orange juice
½ cup sauterne
½ teaspoon salt
¼ teaspoon pepper
¼ teaspoon crushed dried mint
1 tablespoon minced parsley
1 cup seedless orange sections
1 cup seedless green grapes (optional)

Dip chops in flour. In a skillet, quickly sear chops in butter over high heat. Remove chops to a shallow baking dish, and add all the remaining ingredients except orange sections and grapes. Cover and bake at 350° F. for 1 hour. Cool, uncovered, for 20 minutes, then cover and refrigerate. If desired, cover with foil and freeze when dish is completely cold. Reheat in a 300° F. oven for 30 minutes, adding orange sections and grapes during the last 10 minutes.

Serves three to six.

THREE CAKES FROM ONE BATTER

Save taking out the same basic ingredients three times by making one big batch of plain cake batter and giving it three different finishing touches. The tricky part comes when the batter is ready and you want to get it into the cake pans quickly, so make this step go faster by doing all the advance preparation in the order given. Any of the cakes can be frozen when completely cool. None needs frosting.

Recipes

Fudge Ripple Cake

Mai Tai Upside-Down Cake

Blueberry-Lemon Cake

Total Cooking Time: 35 minutes

Basic Cake with Variations

¾ cup (1½ sticks) butter
3 cups granulated sugar
3 eggs
2 cups milk
5¼ cups all-purpose flour, stirred to lighten
6 teaspoons baking powder
1 teaspoon salt
½ cup chocolate chips, or 4 ounces sweet chocolate, melted
3 tablespoons butter (for Mai Tai cake topping)
½ cup brown sugar
About 7 slices canned pineapple
½ teaspoon grated lemon rind
1 tablespoon lemon juice
½ teaspoon grated orange rind
2 tablespoons orange juice
1 cup blueberries, fresh or frozen, not in syrup
1 teaspoon vanilla
1 teaspoon cinnamon sugar (see page 361)
2 to 3 tablespoons dark rum

Bring butter, eggs, and milk to room temperature. Sift flour, baking powder, and salt together three times. Melt chocolate over hot water.

Prepare pans as follows: While preheating oven to 350° F., melt 3 tablespoons butter for Mai Tai cake topping in a 10-inch skillet with an oven-proof handle (cast iron is ideal) or in a 10-inch cake pan. Butter two 9-inch cake pans, line the bottoms with thin, plain paper, and butter the paper, also. Sprinkle brown sugar in hot Mai Tai cake pan, and press the sugar into an even layer with a fork. Lay pineapple slices on brown sugar.

Assemble flavorings. In a cup, mix grated lemon rind with lemon juice. In another cup, mix grated orange rind with orange juice. Measure out blueberries, and mix them with 2 teaspoons of the sifted dry ingredients. Have vanilla ready as well as three bowls of medium size for the batter.

Prepare batter. In the large bowl of an electric mixer, cream butter on medium-high speed until it is light and fluffy. Gradually add granulated sugar. Beat in eggs, one at a time. Reduce speed to medium or medium-low, and add flour mixture in six or more portions alternately with milk, beginning and ending with flour. Mix just long enough to blend each time. Divide the batter evenly between the three medium-size bowls.

For fudge ripple cake, thoroughly mix vanilla into cake batter, and spoon it into a prepared 9-inch cake pan. Spoon melted chocolate lightly over the top, and run a table knife back and forth several times for ripple effect.

For blueberry lemon cake, thoroughly mix lemon rind and juice into cake batter. Fold in blueberries. Spoon batter into prepared 9-inch cake pan. Sprinkle top with cinnamon sugar.

For Mai Tai cake, thoroughly mix orange rind and juice into the batter, and spoon it over the pineapple topping.

Bake the cakes on two shelves placed at the top and middle positions—staggered so that no pan is directly over another—for 35 minutes or until golden brown. Test with a cake tester inserted in the center, which should be dry.

Cool cakes on wire racks for 5 minutes. Remove fudge and blueberry cakes from pans to racks to cool completely. Peel off paper. Loosen sides of Mai Tai cake with a spatula, and invert it onto a large cake dish. The topping usually comes out very neatly, but if one pineapple slice should stick in cake pan, just pick it up with a fork and place it on cake. Pour rum over warm cake.

FILLING THE COOKIE JAR

One basic butter-cookie recipe yields three different flavors, and about 4 dozen cookies.

Basic Butter Crisps

1 cup (2 sticks) butter, softened
1½ cups sifted confectioners' sugar
1 egg
2½ cups all-purpose flour
1 teaspoon baking powder
¼ teaspoon salt

Add for Cherry-Anise Cookies:

¼ teaspoon anise extract
¼ cup candied cherries, finely chopped

Add for Marmalade-Oatmeal Cookies:

¼ cup orange marmalade
½ teaspoon grated orange rind
½ cup quick-cooking oatmeal

Add for Almond-Coconut Cookies:

¼ teaspoon almond extract
½ cup grated coconut
About 18 whole almonds

Cream the butter until light. Gradually add sugar. Beat in egg. Stir flour to lighten it before measuring. Sift flour with baking powder and salt. Stir dry ingredients into butter mixture.

Divide dough into three portions. Add the flavoring ingredients for each portion, except for the whole almonds, which are reserved for later use. Blend well. Chill the dough until it is firm enough to shape, and form each into a roll about 2 inches in diameter. Chill or freeze rolls again until very firm. (Frozen dough will have to soften a bit before slicing.)

When ready to bake, preheat oven to 375° F. Slice dough in ¼-

inch slices and place on ungreased baking sheets, allowing 2 inches space between cookies. Press a whole almond into the center of each slice of the almond-coconut roll. Bake 6 to 7 minutes or until edges are lightly brown. If the cookies seem quite soft, let them cool in the pan for a minute or two until they can be removed with a spatula. Continue cooling cookies on wire racks. They get crisp as they cool.

THREE QUICK FRUIT BREADS

You can make peach, pineapple, and apple breads from one batter for the time and effort it would take to make one bread—for gifts, for coffee breaks, or just to stock the freezer.

Basic Quick Breads

1½ cups (3 sticks) butter, softened,
   or other solid shortening
2 cups sugar
6 eggs
1 cup buttermilk or soured milk (see page 362)
6 cups all-purpose flour
1 tablespoon baking powder
1 tablespoon baking soda
1 teaspoon salt

Butter three 9-inch by 5-inch loaf pans, and line the bottoms with thin, plain paper. Prepare flavoring ingredients (instructions follow) in three separate bowls.

In the large bowl of an electric mixer, cream butter or shortening until light. Gradually add sugar, beating until fluffy. Add eggs, one at a time, beating well after each. Mix in buttermilk or soured milk. Remove bowl from mixer. Stir flour to lighten it before measuring. Sift together flour, baking powder, soda, and salt. Incorporate the flour mixture into the butter-egg mixture in several additions, stirring by hand until just blended.

Divide the batter between the 3 loaf pans, and with a fork, stir into each the flavoring ingredients for each bread. Blend evenly but don't overbeat. Smooth the batter. Bake the breads in the middle shelf of a preheated 375° F. oven for 40 to 45 minutes, or until a cake tester inserted in the center comes out dry. Don't test until breads have risen completely in the center and are golden brown.

Cool breads in pans on wire racks for 10 minutes. Remove from pans, peel off paper, and cool completely on racks.

Peach-Almond Bread

Mix together:
1 cup drained, canned peaches, chopped
½ cup toasted, slivered almonds
½ teaspoon almond extract

Pineapple-Date Bread

Mix together:
8-ounce can crushed pineapple, well drained
½ cup chopped dates

Apple-Cheddar Bread

Mix together:
1 cup chopped, peeled apples
1 tablespoon lemon juice
½ cup coarsely grated cheddar cheese, firmly packed
¼ teaspoon ground cloves

BROWN AND SERVE ROLLS

Want your family to be the envy of all? Just have a supply of homemade yeast rolls in the freezer, ready to brown and serve! This easy recipe produces about seven dozen.

Oldtime Pan Rolls

3 packages dry yeast
1 cup very warm water
1 teaspoon sugar
2½ cups warm water
1 cup nonfat dry milk
⅓ cup sugar
4 teaspoons salt
2 eggs, beaten
12 to 13 cups all-purpose flour, divided
⅓ cup butter, melted and cooled slightly

Sprinkle yeast on 1 cup very warm water mixed with 1 teaspoon sugar in a small bowl. Let set 5 to 10 minutes to proof (bubble). In a very large bowl (a very large pan can be used instead if you don't have an oversize bowl), combine yeast mixture with 2½ cups warm water, dry milk, sugar, and salt. Stir to dissolve dry ingredients. Add eggs and beat to blend. Stir in 6 cups flour. Beat in melted butter. Add 6 cups flour, a cup at a time, to form a soft but manageable dough. If necessary, add a little more flour. Turn out the dough onto a floured surface, and let it rest for 10 minutes. Knead for 10 minutes. (If using dough hooks, divide dough in half and knead each half for 5 minutes.) Place dough in a very large buttered bowl (or divide in half and use two regular large bowls) and turn to grease on all sides. Cover bowl loosely with plastic wrap, and let dough rise until double in bulk, about 2 hours. Punch down. Form dough into four ropes, 1 inch wide. Cut each rope into 3-inch pieces, and roll each piece into a ball. Place the balls so that they are barely touching in eight buttered 8-inch or 9-inch pie pans (cake pans also can be used). Let rise until doubled, about 1½ hours. Ideally, four pans of rolls should be allowed to rise a little faster than the remainder, because you are going to bake four pans of rolls at a time, so if you can arrange to have them rise at slightly different temperatures, do so.

Preheat oven to 350° F. Place shelves in middle positions, and stagger pans so that none is directly over another. Bake four pans of rolls at a time for 18 minutes or until just beginning to brown. Gently turn rolls out onto racks to cool completely, right side up. Do not separate them. Wrap and freeze. To brown, place frozen rolls on a greased baking sheet, and bake in a preheated 400° F. oven for 10 to 12 minutes, or until the desired color is reached.

Sweet rolls: If you like, you can turn half the recipe for pan rolls into sweet, sticky, cinnamon-flavored rolls. After the first rising, divide dough in half. Let the half for sweet rolls rest for 10 minutes, then roll out into a square 1 inch thick. Brush the dough with 3 tablespoons melted butter. Mix ⅔ cup brown sugar with 2 teaspoons cinnamon, and sprinkle the mixture evenly over the dough. Scatter 1 cup raisins or 1 cup coarsely chopped pecans over the sugar. Roll the dough up like a jelly roll, and pinch it together at the seam to seal it. With a sharp knife, cut the roll into 1-inch lengths, and place them, cut side down, barely touching, in four buttered pie pans. Let them rise, and proceed as for pan rolls.

No-Pot-Watching Oven Beef Stock and Chicken Stock

You can cook these two stocks, either both at the same time or one at a time, when you are baking something else (an energy-wise use of oven heat). You will need a Dutch oven for each or an ovenproof pan of equivalent size.

Total Cooking Time: 3 to 4 hours

Oven Beef Stock

About 5 pounds beef and beef bones
1 large onion, chopped
1 stalk celery with leaves, chopped
1 carrot, chopped
1 clove garlic, chopped
About 2 cups canned tomatoes with juice
1½ quarts (6 cups) water
¼ cup chopped fresh parsley
   or 1 tablespoon dried parsley
1 teaspoon dried basil or thyme
1 bay leaf
1 teaspoon salt

Put the beef and bones into a Dutch oven, uncovered, and roast them for 30 minutes in a 450° F. oven. Add onion, celery, carrot, and garlic, and roast the meat and vegetables 15 minutes longer. Reduce heat to 300° F. Remove pan and add the remaining ingredients. There should be enough liquid to just cover the beef and bones. Cook uncovered for 3 hours. Allow the liquid to reduce about 1 inch, but if it goes lower than that add more water as needed.

Strain the stock through a colander lined with rinsed cheesecloth. Cool stock. Remove congealed fat from its surface. Refrigerate the stock, or freeze it in ½-pint or pint containers.

Note: The stock is purposely low in salt so that it may blend more conservatively with any dish in which you may use it. When used, add more salt and pepper to taste.

Yield: about 1 quart.

Oven Chicken Stock

Approximately 4 pounds chicken backs, necks, and/or wings
   (part of this can be a roast chicken carcass)
1 large onion, chopped
1 stalk celery with leaves, chopped
1 carrot, chopped
1½ quarts (6 cups) water
¼ cup fresh chopped parsley
   or 1 tablespoon dried parsley
¼ teaspoon ground sage or thyme
1 bay leaf
1 teaspoon salt

Proceed as for Oven Beef Stock, except for cooking time: reduce roasting time to 45 minutes at 450° F., and simmering time to 2 hours at 300° F.

   Yield: about 1 quart.

Around the World in an Oven

Most of us will never travel around the world, seeing the wonders each country has to offer and sampling native dishes cooked in the countries in which they originated. But we can do the next best thing —prepare those ethnic favorites in our own homes.

Our country is a melting pot of national cuisines, each one an important part of a heritage. As people have come to our shores, they've brought with them not only stories of the places they've left behind, but recipes for dishes which have meant "home" to them. These foods have often been the remaining tie with their native lands, and so they've had special meaning.

Many of these recipes have been passed down from generation to generation with little or no changes, while others have been altered to suit differences in taste and availability of ingredients.

The availability of foods has had a large part in dictating what dishes are prepared in what countries, and the type of cooking for which various regions are known. Ireland, for instance, with its supply of potatoes has an almost unending list of recipes for their use, while wheat dishes abound in Russia. A land-locked country is unlikely to become famous for its fish dishes, and those without grazing land will use little beef. People from sunny lands cook with an abundance of the good, fresh fruits and vegetables they grow. Those not so fortunate have learned to adapt dried fruits and vegetables to their dishes. In most places, people take what's available and turn out masterful meals.

There are countries where the supply and assortment of vegetables and meats is pretty much the same, yet the end results are vastly different. Seasonings and fats are responsible for a large part of this difference. Italian cooking, for instance, with its yummy pastas, and marvelous fruits and vegetables, uses olive oil extensively, and the flavor it imparts is unmistakable. Mexico, with many of the same fruits and vegetables, favors cornmeal and lard, resulting in a distinctive cuisine. And the traditional French cooks use butter so lavishly it's almost sinful (and it is expensive). Spices and herbs are used with varying regularity in different countries. Curry is the favorite in India, the Russians would use dill, and the Italian would probably bypass both these in favor of his beloved basil.

Ethnic cooking is always an interesting experiment, and one in which your oven will prove invaluable. Of course, we have just touched on a few recipes from a few countries—some of the dishes from cuisines of which we're particularly fond. We hope you find your favorite among them.

A HUNGARIAN BOILED DINNER

Peppers, sweet red or green, figure prominently in Hungarian dishes. A pepper and tomato sauce, *Letcho,* frequently served with plain meats, is included in this menu. It's usually prepared in a skillet, but ours is an oven version. This boiled dinner, which is interestingly different from American boiled dinners, serves six.

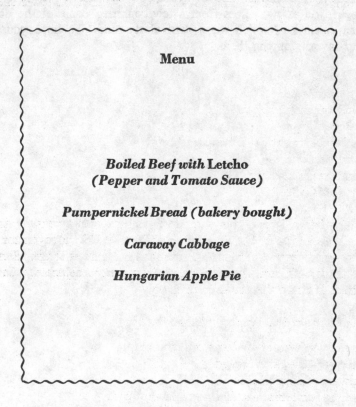

Menu

Boiled Beef with **Letcho**
(Pepper and Tomato Sauce)

Pumpernickel Bread (bakery bought)

Caraway Cabbage

Hungarian Apple Pie

Total Cooking Time: 2 hours and 40 minutes

Plan of Action

Preheat oven to 425° F. While it is heating, oven-sauté vegetables for

Letcho. When oven is heated to 425° F., bake pie on top shelf for 10 minutes. Reduce heat to 350° F. Place beef, covered, on lower shelf. Continue cooking for 40 minutes or until pie is golden brown. Remove pie, and place it on a wire rack to cool. Place *Letcho,* uncovered, on top shelf to cook for 45 minutes to 1 hour. Remove when it reaches the desired consistency. When the beef has cooked for 2 hours, add the carrots and parsnips, re-cover, and cook 30 minutes longer. At the same time, cook cabbage, covered, on lower shelf beside beef.

Boiled Beef with Letcho

3 pound piece boiling beef, such as brisket
2 cups hot water
1 stalk celery, chopped
1 onion, chopped
2 tablespoons chopped fresh parsley
1 teaspoon salt
2 large carrots, sliced
2 parsnips, sliced

Place beef in a Dutch oven with water, celery, onion, parsley, and salt. Cover and simmer on the lower shelf of a 350° F. oven for 2 hours. Add carrots and parsnips, and cook 30 minutes longer. Serve meat sliced with carrots and parsnips. Pass *Letcho* separately. Save the meat broth to use for soup or gravy.

Letcho *Pepper and Tomato Sauce*

4 green peppers, seeded and cut into strips
2 onions, sliced and ringed
2 tablespoons vegetable oil
28-ounce can tomatoes, drained and chopped
1 teaspoon salt
½ teaspoon pepper
½ teaspoon sugar

Oven-sauté peppers and onions in oil in a 2-quart casserole until they are sizzling. Add all remaining ingredients. Cook, uncovered, on the top shelf of a 350° F. oven for 45 minutes to 1 hour, until the sauce reaches desired thickness. Stir occasionally while cooking.

Caraway Cabbage

½ medium-sized head cabbage, shredded
¼ cup beef broth
2 tablespoons butter
1 teaspoon white vinegar
1 teaspoon sugar
½ teaspoon salt
¼ teaspoon pepper
¼ teaspoon caraway seeds

Combine all ingredients in a 3-quart casserole. Cover and cook for 30 minutes at 350° F.

Hungarian Apple Pie

Pastry for double crust 9-inch pie (see page 359)
¼ cup strawberry jam
6 to 8 apples, peeled, cored, and sliced—enough to fill pie pan
½ cup sugar
2 teaspoons cornstarch
⅛ teaspoon salt
½ cup chopped almonds
2 tablespoons almond-flavored liqueur

Divide pastry in half. Roll out half to fit a 9-inch pie pan, and chill it while preparing filling. Preheat oven to 425° F. Prepare apples, and toss them with sugar, cornstarch, salt, almonds, and almond liqueur. Layer strawberry jam in the bottom of chilled crust. Put apple mixture on top. Top with the second half of pastry rolled to fit. Trim, leaving a 1 inch overhang. Turn the extra under the bottom crust. Seal by pressing with the tines of a floured fork. Cut vents for steam to escape. Bake for 10 minutes on the top shelf. Reduce heat to 350° F., and continue cooking for 40 minutes, or until crust is golden brown and apples are tender. (A cake tester inserted through one of the vents can be used to test the apples.)

FORGET ABOUT DIETING WITH THIS DINNER FROM FRANCE

From simple peasant cooking to the haute cuisine of famous restaurants, France is known for dedication to good eating. This menu serves four.

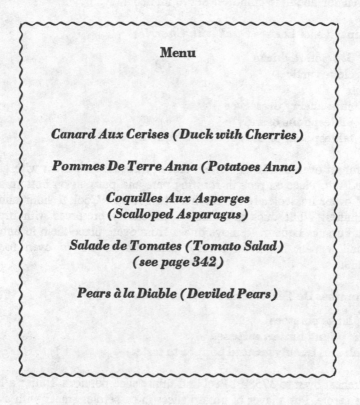

Menu

Canard Aux Cerises (Duck with Cherries)

Pommes De Terre Anna (Potatoes Anna)

Coquilles Aux Asperges (Scalloped Asparagus)

Salade de Tomates (Tomato Salad) (see page 342)

Pears à la Diable (Deviled Pears)

Total Cooking Time: about 1 hour and 35 minutes

Plan of Action

Assemble potatoes Anna. Preheat oven to 450° F. Prepare ducks, and put them on bottom shelf of oven. Immediately reduce heat to 375° F. When ducks have been in oven 5 minutes, put potatoes on top shelf. Make scalloped asparagus. Cut tomatoes and lettuce, and make dressing for salad. When ducks have been in oven for 1 hour, place asparagus on top shelf, continue cooking for another 20 minutes. Finish salad and serve meal. When finished eating, assemble deviled pears, and put them on middle shelf of preheated 375° F. oven for about 15 minutes. Serve immediately.

Canard Aux Cerises *Duck with Cherries*

2 3½ pound ducks
1 clove garlic
Salt
2 cups cherry preserves
2 tablespoons brandy
2 tablespoons orange-flavored liqueur

Preheat oven to 450° F. Wash and dry ducks. Rub them with garlic and salt. Place on rack in roasting pan, and put pan on bottom shelf of oven. Immediately reduce heat to 375° F. Cook 1 hour and 20 minutes. While duck is cooking, mix cherry preserves with brandy and orange liqueur. Remove ducks from oven, place them in another shallow pan, brush on cherry glaze, and return to oven for 15 minutes.

Pommes De Terre Anna *Potatoes Anna*

4 large potatoes
½ pound butter, softened
Salt and freshly ground pepper to taste

Preheat oven to 375° F. Peel and thinly slice potatoes. Butter a large casserole. Put a layer of potato slices in casserole. Smear with a thin layer of butter. Add salt and pepper. Continue layering until all ingredients are used, ending with butter, salt, and pepper. Place on top shelf of preheated oven for 1 hour and 15 minutes, covering with foil if top browns too rapidly. Invert on platter and serve hot.

Coquilles Aux Asperges *Scalloped Asparagus*

1 package frozen chopped asparagus, cooked
2 tablespoons butter
12 large mushroom caps, chopped
1 cup cheese sauce suprême (see page 357)
4 ounces boiled ham, chopped
Salt and pepper to taste
1 cup soft bread crumbs
2 tablespoons butter

Turn oven to 375° F. Put butter in oven-proof dish and place in oven to melt. Add mushrooms and oven-sauté until they're soft. Remove. Mix cheese sauce, ham, asparagus, mushrooms, and salt and pepper. Divide between four ramekins. Top each with ¼ cup bread crumbs. Dot with butter, and place on top shelf of preheated 375° F. oven for 20 minutes.

Pears à la Diable *Deviled Pears*

1 sponge cake
4 large pears, peeled, cored, and quartered
½ cup kirsch
4 egg whites
4 tablespoons confectioners' sugar
2 tablespoons kirsch

Put sponge cake on small, buttered baking sheet or in shallow pan. Mix pears in kirsch and put on top of cake. Beat egg whites until stiff, adding sugar gradually. Frost cake and pears with egg whites. Put on middle shelf of preheated 375° F. oven for about 15 minutes, or until meringue is lightly browned. Warm 2 tablespoons of kirsch, pour over meringue and ignite it with a wooden match. Serve immediately.

Note: This tempting dessert must be assembled and cooked just before serving.

HEALTHY, HEARTY FARE FROM HOLLAND

The Dutch make good use of dried foods, such as split peas, the basis of their favorite winter soup, and dried fruits, which appear in many of their sweets. This cold weather dinner serves six.

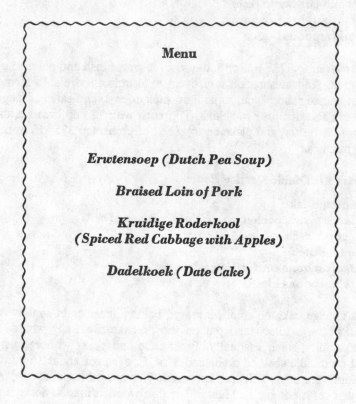

Menu

Erwtensoep (Dutch Pea Soup)

Braised Loin of Pork

*Kruidige Roderkool
(Spiced Red Cabbage with Apples)*

Dadelkoek (Date Cake)

Total Cooking Time: 2½ hours

Plan of Action

Soak split peas for soup overnight; drain. Prepare soup and cake. Place soup, covered, on the lower shelf of a preheated 350° F. oven, cake on top shelf, and cook for 30 to 35 minutes, until cake is golden brown. Remove cake, and stir soup. Oven-sauté vegetables for pork loin and spiced cabbage in their separate baking dishes. Finish assembling pork and cabbage. When the soup has been in the oven for 1 hour, stir it, and place pork beside it. Cook the pork, uncovered, for 30 minutes. Baste and cover pork. When the soup has cooked for 2 hours, add to it the remaining vegetables and other ingredients, cover, and cook 30 minutes longer. At the same time, place cabbage, covered, on top shelf. When cooking is complete, the pork loin should have cooked a total of 1½ hours, the cabbage for 30 minutes.

Erwtensoep *Dutch Pea Soup*

1 cup green split peas
1 teaspoon salt
1 onion, sliced
2 quarts boiling water
2 potatoes, diced
1 carrot, very thinly sliced
2 frankfurters, thinly sliced
½ cup chopped celery tops
¼ cup chopped fresh parsley
Pepper to taste
Pumpernickel bread and butter

Soak peas overnight in water to cover; drain. Place them in a Dutch oven with salt, onion, and boiling water. Cover and cook in a 350° F. oven for 2 hours, stirring occasionally. Add potatoes, carrots, frankfurters, celery tops, parsley, and pepper. If very thick, thin with ½ cup water or more. Cover and cook 30 minutes longer, or until potatoes and carrots are tender. Serve soup with pumpernickel bread and butter.

Braised Loin of Pork

Boneless loin of pork, about 2½ pounds
2 cloves garlic, minced
1 onion, chopped
1 stalk of celery, chopped

1 carrot, chopped
1 green pepper, chopped
2 tablespoons vegetable oil
16-ounce can tomatoes
1 cup beef broth
¼ cup dry white wine
2 tablespoons chopped fresh parsley
1 teaspoon dried thyme leaves
1 teaspoon salt
½ teaspoon dried tarragon
Freshly ground black pepper to taste

In a 12-inch by 8-inch casserole, oven-sauté garlic, onion, celery, carrot, and green pepper in oil until the vegetables are sizzling. Add pork and the remaining ingredients. Bake for 30 minutes on lower shelf at 350° F., uncovered, basting once or twice. Then cover with foil and continue cooking for 1 hour, or until tender. Place the loin on a warm platter. Skim fat from pan juices, and spoon some of the juices over the loin. The rest may be served separately or saved for reheating leftovers.

Kruidige Roderkool *Spiced Red Cabbage with Apples*

1 onion, finely chopped
2 tablespoons butter
1 tablespoon flour
1 small head of red cabbage, shredded
2 apples, peeled and chopped
2 tablespoons cider vinegar
1 tablespoon sugar
1 teaspoon salt
¼ teaspoon ground cloves
¾ cup boiling water

Oven-sauté onion in butter in a 3-quart casserole until the onion is sizzling. Remove from oven and stir in flour. Add the remaining ingredients, cover, and cook the casserole for 30 minutes in a 350° F. oven. Stir before serving.

Dadelkoek *Date Cake*

¾ cup (1½ sticks) butter, softened
½ cup brown sugar
1 egg, beaten
1 teaspoon vanilla
1½ cups all-purpose flour
2 teaspoons baking powder
½ teaspoon salt
1½ cups quick-cooking oatmeal
¾ pound dates, pitted and chopped
6 whole dates, pitted and halved for garnish

Cream the butter until it is light. Gradually add sugar, then egg and vanilla. Stir flour to lighten it before measuring. Sift together flour, baking powder, and salt. Stir oatmeal into flour mixture. With a wooden spoon, stir the dry ingredients into the butter-egg mixture until blended. Spoon a little more than half the dough into a buttered, floured 9-inch square cake pan, and smooth it into a layer with a spatula. Arrange a layer of chopped dates over the dough. Cover with remaining dough, and smooth this into a second layer. (This takes a bit of patience.) Press date halves, cut side down, onto the top as a decoration. Bake in a 350° F. oven for 35 minutes, or until cake is golden brown. Cool in pan on wire rack. Cut in squares to serve.

A FEAST FROM THE MIDDLE EAST

Redolent of the spices that create its unique flavor, *kibbeh* is the hamburger of the Middle East. Serves eight.

Menu

Kibbeh-*Burgers*

Feta Cheese in Grape Leaves

Onion-Topped Pita Bread

Tomato and Pepper Salad (see page 344)

Lemon Sherbet (store bought)

Total Cooking Time: 30 minutes

Plan of Action

In a preheated 375° F. oven, bake *kibbeh* and onion topping on the lower shelf for 20 minutes. Remove onions and quickly spread them on pita bread. Place pitas on top shelf, grape leaves with feta on lower shelf beside *kibbeh*, and continue cooking the dishes for 10 minutes.

Kibbeh-*Burgers*

¾ cup cracked wheat
¼ teaspoon salt
1½ cups boiling water
2 pounds ground lamb or beef
2 tablespoons minced fresh parsley
1 clove garlic, finely minced
1 teaspoon salt
½ teaspoon pepper
½ teaspoon Syrian red thyme
  or regular ground thyme
¼ teaspoon cinnamon
½ cup pine nuts

Mix together cracked wheat and ¼ teaspoon salt in a small bowl. Pour boiling water over wheat. Let the mixture stand until the water is absorbed, about 20 minutes. Put the wheat into a fine-meshed strainer and press out the excess water. Mix the wheat with all remaining ingredients. Pat the *kibbeh* into a layer in an 11-inch by 8-inch baking pan. Mark diamond shapes on the surface of the loaf, then cut all the way through with a table knife. This enables the loaf to cook more quickly. Bake 30 minutes in a preheated 375° F. oven.

Feta Cheese in Grape Leaves

8-ounce jar grape leaves in brine
1 pound feta cheese
Olive oil

Soak the grape leaves in very hot water for 30 minutes. Gently separate them, rinse in cool water, and pat dry. Lay them out, dull side up. Place on each a piece of feta cheese approximately 2½-inch long, 1-inch wide, ½-inch thick. Fold each grape leaf around cheese to make a package, and place seam side down in a 9-inch square baking dish. Brush the tops with olive oil. Cook for 10 minutes in a preheated 375° F. oven.

Onion-Topped Pita Bread

4 large onions, sliced
¾ cup olive oil
1 teaspoon oregano
Salt and pepper to taste
4 large loaves (pieces) pita bread, split

Combine onions, oil, oregano, salt, and pepper in a baking dish, and oven-sauté for 20 minutes in a preheated 375° F. oven. Remove the dish from the oven. Lay the pitas on a baking sheet, concave side up. Divide the onion mixture between the breads, and spread the topping to cover loaves to within 1 inch of the rims. Bake 10 minutes.

AN ITALIAN FAMILY DINNER

A favorite with Italians, dandelions are sold in some vegetable stores, but they also grow wild for the harvesting. (Pick them before they blossom.) Eggplant slices for eggplant parmigiana are usually fried, but in our version, they are broiled instead, using much less oil. This uncomplicated dinner serves six.

Menu

Polpettone con Ricotta
(Meat Loaf with Ricotta)

Melenzana alla Parmigiana
(All-in-the-Oven Eggplant Parmigiana)

Italian Bread (bakery bought)

Cicoria Fina Agliata
(Braised Dandelions with Garlic)

Pasta Frolla di Pignoli (Florentines)

Total Cooking Time: 8 minutes broiling and 30 minutes baking

Plan of Action

Prepare and broil eggplant slices according to instructions. Assemble meat loaf, eggplant, and Florentines. Preheat oven to 350° F., and while it is heating oven-sauté garlic for dandelion dish. Assemble dandelion casserole. Place eggplant and Florentines on top shelf of oven, meat loaf and dandelions on lower shelf. Cook everything 30 minutes. Let meat loaf rest before cutting.

Polpettone con Ricotta *Meat Loaf with Ricotta*

2 pounds lean ground beef
1 cup seasoned crumbs (see page 361)
1 egg
¼ cup beef broth
¼ cup grated Romano cheese
½ onion, very finely chopped
¾ teaspoon salt
¼ teaspoon black pepper
1 pound ricotta cheese
1 egg
¼ teaspoon salt
⅛ teaspoon white pepper
1 tablespoon minced fresh parsley

Mix together beef, crumbs, 1 egg, broth, Romano, onion, ¾ teaspoon salt, and black pepper; blend well. In another bowl, mix ricotta with 1 egg, ¼ teaspoon salt, white pepper, and parsley. Press half the beef mixture into a 9-inch square baking dish. Make a layer of the ricotta mixture on top of beef. Top with remaining beef. The ricotta filling is soft until it is cooked, so pat the meat into flat sheets between your palms, and then place them on top of ricotta. Pinch them together to form a single top layer. Bake the meat loaf for 30 minutes on the lower shelf of a preheated 350° F. oven. Let it rest for about 10 minutes before cutting into squares to serve.

Note: This meat loaf cooks in 30 minutes because it is flat rather than loaf-shaped. You can check for doneness, however, by separating it a bit at the center with a table knife to be sure it is cooked through.

Melenzana alla Parmigiana *All-in-the-Oven Eggplant Parmigiana*

2 medium eggplants
Salt
About ⅓ cup olive oil
2½ cups tomato sauce (see page 256)
½ cup freshly grated Parmesan cheese
½ pound mozzarella cheese

Slice unpeeled eggplant into ½-inch slices lengthwise. Sprinkle them with salt, and drain them for 30 minutes. Rinse and pat dry. Place them on an oiled broiler, and brush them with oil. Broil for 4 minutes or until golden. (You may have to do this in batches.) Turn and brush with oil. Broil 4 minutes. Layer the slices in a 12-inch by 8-inch baking dish with tomato sauce and Parmesan. Top with slices of mozzarella. Bake on the top shelf of a 350° F. oven for 30 minutes.

Cicoria Fina Agliata *Braised Dandelions with Garlic*

2 pounds tender, young dandelion leaves
1 large clove garlic, minced
¼ cup olive oil
¼ cup beef or chicken broth
Salt and pepper to taste

Wash dandelions very well. Trim off any roots, and cut the leaves into thirds. In a 3-quart casserole, oven-sauté garlic in oil until sizzling. Do not brown garlic. Add dandelions, broth, salt, and pepper. Cover and bake at 350° F. on lower shelf for 25 to 30 minutes or until tender.

Pasta Frolla di Pignoli *Florentines*

½ cup (1 stick) butter, softened
⅓ cup sugar
3 eggs
½ teaspoon anise extract
2 cups all-purpose flour
2 teaspoons baking powder

½ teaspoon cinnamon
¼ teaspoon salt
½ cup pine nuts, divided
Confectioners' sugar

Cream butter until light. Gradually add sugar. Beat in eggs, one at a time, then anise extract. Stir flour to lighten it before measuring. Sift together flour, baking powder, cinnamon, and salt. With a wooden spoon, gradually add dry ingredients to butter-egg mixture. With the last of the dry ingredients, add ¼ cup pine nuts. Spread the dough in a buttered 9-inch square baking dish. Sprinkle remaining pine nuts on top, and press them lightly into dough. Bake on the top shelf of a preheated 350° F. oven for 25 to 30 minutes, or until golden. A cake tester inserted in the center should come out dry. Cool in pan on wire rack. When ready to serve, cut into 3-inch "fingers," and sprinkle with confectioners' sugar.

A STICK-TO-YOUR-RIBS GERMAN MEAL

This menu with its frothy dessert is a bit lighter than many German dinners. Yet it's typically German. Serves six.

Menu

Schweinebraten mit Aprikosen und Äpfeln
(Roast Pork with Apricot
and Apple Stuffing)

Gemüsepudding (Vegetable Pudding)

Parslied Potatoes (see page 69)

Erdbeerschnee mit Schlagsahne
(Strawberry Ambrosia Cream)
(see page 348)

Total Cooking Time: about 3 to 4 hours, depending on size of loin

Plan of Action

Make ambrosia cream in advance. Preheat oven to 350° F. Prepare loin and place it on bottom shelf of oven. Prepare vegetable pudding, and when pork has 1 hour left to cook place pudding on middle shelf of oven. Prepare potatoes; when vegetable pudding has been in oven 15 minutes, place potatoes on *upper* shelf (the recipe on page 69 says lower shelf but is for use in that menu) and continue to cook another 45 minutes.

Gemüsepudding *Vegetable Pudding*

2 10-ounce packages frozen cauliflower, thawed to separate
1 4-ounce can mushroom pieces, drained
1½ cups white sauce (see page 357)
4 eggs, separated
Butter
½ cup soft bread crumbs

Mix cauliflower and mushrooms. Make white sauce, and allow it to cool slightly. Beat egg yolks, and mix a little of the white sauce into them before adding yolks to sauce. Beat egg whites until stiff, then fold them into white sauce. Gently mix in cauliflower and mushrooms. Butter a 2-quart casserole. Sprinkle crumbs on butter so they cover sides and bottom of casserole. Put on middle shelf of preheated 350° F. oven and bake for 1 hour, until puffy and set.

Schweinebraten mit Aprikosen und Äpfeln
Roast Pork with Apricot and Apple Stuffing

1 5 to 6 pound pork loin, boned
1 cup dried apricots
2 large apples, peeled, cored, and cut into chunks
1 teaspoon salt
⅛ teaspoon white pepper
1 teaspoon powdered ginger
¼ teaspoon cinnamon
1½ cups water
3 tablespoons flour
1 teaspoon Gravy Master
Salt and pepper to taste
½ cup sour cream

Cut pocket in side of loin. In a medium-sized saucepan, parboil apricots for about 10 minutes to plump them. Mix together apricots and apples and stuff them into pocket in loin. Mix together 1 teaspoon of salt, white pepper, ginger, and cinnamon, and rub this on outside of loin. Tie pocket closed by wrapping string around loin several times. Place loin in roasting pan, fat side up, and roast on bottom shelf of preheated 350° F. oven for 40 minutes per pound, or until meat thermometer reaches 185° F.

Remove roast from oven, place it on platter, and set it aside to rest. Put water in screw top jar. Spoon flour on top of water, cover, and shake to blend. Skim most of fat from roasting pan. Put pan on burner set on medium heat. Gradually pour in flour-water mixture, stirring constantly with a wooden spoon until thickened. Add more water if necessary to thin gravy. Season with Gravy Master, and salt and pepper to taste. Cook at least 5 minutes, stirring occasionally. Remove from heat and stir in sour cream. Slice meat, and either pour gravy over it or serve in gravy bowl.

FROM RUSSIA WITH LOVE

Russians aren't big dessert eaters. They usually prefer to end their meals with a selection of fruit, either fresh or canned—a good idea since their dinners are more than ample fare.

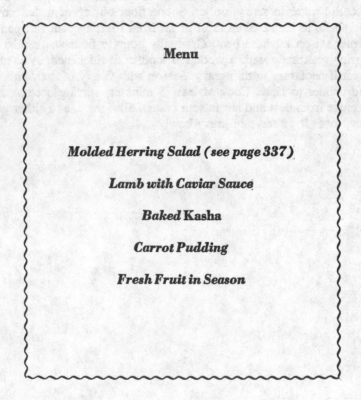

Menu

Molded Herring Salad (see page 337)

Lamb with Caviar Sauce

Baked Kasha

Carrot Pudding

Fresh Fruit in Season

Total Cooking Time: about 2½ to 3½ hours, depending on size of lamb leg

Plan of Action

Prepare and refrigerate herring. Preheat oven to 325° F., prepare lamb and put it on bottom shelf of oven. Mix ingredients for *kasha*, and when lamb has 2 more hours to cook, put *kasha* on middle shelf of oven. Prepare carrot pudding. When *kasha* has cooked 1 hour, add pudding to middle shelf and continue cooking for another hour. During this time, make caviar sauce, unmold herring, and add garnishes.

Lamb with Caviar Sauce

6½ to 7 pound leg of spring lamb
⅛ teaspoon garlic powder
1 teaspoon salt
¼ teaspoon pepper
2 tablespoons butter, melted
⅓ cup lemon juice
½ cup caviar

Rub lamb with mixture of garlic powder, salt and pepper. Put on rack in roasting pan. Roast on bottom shelf of preheated 325° F. oven for 30 minutes per pound, or until a meat thermometer reads 175° F. Mix butter, lemon juice, and caviar just before serving time, and serve them as sauce for lamb.

Baked Kasha

1 cup buckwheat
1 small onion, grated
½ teaspoon salt
1½ cups boiling water
1 cup chicken stock
1 tablespoon butter

Combine all ingredients in greased medium-sized casserole. Mix with fork until butter melts. Cover and bake on middle shelf of preheated 325° F. oven for 2 hours or until water is absorbed.

Carrot Pudding

4 large carrots, cooked and grated
1 small onion, grated
½ teaspoon salt
¼ teaspoon nutmeg
1 tablespoon sugar
1 cup milk
3 eggs, beaten

Mix together all ingredients. Put in 1½-quart casserole and bake on middle shelf of preheated 325° F. oven for 1 hour until set. If top browns too quickly, cover with foil.

A Taste of Merry Old England

Who says the English can't cook! We hope this menu will help dispel that false rumor. Serves four.

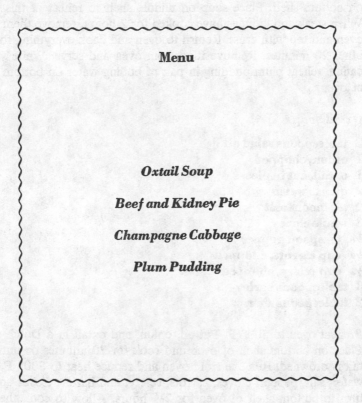

Menu

Oxtail Soup

Beef and Kidney Pie

Champagne Cabbage

Plum Pudding

Total Cooking Time: about 3 hours and 10 minutes

Plan of Action

Day before meal: Preheat oven to 500° F. Place oil, onion, and oxtail in Dutch oven on bottom shelf for 20 minutes. During this time assemble plum pudding. Reduce heat to 300° F. Complete assembling oxtail soup, and place it and plum pudding on bottom shelf of oven for 2½ hours. Store soup and pudding in refrigerator.

Day of meal: Put steak and kidneys in casserole on bottom shelf of preheated 350° F. oven. Assemble cabbage, and when steak and kidneys have been cooking for 1 hour and 50 minutes, put cabbage on bottom shelf. Place soup on middle shelf to reheat at this time. When steak and kidneys have cooked for 2 hours, remove them from oven and top with crust. Return to oven and cook everything for another 20 minutes. Remove food from oven and serve. While you're eating, reheat plum pudding in pan of boiling water on bottom shelf of oven.

Oxtail Soup

3 tablespoons salad oil
1 onion, chopped
1 oxtail, cut in pieces
2 quarts water
2 teaspoons salt
3 whole cloves
⅛ teaspoon pepper
½ cup carrots, chopped
½ cup celery, chopped
3 tablespoons barley
2 tablespoons sherry

Preheat oven to 500° F. Put oil, onion, and oxtail in a Dutch oven. Place on bottom shelf of oven and cook for 20 minutes or until oxtail is browned. Remove from oven and reduce heat to 300° F. Add water, salt, pepper, cloves, carrots, celery, and barley. Cover and return to bottom shelf of oven for 2½ hours. Allow to cool, then refrigerate. Skim fat from top, remove oxtail from bone and return meat to soup, adding sherry before reheating.

Beef and Kidney Pie

3 pounds lean chuck, cubed
1 beef kidney, cleaned and chopped
1 teaspoon salt
⅛ teaspoon pepper

½ cup all-purpose flour
1 large onion, chopped
1 beef bouillon cube
1 cup boiling water
Pastry for one crust pie (see page 359)

Mix together beef and kidney chunks. Mix salt, pepper, and flour. In a 2-quart casserole, put a layer of beef and kidney, a layer of chopped onion, and sprinkle flour on top. Continue to layer until beef, kidney, and flour are used, ending with flour. Dissolve bouillon cube in boiling water and pour over. Cover casserole and place it on bottom shelf of preheated 350° F. oven for 2 hours. Roll out crust. Remove casserole from oven. Remove cover and top with crust, making slits to vent in top. Return to bottom shelf of oven and continue cooking for 20 minutes, or until crust is browned.

Champagne Cabbage

3 tablespoons butter
1 large onion, sliced and ringed
2 large pears, peeled, cored, and chunked
1 small head cabbage, shredded
¾ cup tepid champagne
1 tablespoon honey
1 tablespoon lemon juice
Salt and pepper to taste

Melt butter in Dutch oven. Add onion and pears and sauté, stirring constantly until onions are soft and pears are lightly browned. Add remaining ingredients. Cover and cook on bottom shelf of preheated 350° F. oven for 30 minutes. Remove cover and continue cooking another 10 minutes, or until cabbage is soft.

Plum Pudding

6 tablespoons butter, softened
1 cup brown sugar, firmly packed
5 eggs, well beaten
4 tablespoons flour
2 teaspoons baking powder

1 teaspoon salt
1 teaspoon cinnamon
1 cup raisins
¼ cup citron, chopped
½ cup chopped walnuts
Grated orange zest
2½ cups soft bread crumbs

Grease a large (approximately 8-cup) mold. Cream butter and sugar. Add eggs and mix well. Sift together flour, baking powder, salt, and cinnamon. Add remaining ingredients to flour, and stir into butter-egg mixture. Turn into mold, place mold in a pan, then put pan on bottom shelf of preheated 300° F. oven. Pour boiling water into pan to within 2 inches of top of mold. Bake 2½ hours, adding more boiling water to pan if necessary.

THE FLAVOR OF IRELAND

Pale green, whipped colcannon is often served at Halloween or on All Hallows' Day in Ireland. Irish brown bread is allowed to cool before serving for easier slicing. This dinner serves six.

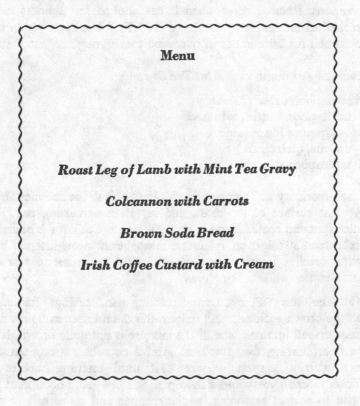

Menu

Roast Leg of Lamb with Mint Tea Gravy

Colcannon with Carrots

Brown Soda Bread

Irish Coffee Custard with Cream

Total Cooking Time: about 2 hours and 40 minutes

Plan of Action

Prepare bread and bake it on top shelf of a preheated 425° F. oven for 20 minutes. Lower heat to 350° F. (leaving bread in oven), and place roast and colcannon on lower shelf. Remove bread after 10 minutes at 350° F., and allow it to cool on wire rack. When colcannon has cooked for 50 minutes, remove it from oven. Cover roast loosely with foil, and place custard on same shelf. Cook custard for 40 minutes or until set. Remove foil from roast when custard is done. Meanwhile, finish preparing colcannon casserole according to recipe directions. Remove roast when it has cooked for 2 hours or has reached an internal temperature of 170° F. While roast rests, reheat colcannon for 20 minutes in oven and make gravy.

Roast Leg of Lamb with Mint Tea Gravy

½ teaspoon dried rosemary
1 tablespoon butter, softened
4 to 5 pound leg of lamb
2 onions, quartered
2 tablespoons water

Crush rosemary and combine it with butter. Rub the rosemary-butter over the surface of the roast, and lay it in a roasting pan. Tuck onions around roast and pour water into pan. Cook for 2 hours in a preheated 350° F. oven, or until a meat thermometer inserted in the center reaches a temperature of 170° F. Allow roast to rest on a warm platter while making gravy.

Mint Tea Gravy: Pour fat from roasting pan, leaving 1 tablespoon fat, the brown sediment, and onions. Stir 2 tablespoons flour and ¾ teaspoon salt into pan, and, if the mixture is not quite brown, brown the flour, stirring, over low heat. Add 2 cups hot, strong tea all at once, stirring constantly over heat until mixture bubbles and thickens. *Strain* gravy into a saucepan. Stir in 1 tablespoon mint jelly. Taste to correct seasoning, adding pepper and more salt to taste. Pass the rest of the mint jelly at the table.

Colcannon with Carrots

4 large potatoes, halved
4 carrots, cut into thirds
½ head cabbage, cut into wedges
2 tablespoons chopped fresh parsley

¼ cup chopped scallion tops (optional)
1 cup water
2 tablespoons butter
1 teaspoon salt
Several dashes of white pepper
Cream
Nutmeg
¼ cup (½ stick) butter, melted

Combine potatoes, carrots, cabbage, parsley, scallions (if using), water, 2 tablespoons butter, salt, and white pepper in a 3-quart casserole. Cover and bake in a 350° F. oven for 50 minutes or until vegetables are tender. Drain, reserving liquid. Purée cabbage in processor or blender, or finely chop it by hand. Mash and whip the potatoes until they are fluffy, adding some of the reserved liquid and cream, as much as is needed for desired consistency. Beat cabbage purée into potatoes. Return this mixture to the casserole. Slice the carrots and place them around the outer edge of the casserole in a ring. Sprinkle all with a little nutmeg. Brush the carrots with some of the melted butter. When ready to serve, reheat the colcannon for 20 minutes at 350° F. Make wells in the surface of the casserole with the back of a spoon, and pour into them the remaining melted butter.

Brown Soda Bread

1 cup whole wheat flour
2 cups all-purpose white flour
¼ cup sugar
2 teaspoons baking soda
1 teaspoon salt
3 tablespoons butter
2 tablespoons lard
About ¾ cup buttermilk or soured milk (see page 362)

Combine dry ingredients in a large bowl and stir well to blend thoroughly. With a pastry blender or two knives, cut in butter and lard until the mixture resembles coarse cornmeal. Add enough buttermilk or soured milk to make a soft dough that can be handled. On a floured surface, knead the dough just a few times to make a smooth ball, and place the ball on a greased baking sheet. With the heel of your hand, gently flatten the ball of dough so that it is about 1½ inches thick. With a floured knife, cut a deep cross across the top. Bake the bread for 20 minutes on the top shelf of a preheated 425° F. oven. Reduce heat to 350° F. and continue cooking for 10 minutes, or until the bottom of the loaf is brown and crusty. Remove bread from baking sheet and cool it on a wire rack before serving. Serve with unsalted butter.

Irish Coffee Custard with Cream

3 cups milk, scalded
6 eggs
¾ cup sugar
¼ teaspoon salt
1 teaspoon vanilla extract
2 tablespoons Irish whiskey
2½ teaspoons instant coffee
½ pint heavy cream, whipped
2 teaspoons sugar

While milk is heating, beat eggs with sugar, salt, vanilla, and whiskey in a medium-sized bowl until well blended. Stir coffee into hot milk to dissolve. Add milk in a slow stream to egg mixture while whisking constantly. Pour the custard mixture into a buttered 2-quart casserole, and place the casserole in a larger baking pan on the lower shelf of a 350° F. oven. Pour hot water into the larger pan to a depth of 1 inch. Bake the custard for 40 minutes, or until a knife inserted 1 inch from the center comes out clean. Cool the custard to room temperature and serve it with cold whipped cream flavored with 2 teaspoons sugar.

A Scottish Lowland Supper

Kale is the vegetable most frequently served in Scotland (not counting potatoes, of course), since it thrives in cool weather. Oatmeal is the favorite grain, but the texture of Scottish oatmeal is lighter than ours. And fish is ever-plentiful. You'll find them all in this homey supper for four.

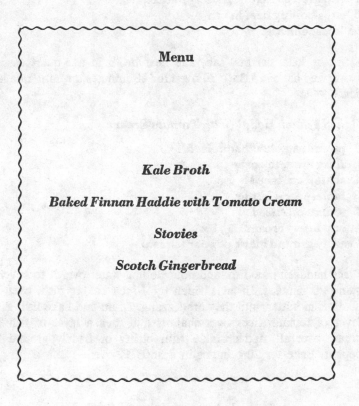

Menu

Kale Broth

Baked Finnan Haddie with Tomato Cream

Stovies

Scotch Gingerbread

Total Cooking Time: 40 minutes

Plan of Action

Preheat oven to 350° F. and, while it is heating, oven-sauté shallots for fish. Place kale and potatoes on lower shelf and cook them for 10 minutes. Place cake on top shelf and continue cooking for 10 minutes. Place finnan haddie beside cake, and cook everything 20 minutes longer.

Kale Broth

1 pound kale, well-washed and shredded
1 cup grated carrots, loosely packed
3 cups boiling beef broth
½ teaspoon salt

Combine kale, carrots, salt, and beef broth in a 3-quart casserole. Cover and bake in a 350° F. oven for 40 minutes, or until kale is tender.

Baked Finnan Haddie with Tomato Cream

2 pounds smoked haddock fillets
Boiling water to cover
4 shallots, minced
2 tablespoons butter
2 tomatoes, sliced
1 cup heavy cream
Freshly ground black pepper to taste

Place haddock in a dish, and pour boiling water over it to cover. Let stand 20 minutes. In an 11-inch by 7-inch baking dish, oven-sauté shallots in butter until they are sizzling. Drain and flake fish. Place a layer of tomato slices over shallots and then a layer of fish. Pour cream over all, and sprinkle with plenty of freshly ground black pepper. Bake for 20 minutes in a 350° F. oven.

Stovies

4 large potatoes, peeled and very thinly sliced
1 onion, thinly sliced and separated into rings
¼ cup butter
½ teaspoon salt
¼ teaspoon white pepper
1 cup boiling beef broth

Layer potatoes, onions, and dots of butter in a 2-quart casserole. Mix salt and pepper with broth, and pour it over potatoes. Cover and bake for 40 minutes, or until quite tender, in a 350° F. oven.

Scotch Gingerbread

The fresh ginger is especially tangy—and the recipe uses no eggs!

½ cup butter, softened
¼ cup brown sugar
½ cup dark molasses
½ cup oatmeal
1½ cups all-purpose flour
1 teaspoon baking soda
¼ teaspoon salt
1½ tablespoons grated fresh ginger
   or 1 teaspoon ground ginger
¼ cup chopped candied citron
⅓ cup soured milk (see page 362)
Lemon sherbet (optional)

Cream butter until light, and gradually beat in sugar, then molasses. Blend or process oatmeal in a blender (or food processor fitted with steel blade) until oatmeal is lighter in texture but still coarse—this takes only about two on-off turns of the motor. Sift together flour, baking soda, salt, and ground ginger (if not using fresh ginger). Blend with oatmeal. Stir dry ingredients into butter-molasses mixture. If using fresh ginger, stir that in with the citron. Add milk last, and spoon the batter into a buttered 9-inch square pan. Bake 30 minutes in a preheated 350° F. oven, or until a cake tester inserted in the center comes out clean. Cool on wire rack. Cut into squares and serve from pan. If desired, top with lemon sherbet.

Oven Magic, Mexican Style

Easy and spicy, this south of the border dinner for six requires very little watching. A pitcher of Margaritas could help while away the time once everything is safely in the oven.

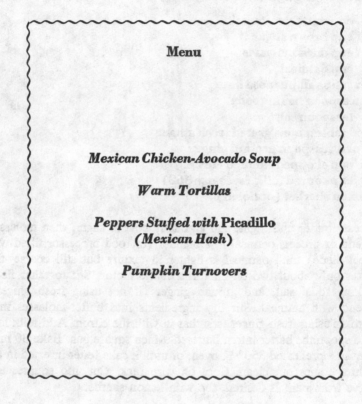

Menu

Mexican Chicken-Avocado Soup

Warm Tortillas

Peppers Stuffed with Picadillo (Mexican Hash)

Pumpkin Turnovers

Total Cooking Time: about 3 hours

Plan of Action

Preheat oven to 400° F. While it is heating, oven-sauté onion and celery for soup. Bake turnovers for 20 to 25 minutes on the top shelf of oven while assembling soup and peppers. Remove turnovers and place soup on lower shelf. Cook 2 hours. Add remaining vegetables to soup and cook 30 minutes longer. At the same time, cook peppers on top shelf: 20 minutes covered, then 10 minutes uncovered. Warm tortillas during this last 10 minutes. Add cilantro (coriander leaves) and avocado to soup before serving.

Mexican Chicken-Avocado Soup

1 large onion, chopped
2 stalks celery, chopped
2 tablespoons chicken fat
3 to 3½ pounds chicken pieces
8 cups boiling water
16-ounce can tomatoes, chopped, with juice
1 teaspoon salt
¼ teaspoon pepper
2 large carrots, sliced
1 zucchini, sliced into half-rounds ½-inch thick
16-ounce can shelled beans, drained
1 tablespoon chopped fresh cilantro or parsley
1 ripe avocado, peeled, pitted, and thinly sliced

Oven-sauté onion and celery in chicken fat in a Dutch oven until the vegetables are transparent. Add chicken, water, tomatoes, salt, and pepper. Cover and cook the soup at 350° F. for 2 hours. Add carrots, zucchini, and beans. Re-cover, and cook 30 minutes longer. Taste to correct seasoning, adding more salt if desired. Add cilantro or parsley and avocado slices just before serving.

Warm Tortillas: Wrap the contents of an 11-ounce can of tortillas in foil, and heat them in a 350° F. oven for 10 minutes.

Peppers Stuffed with Picadillo (Mexican Hash)

6 large green peppers
1½ pounds ground pork or beef
1 apple, peeled and grated
½ cup raisins
2 tablespoons tomato paste

2 canned whole green chilies, seeded and chopped
1 tablespoon capers
1 clove garlic, minced
1 teaspoon salt
½ teaspoon ground cumin
¼ teaspoon pepper
¼ teaspoon cinnamon
¼ cup water

Cut the tops off peppers, seed them, and stand them in a casserole that will hold them snugly. In a large skillet over high heat, quickly sear meat. Drain fat. Add all the remaining ingredients except water, and stir to blend thoroughly. Use this mixture to stuff peppers. Pour water into casserole, cover, and bake for 20 minutes at 350° F. Uncover, and bake 10 minutes longer or until peppers are fork-tender.

Pumpkin Turnovers

15-ounce can pumpkin
1 cup brown sugar
1 tablespoon melted butter
1 tablespoon rum
½ teaspoon ground cloves
½ teaspoon ground allspice
Pastry for double crust 9-inch pie (see page 359)
Milk
Granulated sugar

Mix pumpkin with brown sugar, butter, rum, and spices. Divide pastry into 12 portions. Roll each into a 6-inch circle. Place 2 full tablespoons pumpkin filling in each circle, fold to form turnover, and seal edges with a fork. Cut a vent at the top to allow steam to escape. Brush the turnovers with milk, and sprinkle them with granulated sugar. Bake on two greased baking sheets in a preheated 400° F. oven for 20 to 25 minutes or until golden brown. Cool on wire racks.

Accompaniments

Although this is a book on oven cooking and how to use your oven for maximum efficiency, it is also a book offering complete meals and menus. And there are some non-oven-cooked foods without which our meals just wouldn't be complete, balanced, or as tasty as we can make them. For this reason, we have included accompaniments.

Since we don't use canned soups and sauces, choosing to avoid the additives and the high salt content in most of these commercial products, we have included recipes for the piquant sauces and gravies we use in their place. Some of these are made on top of the range. We feel the superiority to their canned counterparts more than warrants their inclusion.

A book of complete meals without any salads would offer dreary fare indeed. So we have included crisp greens and inviting slaws where our menus call for them.

Beverage recipes are included on occasion, and we have yet to find a beverage that we can cook to our satisfaction in an oven (although we've not stopped looking).

Some meals are more filling than others, and seem to need light endings—the frothy kind of desserts you whip up without cooking. When our meals are improved by this touch, we would be doing a disservice not to provide it.

So, while it's true this book is about oven cooking, we're happy to round it out with these few non-oven accompaniments.

BEVERAGES

Banana Punch

4 bananas, peeled and quartered
2 cups milk
2 cups half-and-half
3 tablespoons honey
½ cup crushed ice

Blend all ingredients in blender in two batches.
Note: This is a good drink for breakfast skippers. It's quick and easy as well as nutritious.
Yield: 6 glasses.

Nippy Tomato Cocktail

1 28-ounce can tomato juice
4 tablespoons catsup
2 tablespoons creamed horseradish
1 tablespoon Worcestershire sauce
1 cup clam broth
½ teaspoon celery salt

Mix all ingredients in blender. Chill well, and serve over ice.
Note: This eye-opener can be served with vodka or gin. The horseradish may be adjusted according to taste.
Yield: 6 glasses.

Strawberry Champagne Punch

Serve with a strawberry in each glass.

12 cups cranberry juice
3 cups orange liqueur
3 bottles champagne
1 pint strawberries, washed but not hulled

Mix cranberry juice and orange liqueur, and chill. When ready to serve, pour cranberry-orange mixture into punch bowl. Slowly pour in champagne, and mix well. Add ice and then strawberries.
Yield: about 40 servings.

Accompaniments

APPETIZERS

Liptauer Cheese

Paprika gives the rosy color to this cheese spread from Hungary and Austria.

2 8-ounce packages cream cheese, softened
½ pound cheddar cheese, coarsely grated
¼ cup sour cream
¼ cup (½ stick) butter, softened
2 tablespoons finely chopped scallions with green tops
2 teaspoons Dijon mustard
2 teaspoons to 1 tablespoon sweet Hungarian paprika, or regular paprika to taste

Combine all ingredients and blend well, either by hand or with an electric mixer or food processor. Store the spread in a covered crock or jar and refrigerate until needed. Liptauer is better if made two or three days ahead and allowed to ripen before serving.

Yield: about 3 cups.

Meatless Antipasto

8 large mushrooms, sliced
1 6-ounce jar marinated artichoke hearts, drained
¼ cup pitted ripe olives
¼ cup stuffed green olives
8 hard-boiled eggs, halved
4 slices provolone cheese, quartered
4 large lettuce leaves
Vinegar
Olive oil

Arrange mushrooms, artichoke hearts, olives, tomatoes, and cheese on lettuce leaves on four salad plates. Serve with vinegar and oil for dressing.

Serves four.

Melon Compote

1 ripe cantaloupe melon
1 ripe honeydew melon
2 ripe bananas
3 cups freshly squeezed orange juice, strained

Cut cantaloupe in half. Discard seeds and stringy matter, and scoop out melon balls. Do the same with the honeydew. Peel and slice bananas. Mix fruit and pour orange juice over it.

Serves four.

Rolled Watercress Sandwiches

1 small bunch watercress
1 3-ounce package cream cheese, softened
¼ teaspoon salt
12 slices thin white bread

Wash watercress and set aside to dry. Reserving 12 pieces for garnish, remove stems from remaining sprigs. Chop watercress and mix it and salt into softened cream cheese. Remove crusts from bread and roll slices even thinner with a rolling pin. Spread each slice with a thin layer of watercress and cream cheese. Roll up as you would a jelly roll. Insert a sprig of watercress in one end of each roll. Store tightly covered in refrigerator.

Yield: 12 sandwiches.

SALADS AND SALAD DRESSINGS

Boston Salad

3 small heads Boston lettuce
Rings of sweet onion (Spanish or Bermuda)
⅔ cup sweet vinaigrette (see page 345)
1 cup herb-flavored croutons (optional)

Separate and wash lettuce leaves in cold water. Shake them dry, wrap loosely in tea towels and chill.

When ready to serve, tear lettuce into bite-size pieces. Combine lettuce with remaining ingredients, and toss to coat leaves with dressing. If desired, top with croutons.

Yield: 6 generous servings.

Molded Herring Salad

1 pound salted herring fillets
1 cup sour cream
1 small onion
1 hard-boiled egg
Several sprigs of parsley

Finely chop herring fillets. Mix herring and ½ cup of the sour cream and press this into a small, greased fish-shaped mold. Chill thoroughly. Turn out of mold onto plate. Peel, slice, and ring onion, then place around herring. Finely chop egg and sprinkle over fish. Garnish with parsley and serve with remaining sour cream.

Serves four.

Carrot Slaw

1½ pounds carrots, scraped and coarsely grated
½ teaspoon salt
¼ teaspoon white pepper
2 teaspoons sugar
2 tablespoons vinegar
½ cup mayonnaise (or more, to your taste)
Lettuce leaf cups

Combine all ingredients except lettuce leaves. Spoon slaw into lettuce leaf cups when ready to serve.

Note: Raisins or drained crushed pineapple can be added to carrot slaw.

Serves six to eight.

Chick-Pea and Mushroom Salad

1 cup chick-peas
1 cup chopped mushrooms
1 small onion, ringed
4 lettuce leaves
1 cup mayonnaise
¼ cup catsup
1 hard-boiled egg, chopped

Mix chick-peas, mushrooms, and onion rings, and arrange them on lettuce leaves on four salad plates. Mix together mayonnaise and catsup, and pour over salad. Garnish with chopped egg.

Serves four.

Cool Green Salad

¼ cup mayonnaise
¼ cup sour cream
1 tablespoon horseradish sauce
Salt to taste
1 10-ounce package frozen peas, cooked and chilled
1 large cucumber, peeled, seeded, and chopped
4 lettuce leaves

In a medium-sized mixing bowl, combine mayonnaise, sour cream, horseradish, and salt. Add peas and cucumber, and mix well. Chill and serve on lettuce leaves.

Serves four.

Crunchy Vegetables Vinaigrette

½ pound mushrooms, thinly sliced
1 small zucchini, sliced into thin half rounds
1 small head cauliflower, separated into florets and sliced

1 box cherry tomatoes
1 bunch scallions, chopped
1 celery heart with leaves, chopped
1 carrot, very thinly sliced
6 radishes, thinly sliced
2 green peppers, seeded and cut into strips
1 pepperoni, peeled and thinly sliced
2 tablespoons chopped fresh parsley
1 cup sweet vinaigrette (see page 345)
1 teaspoon Dijon mustard
6 medium loaves (slices) Syrian bread

Combine vegetables, pepperoni, and parsley in a container. Blend vinaigrette and mustard, and pour the dressing over the vegetable mixture. Cover and store overnight in the refrigerator to marinate. Serve on loaves of Syrian bread instead of plates (don't overload them). Provide forks. The idea is to eat the salad, and then eat the "plate," which will have absorbed all the delicious juices.

Serves six.

Ditalini Salad

4 cups cooked ditalini macaroni
½ head of lettuce, torn in small pieces
1 large cucumber, peeled, seeded, and chopped
3 large tomatoes, peeled, seeded, and chopped
1 stalk celery, chopped
¼ cup chopped radishes
1 cup mayonnaise

Mix all ingredients well. Chill.
Serves six.

Feta Cheese Salad

3 cups shredded lettuce
½ pound feta cheese
12 Greek olives
1 large tomato, cut into eighths
8 to 12 raw red onion rings

8 anchovy fillets, rinsed
Pinches of crushed dried mint
About 4 tablespoons olive oil
About 4 teaspoons lemon juice
Pita bread

On four salad plates, make beds of shredded lettuce. On these arrange slices of feta cheese, olives, tomato wedges, and onion rings. Top with crossed anchovy fillets, and sprinkle each with mint. Cover plates with plastic wrap until needed. Just before serving, drizzle on olive oil and lemon juice to taste. Pass pita bread at the table.
 Serves four.

Mushroom-Watercress Salad

2 bunches watercress, washed, and trimmed
1 head iceberg lettuce, broken into bite-sized pieces
2 cups mushroom slices
1 cup diced feta cheese
5 tomatoes, peeled and sliced
1 cup sweet vinaigrette dressing (see page 345)

Just before serving, toss all ingredients together.
 Serves ten.

Nutty Salad

¼   cup vegetable oil
¼   cup lime juice
Salt and pepper to taste
½   head lettuce, torn in small pieces
1   cup seedless grapes
½   cup unsalted peanuts
1   seedless orange, peeled and sectioned

To make dressing, mix oil, lime juice, and salt and pepper. In small salad bowl, combine lettuce, grapes, and peanuts. Add dressing and toss to coat all pieces. Arrange orange sections on top.
 Serves four.

Peanut Slaw

1½ cups mayonnaise
2 teaspoons peanut butter
1 large head of cabbage, grated
1 small onion, grated
1 large carrot, grated
½ cup unsalted peanuts, chopped

Blend together mayonnaise and peanut butter. Combine remaining ingredients. Refrigerate and toss lightly with dressing just before serving.

Serves ten to twelve.

Pickled Beets

2 16-ounce cans small whole beets
½ cup juice from beets
1 onion, finely chopped
½ cup wine vinegar
¼ cup sugar
1 teaspoon dried dill
½ teaspoon celery salt
Pepper to taste

Drain beets, reserving ½ cup juice. Combine beets with onion in a bowl. Pour juice into a small saucepan. Add all the remaining ingredients. Heat, stirring, until sugar is dissolved. Pour the dressing over the beets. Chill beets in refrigerator. The flavor improves with marinating.

Serves eight.

Popeye Salad

1 small bunch spinach
4 ounces Monterey Jack cheese, cubed
½ cup mayonnaise
¼ cup sour cream
1 tablespoon Dijon mustard
½ teaspoon salt

⅛ teaspoon pepper
2 hard-boiled eggs, sliced

Wash spinach well. Dry it and tear into bite-sized pieces. Toss spinach with cubed cheese and chill. Combine mayonnaise, sour cream, mustard, salt, and pepper. Just before serving, pour dressing over spinach and garnish with egg slices.

Note: Gritty spinach can ruin a salad. Wash the spinach several times until you're certain all the sand is removed.

Serves four.

Red Cabbage Slaw

1 small head red cabbage, grated
1 8-ounce can crushed pineapple, well-drained, juice reserved
1 small onion, grated
1 cup mayonnaise
2 tablespoons pineapple juice (reserved, from can)
½ teaspoon salt
¼ cup chopped walnuts

In a glass bowl, combine cabbage, pineapple, and onion. Blend mayonnaise, pineapple juice, and salt in a small mixing bowl. Fold dressing into cabbage combination and chill well. Just before serving, add nuts and mix well.

Serves four.

Salade de Tomates *Tomato Salad*

2 large tomatoes, cut into wedges
½ head lettuce, broken in pieces
⅔ cup olive oil
⅓ cup cider vinegar
½ teaspoon sugar
½ teaspoon salt
⅛ teaspoon garlic powder
1 teaspoon paprika
⅛ teaspoon pepper
1 teaspoon Worcestershire sauce
2 hard-cooked eggs, sliced

Arrange tomato wedges on top of lettuce in large salad bowl. Combine oil, vinegar, sugar, salt, garlic powder, paprika, pepper, and Worcestershire sauce in jar and shake. Pour enough of this over salad to dampen, and toss to coat all pieces. Put egg slices on top and serve immediately.

Serves four.

Simple Salad with Paprika Dressing

½ large head iceberg lettuce
2 large tomatoes, quartered
4 large mushrooms, sliced
1½ teaspoons dill
2 hard-boiled eggs, sliced

Combine first four ingredients, tossing to coat with dill. Arrange egg slices on top. Serve with Paprika Dressing.

Serves four.

Paprika Dressing

1 tablespoon lemon juice
1 tablespoon sugar
½ cup mayonnaise
⅛ teaspoon salt
1 teaspoon milk
1 teaspoon paprika

Mix lemon juice and sugar to dissolve sugar. Add remaining ingredients, blending well.

Sliced, Herbed Tomatoes

2 large, ripe tomatoes
½ teaspoon crushed oregano
Olive oil

Slice tomatoes and arrange them on a plate. Sprinkle oregano over tomato slices and dribble on olive oil.

Serves four.

Spinach-Bacon Salad

2 pounds tender fresh spinach
6 slices crisply cooked bacon, crumbled
½ cup sweet vinaigrette, or more, to taste (see page 345)
2 hard-boiled eggs, finely chopped

Wash each leaf of spinach on both sides under cool running water. Remove stems and discolored leaves. Wash the leaves a second time to be sure there isn't a speck of lingering sand on them. Shake off excess moisture, and store the spinach in a loosely wrapped towel in the refrigerator.

In a large bowl, toss the spinach with bacon and vinaigrette. Sprinkle egg on top before serving.

Note: Finely chopped raw onion may be tossed with the salad, if desired.

Serves six.

Tomato and Pepper Salad

4 large green peppers, seeded and sliced
4 large firm tomatoes, sliced
2 tablespoons chopped fresh flat parsley
¼ teaspoon dried mint
1 cup Greek black olives
⅔ cup sweet vinaigrette (see page 345)

Cut the pepper into very thin slices, 2 inches long. Cut the tomatoes into very thin half rounds. Toss the vegetables with parsley, mint, olives, and sweet vinaigrette. This can be done ahead and refrigerated, since marinating improves the flavor. Before serving, taste to correct seasoning; add salt, pepper, or more mint, according to your taste.

Serves eight.

Vinaigrette

1¼ cups olive oil,
     or half olive oil and half vegetable oil
½ to ¾ cup wine vinegar (to taste)
1 teaspoon salt

1 teaspoon dried basil or dill weed (optional)
½ teaspoon pepper
¼ teaspoon dry mustard, or 1 teaspoon Dijon mustard
1 clove garlic, peeled, whole (optional)

Combine all ingredients in a large cruet or jar. Cover and shake to blend. (Always shake dressing again before using.) A medium bowl of salad requires ⅓ to ½ cup dressing.

Yield: about 2 cups.

Sweet Vinaigrette

Use it whenever you want a sweet pickled quality, such as in a vegetable salad.

1¼ cups olive oil,
  or half olive oil and half vegetable oil
½ to ¾ cup wine vinegar
2 teaspoons sugar
1 teaspoon celery salt
1 teaspoon dill weed or dried basil, crushed
½ teaspoon pepper
¼ teaspoon dry mustard (optional)
1 teaspoon paprika (optional—use it for color)

Put all the ingredients into a jar or bottle. Cover and shake to blend. Always shake well before using.

Yield: about 2 cups.

DESSERTS

Almond Peaches

4 fresh peaches
  (or 1 16-ounce can peach slices)
1 tablespoon sugar (for fresh peaches only)
¼ teaspoon almond extract
¼ cup slivered almonds

Peel and slice fresh peaches. Do this over a bowl so that you'll catch the juice. Put sugar and almond extract into juice in bowl and mix. Add peach slices, stirring to coat them with sugar and almond extract. Serve topped with slivered almonds. If using canned peaches, omit sugar.

Serves four.

Apricot Granita

28-ounce can pitted apricot halves in syrup
¼ cup Galliano

Purée apricots with syrup in a blender or processor fitted with steel blade. Mix in liqueur. Pour the mixture into a glass baking dish or stainless steel bowl. Cover and freeze the purée until it is solid, about 3 hours.

Granitas are supposed to be icy and grainy, as well as flavorful and refreshing. To serve, scrape the surface of the frozen purée with a fork to free icy grains, and spoon them into sherbet glasses. Serve immediately.

Serves four.

Biscuit Tortoni

1 quart vanilla ice cream, softened
1 cup crushed macaroons, divided
½ cup chopped toasted almonds
2 tablespoons chopped maraschino cherries
2 tablespoons sweet sherry or rum
6 maraschino cherries, cut in half

Mix softened ice cream with ½ cup macaroon crumbs, almonds, chopped cherries, and sherry or rum. Spoon the mixture into 12 paper-lined muffin cups. Garnish with cherry halves and the remaining ½ cup macaroon crumbs (sprinkle them around the rim of each). Freeze until firm, and keep them frozen until ready to serve. If kept for any length of time, cover with freezer wrap.

Blender Mocha-Rum Pots de Crème

12 ounces German sweet chocolate
½ cup boiling water
⅔ cup sugar
2 teaspoons vanilla
2 teaspoons instant coffee
2 tablespoons rum
2 eggs
½ pint (1 cup) heavy cream
1 pint vanilla ice cream (optional)

Break chocolate into small pieces, place in blender, and grate them with on-off turns of the motor. Add boiling water, and blend until melted and smooth. Blend in sugar, vanilla, coffee, and rum. Blend in eggs, then cream. Pour into six or eight sherbet glasses or custard cups. Chill until firm. If desired, serve with a small scoop of vanilla ice cream on top.

Blue Cheese Pears

6 fresh pears
8-ounce package cream cheese, softened
4 ounces blue cheese, mashed
Chopped pecans or pistachios

Cut pears in half; peel and core them but leave stems intact. Blend cream cheese and blue cheese, and whip the mixture until it is fluffy. Divide the cheese between the pears, spreading it like a sandwich filling. Press the pear halves back together. Roll the pears in chopped nuts to press them into the edges of cheese filling. Refrigerate until 30 minutes before serving.

Chocolate-Cherry Ricotta Dessert

1 pound whole-milk ricotta cheese
½ cup sugar
3 ounces semi-sweet chocolate, shaved
8 candied cherries, finely chopped
1 tablespoon candied citron (optional)
¼ cup sliced almonds
¼ teaspoon almond extract

Combine all ingredients and blend well. Spoon the mixture into four dessert dishes, cover them loosely with plastic wrap, and refrigerate until serving time.

Erdbeerschnee mit Schlagsahne Strawberry Ambrosia Cream

1 pint strawberries
1 package unflavored gelatin
¼ cup hot water
½ cup sugar
1 cup heavy cream
1 teaspoon almond extract
2 tablespoons light rum
3 egg whites
3 macaroons, crushed

Wash and hull strawberries. Dissolve gelatin in hot water. Add sugar. Beat cream, almond extract, and rum until stiff. Mix in gelatin. Place in refrigerator. When gelatin begins to thicken, beat egg whites until stiff, and fold them into gelatin. Fold in macaroon crumbs. Chill well before serving topped with strawberries.

Serves six.

Grape Almond Crème Dessert

½ pound seedless white grapes
½ pint heavy cream
2 tablespoons confectioners' sugar
A few drops almond extract
8 whole almonds

Wash grapes and set aside to dry. Whip cream until it stands in peaks. Add sugar and almond extract, and beat just long enough to blend; mix in grapes. Divide between four parfait glasses and chill. Just before serving top each with two almonds.

Note: Cream whips better if it, as well as the bowl and beaters, is chilled well first.

Grasshopper Sundaes

1 pint chocolate ice cream
4 jiggers green crème de menthe
½ cup heavy cream, whipped
4 green maraschino cherries
Shaved semi-sweet chocolate

Divide ice cream between four dessert dishes. Pour crème de menthe over ice cream. Top with whipped cream. Garnish with cherries and shaved chocolate.

Instant Raspberry Ice Cream

⅔ cup heavy cream
¼ cup sugar
10-ounce package frozen raspberries in syrup,
    broken up but not thawed

In a blender or processor fitted with steel blade, whip cream and sugar until thickened and double in bulk. Do not overbeat. With the motor running, add frozen chunks of fruit, and blend until the mixture is smooth. Spoon the ice cream into sherbet glasses and serve it immediately. Fresh raspberries and mint leaves make a pleasing garnish.

Serves four.

Layered Fruit Compote

20-ounce can pineapple chunks in syrup
1 small cantaloupe cut into melon balls
1 cup halved strawberries
½ pound seedless green grapes, stems removed

2 bananas, sliced
2 seedless oranges, peeled and sliced into half rounds
1 cup blueberries
12 whole strawberries
¼ cup kirsch or fruit-flavored brandy

Drain pineapple, reserving syrup. In a large deep glass bowl, layer fruit in the order given, beginning with pineapple chunks. At the top make a ring of blueberries and place the whole strawberries in the center. Mix the kirsch or brandy with the reserved syrup and pour it over all. Chill compote in the refrigerator until needed.
Serves six.

Lime Ice Cream Pie

1½ cups graham cracker crumbs
1 tablespoon sugar
½ teaspoon flour
¼ cup melted butter
1 3-ounce package lime gelatin
1 cup boiling water
1 pint vanilla ice cream, softened

Mix together graham cracker crumbs, sugar, and flour. Add butter and blend thoroughly. Grease 9-inch pie plate, and press crumb mixture on bottom and sides to form crust. Chill for 1½ hours. Dissolve gelatin in boiling water. Add ice cream a little at a time, stirring until ice cream has melted and mixture is smooth. Pour into chilled pie crust, and refrigerate for at least 2 hours before serving.

No-Bake Mocha-Rum Balls

2½ cups graham cracker crumbs
1 cup walnuts, finely chopped
1 cup confectioners' sugar
¼ cup cocoa
2 tablespoons instant coffee (see Note)
2 tablespoons rum
3 tablespoons light corn syrup
Additional confectioners' sugar

Blend well together the crumbs, walnuts, sugar, cocoa, coffee, rum, and syrup. Roll dough into 1-inch balls, and roll each ball in additional confectioners' sugar. Chill on cookie sheet for 3 hours before storing in a jar. Keep refrigerated overnight before serving.

Note: If you substitute freeze-dried coffee for instant, dissolve it first in a tablespoon or so of hot water.

Yield: 6 dozen cookies.

Papaya Ice Cream

Exotic and easy to make!

2 ripe papayas
¼ cup orange juice
½ cup sugar
½ pint (1 cup) heavy cream
12 macaroons (optional)

Peel and cut up papayas over a bowl to catch all the juice. Purée the fruit in a blender or processor. Add orange juice and sugar. Gradually add cream. Freeze 1 hour, then whip in an electric mixer or by hand until smooth. Freeze again for 1 hour, and again whip until smooth. Cover and freeze for several hours or overnight. Allow the ice cream to ripen in the refrigerator for 15 minutes before serving. Spoon the ice cream into six sherbet dishes or champagne glasses, and, if desired, accompany each serving with 2 macaroons.

Papaya Whip

3 egg whites, beaten
½ cup confectioners' sugar
1 cup puréed papaya

Beat egg whites until peaks form. Slowly add sugar, beating constantly. Mix in papaya pulp with wooden spoon. Put whip in parfait glasses and chill for a short time before serving.

Serves four.

Pears Helene

½ cup semi-sweet chocolate chips
2 tablespoons vanilla sugar (see page 362)
  or 2 tablespoons regular sugar plus ½ teaspoon vanilla
  extract
½ cup heavy cream
1 pint French vanilla ice cream
8 chilled, drained canned pear halves

In a small heavy saucepan, melt chocolate in the heat that remains in turned-off oven after cooking.

When ready to serve, warm chocolate over low heat. Gradually stir in sugar and cream. Bring the mixture to a boil, stirring constantly. Remove from heat.

Place a scoop of ice cream in each of four dessert dishes. Lay pear halves alongside. Top with chocolate sauce.

Plum Perfect Pound Cake

10-ounce frozen pound cake, thawed
30-ounce can plums in heavy syrup
6 tablespoons Curacao
½ pint heavy cream, whipped
2 teaspoons sugar
½ teaspoon grated orange rind

Lay a slice of pound cake on each of six dessert plates. Top each with 2 plums (if they are not already pitted, remove pits) and 2 tablespoons of the syrup. Spoon 1 tablespoon Curacao on each serving. Beat sugar and grated orange rind into whipped cream. When ready to serve, spoon a topping of whipped cream onto each serving.

Triple Coffee

½ pint heavy cream
2 teaspoons vanilla sugar (see page 362)
  or regular sugar
1 teaspoon instant coffee

1 **pint coffee ice cream**
¼ **cup coffee-flavored liqueur**

Whip the cream until stiff. Beat in sugar and coffee powder. Place a scoop of coffee ice cream in each of four dessert dishes. Pour a tablespoon of coffee-flavored liqueur over each scoop. Top with whipped cream.

Wine Jelly

2 **envelopes unflavored gelatin**
1 **cup sugar**
1 **cup water**
1 **cup orange juice**
½ **cup port**
½ **cup sherry**
¼ **cup kirsch**
¼ **cup brandy**
Whipped cream

Mix gelatin and sugar in a small saucepan. Add water and stir over low heat until the gelatin and sugar are completely dissolved. Pour the mixture into a bowl and blend in all the remaining ingredients except cream. Chill until set. Spoon the jelly into six champagne glasses and top with whipped cream.

SAUCES

Blender Blond Cumberland Sauce with Fruit

11-ounce can mandarin orange sections
Juice of 1 lemon
½ teaspoon grated lemon rind
⅓ cup apple jelly
⅓ cup dry vermouth or dry white wine
½ teaspoon dry mustard
¼ teaspoon ground ginger
1½ tablespoons cornstarch
¼ cup golden raisins
3 slices canned pineapple, cut into small pieces

Drain oranges, reserve sections, and pour the juice into blender container. Add lemon juice, rind, jelly, wine, dry mustard, ginger, and cornstarch. Process until thoroughly blended. Pour the mixture into a saucepan, and bring it to a boil, stirring constantly. Cook 1 minute. Add orange sections, raisins, and pineapple.

Yield: about 2½ cups.

Fudge Sauce

2 cups milk
½ cup marshmallow fluff
½ cup cocoa
1½ pounds semi-sweet chocolate, in chunks
½ pound milk chocolate, in chunks

In top of double boiler over boiling water, heat milk until hot. Add marshmallow, cocoa, semi-sweet chocolate, and milk chocolate. Stir constantly until chocolate is melted, and all ingredients are well blended.

Note: This sauce, which may be served either hot or cold, will keep for up to a month when refrigerated.

Yield: about 6 cups.

Raisin-Nut Sauce

1½ cups water
½ cup dark brown sugar, firmly packed
¼ cup lemon juice
2 teaspoons Dijon mustard
2 teaspoons cornstarch
½ teaspoon salt
⅓ cup raisins
⅓ cup pine nuts

Mix together in a blender or by hand water, sugar, lemon juice, mustard, cornstarch, and salt. In a saucepan, bring the mixture to a boil, stirring constantly. Add raisins and nuts.

The sauce can be reheated in a 1-quart casserole, covered, in a 350° to 400° F. oven for 15 minutes, or over hot water in a double boiler.

Yield: about 3 cups.

Red Garlic Sauce

¼ cup beef stock or broth
2 slices light rye bread, crusts removed, cubed
3 cloves garlic, sliced
7- or 7¼-ounce jar pimentos, undrained
2 tablespoons minced parsley
1 teaspoon dried basil
½ teaspoon salt
¼ teaspoon hot pepper sauce
½ cup olive oil

Purée all the ingredients except oil in a blender or processor. With the motor running, add the oil in a thin stream. Refrigerate the sauce in a covered jar until needed.

Note: If a blender is used, you may need a little more beef stock to purée the solid ingredients. The sauce can also be made by hand in the manner of a *pesto,* using mortar and pestle, in which case the garlic should be minced rather than sliced.

Sauce Béchamel

3 tablespoons butter
1 small onion, finely chopped
   or 3 shallots, minced
3 tablespoons all-purpose flour
2 cups milk
½ teaspoon salt
¼ teaspoon white pepper

Melt butter in a medium-size heavy saucepan. Sauté onion (or shallots) until just limp. Stir flour into warm (but not sizzling hot) butter. Stirring constantly with a wooden spoon, cook the roux for 2 or 3 minutes over low heat. Meanwhile, in a separate saucepan, heat the milk to scalding. Slowly add the hot milk to the roux, stirring constantly until thickened and smooth. Cook over very low heat for 15 minutes, stirring occasionally. Strain if a smoother sauce is desired.
   Yield: about 1¾ cups.

Sauce Velouté: Replace the hot milk in béchamel with hot, well-flavored stock or clear broth. If you don't have stock on hand, use a tinned broth that is not overly salty. If it is condensed, dilute it before using in this recipe.

Sauce Suprême: Use a combination of hot stock and hot half-and-half for the 2 cups of liquid required in the béchamel recipe.

Mustard Sauce: Make the basic béchamel. Just before removing it from the heat, whisk in 2 teaspoons Dijon mustard, ½ teaspoon dried dill, and 2 tablespoons white vinegar.

Tarragon Sauce: Make the basic béchamel. Whisk in 1 teaspoon dried or 2 tablespoons fresh snipped tarragon and ¼ cup white wine. Cook 5 minutes longer.

Herb Sauce: Make the basic béchamel. Whisk in 2 tablespoons minced fresh flat-leaved parsley and either 2 tablespoons minced celery leaves or 1 tablespoon snipped fresh chives.

Mushroom Sauce: Sauté ½ pound sliced fresh mushrooms in 2 tablespoons butter over high heat until mushrooms are browned and liquid has evaporated. Drain excess butter. Make the basic béchamel

or sauce suprême, and stir in mushrooms. Cook 5 minutes longer.
Yield: about 3 cups.

Cheese Sauce Suprême: Make the basic béchamel, reducing salt to ¼ teaspoon. Stir in 1½ cups coarsely grated Gruyère or cheddar cheese until it is just melted. If desired, whisk in ½ teaspoon Dijon mustard.

Spanish Sauce

12 ounces fresh mushrooms with stems
½ cup butter
½ cup flour
2 cups half-and-half
24 stuffed Spanish olives, halved
⅛ teaspoon garlic powder
3 teaspoons chopped dill
½ teaspoon tarragon
½ teaspoon thyme
½ teaspoon salt

Wash and slice mushrooms. In a large skillet, melt butter. Sauté mushrooms. Remove with slotted spoon. Stir flour into butter to form a paste. Gradually add half-and-half, stirring constantly until sauce begins to thicken. Cook about 5 minutes, stirring. Add other ingredients, mixing well until olives are heated through.
Yield: about 4 cups.

White Sauce

3 tablespoons butter
3 tablespoons flour
1½ cups milk
½ teaspoon salt
⅛ teaspoon white pepper

In a medium-sized saucepan, melt butter. Work in flour with the back of a wooden spoon to form a paste. Cook 2 minutes. Slowly add milk, heating over medium heat and stirring constantly until mixture thickens. Add salt and pepper, and continue to cook for five minutes.
Yield: about 1½ cups.

BUTTERS

Anchovy Butter

½ cup (1 stick) soft butter
½ can rolled anchovies with capers, drained and minced
1 tablespoon lemon juice

Blend all ingredients well. Refrigerate in a covered jar or crock until needed.

Herb Butter

1 cup (2 sticks) unsalted butter, softened
¼ cup chopped fresh parsley
¼ cup chopped fresh chives or watercress
¼ cup chopped fresh dill or thyme

Combine all ingredients and blend them well. Spoon the mixture into a crock or other server, cover, and refrigerate or freeze until needed. Allow the butter to become room temperature before serving.

Note: Use only fresh herbs, but feel free to make substitutions. Fresh tarragon, basil, marjoram, celery tops, or scallion tops may all be used in place of other herbs.

PASTRY

Pastry for single crust 9-inch pie shell:

1½ cups all-purpose flour
¼ teaspoon salt
½ cup shortening
   (butter, lard, or a combination of the two also can be used)
3 to 4 tablespoons ice water

Pastry for double crust 9-inch pie shell: . .

2½ cups all-purpose flour
½ teaspoon salt
¾ cup shortening
6 to 7 tablespoons ice water

Combine flour and salt in a medium-size bowl. Cut in shortening with a pastry blender or two knives until the mixture is coarsely blended and shortening is the size of small peas. Sprinkle water over mixture, a tablespoon at a time, mixing lightly with a fork. Use just enough water so pastry holds together when pressed. Handle pastry gently and keep everything cold. If using shortening, roll pastry out on a lightly floured surface. If using butter and/or lard, chill the pastry in the refrigerator for 30 minutes before rolling out.

Chill the pastry-lined pie pan while preparing filling, unless the recipe calls for a prebaked pie shell. If it is a double crust pie, chill the dough for the top crust also while preparing filling.

Pizza Dough

1⅓ cups very warm water
1½ packages dry yeast
1 teaspoon sugar
3⅓ cups all-purpose flour
1½ teaspoons salt
1 tablespoon olive oil

Combine water, yeast, and sugar in a small bowl, and let the mixture stand for 10 minutes to proof (bubble). Pour the mixture into a medium-size bowl. Stir in flour, salt, and oil. Mix to form dough. Knead for 10 minutes on a floured surface. (Note: if using dough hooks, 5 minutes' kneading is sufficient. If using a processor, mix dry ingredients in workbowl with steel knife. Add liquid in two additions, mixing with on-off turns until dough forms a ball. Let processor run 40 seconds to knead.)

Place the dough in an oiled bowl, turning to coat with oil. Cover bowl with plastic wrap and let dough rise until double in bulk, 1 to 1½ hours. Punch down, and proceed with recipe.

MISCELLANEOUS

Blanched, Toasted Almonds

1 cup whole almonds
Water to cover
2 tablespoons butter

Combine almonds and water in a small saucepan. Bring to a boil. Remove pan from heat, drain. Slip almonds out of skins while still warm. Dry them. In a small skillet, melt butter. Toast almonds, stirring constantly, until they just begin to change color. Remove from heat. (They will continue to darken, so don't overcook.)

Cinnamon Sugar

¼ cup granulated sugar
2 teaspoons cinnamon

Blend the ingredients well, and store the mixture in a shaker.

Seasoned Crumbs

½ loaf Italian bread, or any white bread
½ cup grated Parmesan cheese
¼ cup chopped fresh parsley
  or 2 tablespoons dried parsley
1 teaspoon paprika
½ teaspoon celery salt
½ teaspoon pepper
½ teaspoon basil
½ teaspoon dried thyme leaves or oregano
1 clove garlic, minced

Cube bread. Reduce it to crumbs in any of the following ways: in batches in a blender, using on-off turns of the motor; in batches in a processor fitted with steel blade, using on-off turns; by hand toast bread cubes in a low oven, cool, scoop the cubes into a plastic bag, and crush them with a rolling pin.

Mix crumbs with remaining ingredients, blending well. Store in plastic container in the refrigerator or freezer. Seasoned crumbs are easy to use even when frozen, since they remain separate and free-flowing. If desired, toast crumbs lightly in a warm oven, 250° F.

Yield: about 5 cups.

Soured Milk

Soured milk may be used in place of buttermilk: To every cup of milk needed, add 1 tablespoon lemon juice or vinegar, stir, and allow the mixture to stand at room temperature for 15 minutes.

Vanilla Sugar

1 vanilla bean, split in half lengthwise
1 pint (2 cups) sugar

Combine bean and sugar in a jar. Cover and allow the flavor to ripen for several days before using the sugar. As sugar is used, add more sugar to the jar. The bean will continue to be aromatic for months.

Use vanilla sugar whenever both sugar and vanilla are called for in a recipe. The flavor is superior to that of vanilla extract.

Metric Measure Conversion Table
(Approximations)

When You Know (U.S.)	Multiply by	To Find (Metric)
	WEIGHT	
ounces	28	grams
pounds	0.45	kilograms
	VOLUME	
teaspoons	5	milliliters
tablespoons	15	milliliters
fluid ounces	30	milliliters
cups	0.24	liters
pints	0.47	liters
quarts	0.95	liters
	TEMPERATURE	
degrees Fahrenheit (°F)	subtract 32° and multiply the remainder by 5/9 or .556	degrees Celsius or Centigrade (°C)

Index